Lisa Raggio

Sherie Seff

Rebecca Gilchrist

Katherine Meloche

Buddy Powell

JoElla Flood

Albert Insinnia

Nancy Robbins

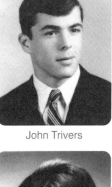

John Trivers

Marcia Mitzman

Forbesy Russell

Derek Kucsak

Sandra Zeeman

David Frank

Liz Myers

Jim Shankman

Peggy Lee Brennan

Mary Gordon Murray

Michael Brindisi

Praise for
Grease, Tell Me More, Tell Me More

"A rare and exuberant exploration and reminiscence of a unique and memorable piece of theater history, all in the words of the people who made it happen."

—**John Rubinstein**, *Children of a Lesser God*

"This is one of my absolute, all-time favorite show biz books! A page-turning story of the dramatic ups and downs of the little show that could and all the incredibly creative minds that were a part of making it a worldwide sensation. The 'worse thing you could do' is not read it!"

—**Seth Rudetsky**, Host of *On Broadway*, SiriusXM

"OMG! What a fun read! For anyone who loves the theater, *Grease, Tell Me More, Tell Me More* is a wonderful adventure of great stories and surprises. And it reads like 'Greased Lightning'"

—**Marsha Mason**, *The Goodbye Girl*

"I love this terrific book. If you're a fan of musical theater lore, you'll love getting the inside scoop. . . . In these vividly recalled stories, what remains paramount is the bond of love shared by everyone connected to this unique and beloved musical. *Grease, Tell Me More, Tell Me More* took fifty years to write—and it was so worth the wait!"

—**Danny Burstein**, *Moulin Rouge!*

"Solid gold! Infectious stories from the inside of the making of a Broadway hit! I couldn't put it down! *Grease, Tell Me More, Tell Me More* is a must-read for *Grease* fans. You'll want more."

—**Glenn Casale**, Director, *Peter Pan*

"This incredible collection of stories not only sheds light on our audience's affinity for the musical but also serves as a touching testimony of how a collaborative community of artists can transform a few good ideas into theater history."

—**Scott Klier**, Producing Artistic Director,
Broadway Sacramento

Grease
TELL ME MORE, TELL ME MORE

Stories from the Broadway
Phenomenon That Started It All

EDITED BY

TOM MOORE | ADRIENNE BARBEAU | KEN WAISSMAN

CHICAGO
REVIEW
PRESS

In the five decades since *Grease* opened,
we have lost many friends and collaborators.
Each played a unique part in our story, and their contributions
to *Grease* and to our lives will never be forgotten.
This book is dedicated to all of them.

Published by Chicago Review Press Incorporated
814 North Franklin Street
Chicago, Illinois 60610
ISBN 978-1-64160-758-2

Library of Congress Control Number: 2022932902

Typesetting: Nord Compo

Printed in the United States of America
5 4 3 2 1

CONTENTS

PROLOGUE

One summer night in the middle of the 2020 COVID-19 pandemic, the original Broadway *Grease* company gathered on a Zoom call. Telling stories becomes central to every alumni reunion, and *Grease* was no exception. We never tire of sharing stories, as the memories are fiercely treasured. Even when stories are repeated over and over, we laugh at all the same things as if for the first time.

One thing that unexpectedly came out of that reunion was the wish to commemorate the show for its fiftieth anniversary on February 14, 2022. We realized one way to do that would be to put our memories into book form.

The genesis of *Grease* is a quixotic one, and its improbable success is a legendary tale. We wanted to share what it was like to create and be part of this showbiz phenomenon.

Most Broadway shows produce some enduring friendships, but *Grease* was unique in that for almost everyone involved, it was our first big break at the beginning of our professional careers, and we were all approximately the same age.

The word Rydell High alumni use most often when referring to their fellow *Grease* actors, musicians, crew, and staff is *family*. Before these hundreds of artists became one big Broadway family, however, they were each part of a unique *Grease* company, or family—and that is how we tell our story.

One Broadway show, eight national tours, from February 14, 1972, until it closed on April 13, 1980, after a record-breaking 3,388 performances.

Tom Moore, Adrienne Barbeau, Ken Waissman

1 | *In the Beginning . . .*

JIM JACOBS (*Author/Composer*): In 1969 I was having a cast party in my apartment and practically everybody had left, but Warren Casey was still there, along with some deadbeats lying around listening to Led Zeppelin, smoking weed and drunk, of course, and I go to this closet where I had a shopping bag full of my old 45s from the '50s and came out and said, "I'm putting on Dion and the Belmonts." I go over, sit next to Warren, and say, "How come there's never been a Broadway show, man, with rock and roll music?" Those exact words.

Warren looked at me like I was nutty and said, "Yeah, well, that's a fun idea, but what the hell would it be about?" I said, "I have no idea. Maybe it should be about the people I went to high school with. And because everything in those days was greasy, because the hair was greasy and the food was greasy, and there were all these guys who had cars and they were always under the hood, man, and they'd come out all greasy . . . it could be called *Grease*."

Warren looked at me and said, "Yeah, yeah. OK, you're drunk, it's three o'clock in the morning, let's all go get a tattoo of an executioner with an axe. I'm goin' home."

Warren was a very close-lipped guy. But I found him the funniest person I had ever known. A latter-day Oscar Wilde of the welfare state. An American Joe Orton. We could have each other in hysterics for hours on end. There were never two more different kind of guys, but we made a great team.

I was part of Chicago's community theater scene while working a day job in advertising. Warren, at that time, was working for Mary Cell Corsetry—a

1

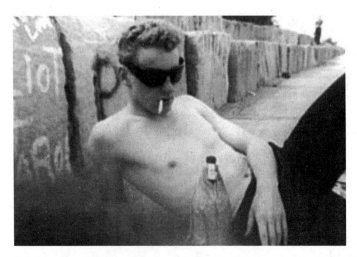

Jim Jacobs at Foster Beach on Lake Michigan.

women's underwear store. When people asked Warren, "What do you do?" he'd say, "Oh, I'm in bras and panties. . . ."

A few weeks after that party where I replaced Led Zeppelin with '50s rock 'n' roll, Warren calls me up and says, "I started working on a scene and a song for that show you were talking about the other night." I said, "What show?" I didn't have a clue what he was talking about. "You remember . . . *Grease.* You said we would call it *Grease.*" I said, "You're writing a scene?" He said, "Yeah, it's a girls' pajama party. And I'm writin' it now. It's called 'Freddy, My Love.'" I knew right away he was spoofing "Eddie My Love" by the Teen Queens. So that was it. I went down to my office and instead of writing direct mail and ads and shit for *Advertising Age,* I just started writing names of characters and making up songs. I started thinking of the drive-in movie, hamburger joints, a rumble, pajama parties, tattoos . . . scenes like that.

Around the same time, this actress-teacher friend of mine calls me up one day and says, "Do you think you could teach my drama class for me?" I said, "I don't know anything about teaching." She said, "Well, just fake it for one week. You'll think of something. Oh, and you get thirty dollars!"

So I came up with *auditioning for a play.* I brought in the pajama party scene and picked out five girls and said, "OK, you'll play Marty, you're gonna be Jan, etc." They start reading the thing—it was the first time I had ever heard it read—and all the people in the class start laughing their asses off. I mean, really howling at the lines; I got goose bumps. *Holy shit, what the fuck!* I called up Warren and said, "Warren, we have a play! We really have a fuckin' play!"

Jim Jacobs.

Warren Casey.

An early version of Grease *was first performed on weekends by an amateur cast at the Kingston Mines Community Theatre, in a converted trolley barn in Chicago, February 1971 to November 1971.*
—TOM MOORE

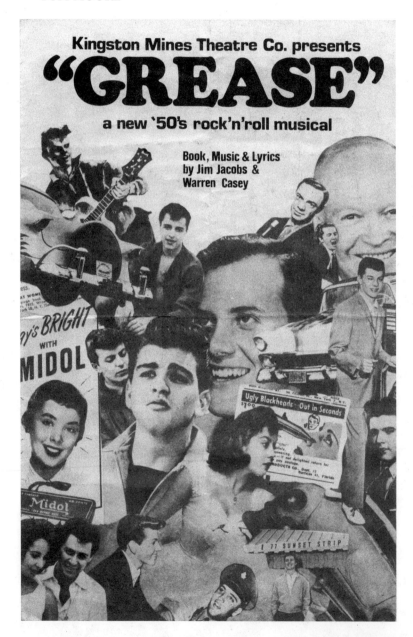

"Could This Be Magic?"

KEN WAISSMAN (*Producer*): In August 1971 a Baltimore high school friend and college roommate, Phillip Markin, called me from Chicago. He and his wife Suzy had happened upon a small, ninety-seat community theater that was presenting a show about high school kids in the 1950s. Phil knew I was looking for a new show to produce.

"It's about the kids with the ducktail haircuts and black leather jackets who hung out in the back of our high school," my Baltimore friend reported. "It's called *Grease*."

In high school and college, Phil was known as the ultimate pessimist. He never had a positive word to say about anything. I figured if he, the champion glass-half-empty guy, is showing enthusiasm for this, I better fly out and see it.

Off to Chicago I went. The theater was in the basement of what had once been a trolley barn. There were no seats, just the cement floor. An usher handed us some newspapers to sit on. I looked at the stage (which was level with the floor) and saw homemade brown paper scenery depicting a mythical Rydell High. I could see the drip marks left by the poster paint.

However, once the show began, I saw my own high school yearbook coming to life. I knew every one of the characters onstage. They each mirrored people I remembered from my high school in Baltimore. I felt their fears, their bravado, and their need to fit in.

Danny and Sandy existed as part of the ensemble but weren't fully developed as central characters. At this stage, the book was way overwritten: 70 percent book, 30 percent music.

The band was basically winging it, slamming through lyrics and often drowning out voices. However, the wit of "Beauty School Dropout" and "It's Raining on Prom Night" and the joy of songs like "We Go Together" and "Greased Lightnin'" came through, sounding original but at the same time like songs I remembered from the '50s.

As rough as the show was at this point, I believed from what I saw that the authors, with the right guidance, had the talent to expand the score and do the rewrites necessary to transform this pint-size show into a Broadway-size musical.

After the performance, I met with Jacobs and Casey and expressed my enthusiasm. I told them if they were willing to move to New York to rework the show, focus the book, and flesh out the musical score, my partner and I would produce it. (My producing partner, Maxine Fox, flew out to Chicago the next day and saw the final performance of the run.)

I told the authors that the authenticity they managed to create in the characters, the feeling that when the show is over the actors, still in their costumes, would jump into an old jalopy and go out for hamburgers, made the *Grease* experience indelible. I told them if we produced it, we would keep that in mind with every single choice we made for the New York production.

2 | *"Move It"*

KEN WAISSMAN (*Producer*): Once back in New York, the next step was for Maxine and me to meet with Jacobs and Casey's agents at International Creative Management—ICM: Steve Sultan, a buttoned-up attorney, and Bridget Aschenberg, a matronly middle-aged woman whose hair always looked like it just came in from a windstorm. Although Jim and Warren became ICM clients because of the Kingston Mines production, Bridget had never seen it and hadn't heard the music. Nonetheless, she decided that the director and choreographer should be Michael Bennett, then a young, up-and-coming Broadway choreographer who would later go on to direct and choreograph the groundbreaking musical *A Chorus Line.* He just happened to be an ICM client. She indicated that if we had Michael Bennett on board, it would be easier for them to recommend that Jim and Warren give us the producing rights.

Maxine and I admired Michael Bennett, but his kind of choreography depended on trained dancers and wouldn't be right for *Grease.* "Come on, Bridget, this isn't our first rodeo," I told her. "We may look like kids, but you know very well we've already produced two hit productions" (*Fortune and Men's Eyes* and *And Miss Reardon Drinks a Little*).

I went on to tell her and Sultan that we weren't going to have a singing and dancing chorus. The principals would be cast mainly for their acting and singing abilities and would move well enough to do the dance numbers. "In fact, Bridget, we've already decided that Pat Birch should be the choreographer." (I had thought about Pat while sitting in the Kingston Mines Theatre in Chicago watching the show.

LEFT: Ken Waissman and Maxine Fox. RIGHT: Pat Birch.

Pat had choreographed the off-Broadway hit *You're a Good Man, Charlie Brown*, which Maxine cast, as well as *The Me Nobody Knows*, a hit off-Broadway musical about inner-city kids, cast with kids who acted, sang, and danced like real kids, not trained professionals. She'd be just the right choice for the authenticity the authors were going for.)

Dick Clark had also made an offer to produce *Grease*, as did the rock 'n' roll concert promoter Sid Bernstein. However, in the end, Jim and Warren awarded Maxine and me the rights. Thus began *Grease*'s journey to worldwide fame.

JIM JACOBS (*Author/Composer*): Pat Birch was an easy yes as choreographer. I knew Pat could do *Grease* 'cause I saw what she did with the kids in *The Me Nobody Knows*. I figured if she could get these inner-city kids to do those routines, she could definitely do our show. If she wasn't familiar with the Swim, the Snake, the Grind, the Fish, the Madison, or the Continental, she would find out. Warren and I were at ease with her.

"Good Timin'": Hiring the Team

KEN WAISSMAN: With everyone agreeing to our choice of choreographer, we focused on finding the right director.

JIM JACOBS: Even before we made a decision on producers, we were searching for directors. Warren and I were never happy with the director at the Kingston Mines in Chicago. In fact, when we didn't hire him for New York, we ended up in a lawsuit.

We wanted someone—a guy with more of a street kind of thing, you know? We were meeting a lot of directors, and when we tried to talk to them about the '50s, they'd say things like "Oh, like *Blackboard Jungle?*"—stuff like that. And we'd say, "No, man, this is more like *Rebel Without a Cause.*" These guys didn't know anything about the real '50s rock 'n' roll scene. *Jeez, isn't there anyone out there who can recreate our specific '50s world?*

KEN WAISSMAN: After meetings with a number of potential directors, I suddenly remembered a young director named Tom Moore. Two years before, Maxine and I had attended a performance of *Welcome to Andromeda* that he directed at the American Place Theatre. We were knocked out by how totally real the characters were. I had to pinch myself to remember they were actors. This is what we wanted for *Grease*.

TOM MOORE (*Director*): Not long out of the Yale School of Drama, I was supporting myself with temp work as a typist at Sloan Kettering Hospital, basically telling people they should pay their bills before they died.

However, a talented young Yale playwright named Ron Whyte, with whom I had earlier collaborated, had written a new play called *Welcome to Andromeda*, and Wynn Handman, the artistic director of the American Place Theatre, offered us their theater for two showcase performances.

KEN WAISSMAN: When Maxine and I decided to form our producing partnership, we took a full-page ad in *Variety*. The headline read, CAN YOU USE TWO PRODUCERS WITH THE FOLLOWING EXPERIENCE? We proceeded to list the logos of the various shows we had worked on. The ad appeared in the April 16, 1969, edition of *Variety*. Immediately, the phone started ringing.

TOM MOORE: Bob Satuloff, a close friend of the playwright, saw an ad in *Variety* placed by producers seeking new material and immediately called Ron's agent, who quickly called the young producers.

KEN WAISSMAN: One call was from a legitimate New York agent, Ellen Neuwald. She represented a playwright named Ron Whyte. His play *Welcome to Andromeda* was being performed as a weekend showcase at the American Place Theatre.

TOM MOORE: *Welcome to Andromeda* is a two-character play about a quadriplegic who wants to kill himself and the nurse who spends the entire ninety minutes of the play trying to convince him to go on living. Throughout the play, taking place in one small room, only one of the characters moved.

KEN WAISSMAN: Watching the play, I had to keep reminding myself that these were actors. They seemed so real it was eerie. With one character confined to a hospital bed and the other the only character who could move, Moore created an energy level that kept it from being a static portrayal. I was also impressed by the amount of humor he was able to realize from the depressing premise. We met Ron and Tom after the performance and congratulated them.

TOM MOORE: We hit it off instantly and talked for quite some time, but that was that. Our two performances ended and I searched for a job, eventually ending up working with Gordon Davidson at the Mark Taper Forum in L.A.

KEN WAISSMAN: When I spoke to Ellen Neuwald the next day, I told her we enjoyed the play but didn't think we could make it work commercially; I also told her how impressed we were with Tom's work and that we looked forward to seeing him again. A few months later when I was in California, Tom and I met for lunch at the Music Center in downtown L.A. Three hours passed and we were still talking. I told Maxine later that day that I knew at some point we would work with Tom.

TOM MOORE: After my stint at the Mark Taper I went back to New York, but less than six months later, feeling discouraged with the theater and wanting to explore film, I was offered a spot in the recently established American Film Institute.

Several months later, however, as I was preparing to direct an AFI film project, I received a call from New York. The call came in to the dean's office, as there were no cell phones in those days and I had no permanent home. The young producers, who I now knew as Ken and Maxine, said they had a new project and wanted me to fly in and meet the writers, Jim Jacobs and Warren Casey.

I remember being shocked and telling my fellow students that I had just received a call out of the blue asking me if I would be interested in this very oddly named musical, *Grease*. A script was overnighted.

Based on the one-act, two-character play they had seen at American Place, with no music and a character who couldn't move, and one three-hour lunch in Los Angeles, these intrepid producers were considering me for a big, splashy, first-of-its-kind '50s rock 'n' roll musical. I was in a state of disbelief as I boarded the plane.

MAXINE FOX (*Producer*): Tom flew in from Los Angeles. First, we had him meet Jim and Warren and hear the score.

TOM MOORE: Sung mostly by Jim on his guitar, the score was kind of irresistible.

JIM JACOBS: So Ken and Maxine bring in Tom Moore—young, collegiate, very white bread, not long out of Yale—and he already rates four aces in that he was at least the right age compared to everyone else we had seen. And Tom knew the difference between *Blackboard Jungle* and *Rebel Without a Cause*. Being from the Midwest was another ace. We instinctively thought he would be really good at helping us to rewrite and shape the script, which we knew was important. He also rated an A+ in my eyes when he said, "These are the people that used to scare the crap outta me in high school."

MAXINE FOX: The next morning we arranged for Tom to meet Pat Birch. His taxi got caught in traffic coming across town from the West Side. Pat became antsy waiting. She had a meeting scheduled at the Juilliard School with John Houseman, founding director of Juilliard's drama division. You didn't keep John Houseman waiting.

Finally, Tom arrived.

TOM MOORE: I apologized to everyone for being late and said the taxi was stuck in traffic, but what really happened was that I took the bus to try to save money. In those days, I was eating on a few dollars a day.

KEN WAISSMAN: Tom and Pat sat next to each other on a couch in her living room and began talking. Maxine and I sat silently across the room. Within moments, the two hit it off and were animatedly talking about the show's possibilities. Somehow, Pat's urgency about leaving to meet Houseman vanished. It was as if they had known each other for years.

TOM MOORE: Within minutes Pat and I made an extraordinary connection. A perfect match.

KEN WAISSMAN: Next we took Tom to Joe Allen Restaurant in the theater district to have lunch with Jim and Warren.

TOM MOORE: We talked for some time and I liked them both, but I had no idea how they felt about me. I complimented them greatly on the music and gave my honest critique on the script, which I thought needed a lot of work and restructuring.

KEN WAISSMAN: After the meeting, Maxine and I drove Tom to the airport for his flight back to Los Angeles. In the car, Tom expressed very positive, enthusiastic feelings about Pat Birch, saying he'd love to work with her. However, he had big doubts that he was the right director for *Grease*. He wasn't attracted to the 1950s and hadn't connected with the greaser kids when he was in high school. He found the characters in *Grease* unlikable. I told him he'd make them appealing through his work with the authors on the book, his casting, and his direction. I asked him to reread the script draft on the plane.

TOM MOORE: I got on the plane and the doors closed. I looked at the script and started to read it again, this time clearly realizing its possibilities. And I began to panic. *What have I done? I've turned down my chance at a New York production. This could be one of the greatest mistakes of my life.* Mildly hyperbolic, as I was only twenty-seven. My mind churned for the whole six and a half hours of the flight. When the doors opened and we finally disembarked, I ran to the nearest pay phone, reached Ken, and said, "I've reread the script, already have ideas, and if you and the guys are still interested, I would very much like to be considered as your director."

KEN WAISSMAN: "I hope I didn't talk you out of hiring me," he said.

MAXINE FOX: Unfortunately, we had another hurdle to overcome.

JIM JACOBS: Warren had some concerns about Tom after our first meeting. He joked, "Maybe Tom should play Eugene."

KEN WAISSMAN: We brought Tom back to New York for another meeting with Jim and Warren, and asked him to focus on Warren.

JIM JACOBS: At the second meeting, our confidence in Tom grew. He definitely wasn't a "street director," but those guys that were really into guerrilla street theater in Chicago, they weren't right either; and they were usually fucked up on drugs and yuppie bullshit. And I reminded Warren that taking on two wealthy Jewish kids from suburban Baltimore to be our producers hadn't hit us as exactly quite the right thing either, you know.

"Well, Warren, do you want to keep looking or should we say yes and just get the fuckin' show on?" The positives definitely seemed to outweigh the negatives, and we had been fartin' around with it for a long time. So we said yes, and it turned out great. A really good collaboration.

KEN WAISSMAN: We had our director.

TOM MOORE: Extraordinary luck and serendipity. *Grease* would change my life forever.

Tom Moore.

"Be-Bop-a-Lula"

KEN WAISSMAN: To complete the creative team, we needed to find a music director. The first candidate was well known for accompanying Bette Midler at the Continental Baths. A very talented, nice enough guy, but my gut feeling told me he wasn't right for us. His name was Barry Manilow.

Next a larger-than-life guy burst into our office with a huge laugh that bounced off the walls. His name was Louis St. Louis. After fifteen minutes of knowledgeable talk about '50s rock 'n' roll and greasers, Maxine and I knew he was the right one.

We took him over to meet Tom Moore and Pat Birch, who were preparing for another round of auditions at the old Helen Hayes Theatre. The three hit it off immediately.

JIM JACOBS: In walks Louis St. Louis. Came from Detroit. A gay Italian guy who thinks he's Black and knows everything there is about pop music. You couldn't get anything past him—one reference from the ghetto and he knew what it was immediately. How could anyone have been any more perfect than Louis St. Louis? He was tops.

3 | *Finding a Theater*

KEN WAISSMAN (*Producer*): My producing partner Maxine Fox and I believed the initial New York audience for *Grease* would be people in their late twenties and early thirties who would have been in high school in the late 1950s and early 1960s. However, in 1971 Broadway catered to a much older generation. Opening directly on Broadway felt too risky.

With a cast of sixteen, *Grease* was too big to work economically in any of the off-Broadway 199-, 299-, or 499-seat theaters. We were in a bind. Then I remembered the Eden Theatre on the corner of East Twelfth Street and Second Avenue, where *Once Upon a Mattress*, starring Carol Burnett, and *Man of La Mancha* played before they moved uptown to Broadway proper. Maxine and I met with the owner, pitched *Grease*, and handed him a check for the theater deposit.

Even though the Eden was a Broadway-size theater, it was classified as off-Broadway. Using off-Broadway rates, we put together a production budget of $110,000, about 20 percent of the cost of an uptown musical back then. We raised the capitalization in two months.

The Eden

DOUG SCHMIDT (*Set Designer*): I had been sent to look at a future home for a raucous little new off-Broadway musical we were starting to work on called *Grease*, scheduled to open on Valentine's Day a scant eight weeks hence. So on a sunny but stunningly bitter cold and windy day in mid-December 1971, my assistant Paul Zalon and I alighted a cab at Twelfth

Street and Second Avenue in front of the raffish and decidedly shabby Eden Theatre near Union Square.

I knew that the theater had been the original home of the notorious nude revue *Oh! Calcutta!*, but other than that I knew nothing of the Eden's storied past. Shivering as we pounded on the stage door, that ignorance was soon to be dramatically informed.

After what seemed like an eternity huddled in the blinding arctic wind, we heard a bolt being drawn. The heavy door slowly opened and we were met by Abe, the stage doorman and custodian. The wizened, stooped gentleman ushered us onto the stage, lit only by the ghost light that did nothing to illuminate anything beyond the footlights. Wordlessly, he disappeared for a moment. Suddenly the cold dark maw beyond the proscenium flickered to life as the houselights came on, revealing a vast auditorium and full balcony aglow with the warm reflection of faded gold leaf and painted woodwork. I don't know what I expected, but it certainly was not to find a full Broadway-style theater with 1,100 seats, seemingly untouched by time.

My involuntary reaction was to gasp and ask, "When was this place built?"

"Nineteen twenty-six," came an immediate response in a profoundly thick Middle European accent. Sensing eager ears, he launched into an oral history of the Yiddish Art Theatre movement in the early 1900s through its demise in the late '40s. He said he had been the stage doorman since shortly after the theater opened in 1927 in what was then known as the Yiddish Rialto. The theater was purpose-built for Maurice Schwartz, a charismatic actor and manager who ran his own company, the Yiddish Art Theatre Company. Productions in this venue over the years and under different managements ranged from the sacred to the profane, from *The Ten Commandments* to *This Was Burlesque*. *Grease* fit neatly into that last category.

As the wind pummeled every door and window in the place, our interlocutor confided that, in fact, Maurice Schwartz's spirit still roamed the old building, and he and others had felt his presence or actually encountered him on several occasions. "But he only appears if the show is going to be a success." With that, a huge blast of wind caught a loose flap of one of the hinged smoke vents high above the stage, slamming it open as a shaft of blindingly bright sunlight stabbed through the fly loft's dust-filled air, pinning the three of us in a pool of light something like a celestial super trooper. "Ah! The ghost of

Schwartz!" he mused. "Looks like you fellows are going to have a big hit." And though far from obvious at the time, the rest, as they say, is history.

TOM MOORE (*Director*): We were exceptionally fortunate in our designers: Doug Schmidt (set), Carrie Robbins (costumes), and Karl Eigsti (lighting). Ken and Maxine brought us all together, and it was the perfect combo, leading not only to a great collaboration on *Grease* but also to an extraordinary number of collaborations with each of us since. They never disappoint.

Doug Schmidt (set designer) and Carrie Robbins (costume designer).

4 | *Burger Palace Boys and Pink Ladies*

JIM JACOBS (*Author/Composer*): As an actor, I had been in a lot of shows in Chicago over eight years, but none of my greaser friends ever came to see me in any of them. So I decided the best way to get them to see something of my "new world" was to write a show about them. And I was right: they came, they saw it, and they loved it. And of course their first question was, *Which one am I?*

The characters in *Grease* are based on real people and named after guys I knew, but they are never one and the same.

The Pink Ladies were another story. The real-life Pink Ladies were a genuine girl gang at my high school for about six or seven years (roughly 1954 to 1962). All their character names are totally our creation.

"Don't Be Cruel"

TOM MOORE (*Director*): Any good director will tell you that casting is at least seventy to ninety percent of a director's work. No matter how exceptional the material or exciting the concept, without a brilliant group of actors to present it, the effort will be mediocre at best. Even at twenty-seven, I knew that the success of this project would very much depend on those sixteen actors.

Maxine acted as the casting director and set up the auditions. I think we had one assistant, who would bring the actors into the room and read with them. The casting would be done by myself, the choreographer, the music director, the producers, and of course, the authors. I sought consensus, as everyone in that room wanted a successful show and each had different needs the actors had to fulfill. Sometimes it took several auditions, but eventually each actor was universally approved. Unlike many musicals, we were looking for actors first, then singers, then dancers.

Here's how it went. The actor came into the room, having been told to bring two monologues: one serious and one comic. (I'm embarrassed to say, having just gotten out of Yale, I may have even asked for a classic scene!) We didn't yet have a completed script, so they couldn't read from that. They would then sing two songs: one ballad and one upbeat number. If they made it through the first two requirements, they were asked to come back later that day for a dance audition. It was an exhausting day for the actors, but an exhilarating day for all of us, as *Grease* would momentarily and in bits and pieces come to life.

Having survived the day, the actors approached the dance auditions with fear and dread, but fortunately the choreography was in the brilliant hands and mind of Pat Birch. Pat could find a way to make anyone dance, since she worked from character and what that particular actor brought to the table, or the dance floor as the case may be. Pat and I would then confer about who we were most interested in, and off she went. I loved that part. I could just sit back and watch.

While watching those dance auditions, a director is given a chance to observe the actors and see how they work, how they respond to changes, and maybe most importantly whether they can keep a sense of humor during a grueling process.

The auditions went on for close to a month. We were nothing if not thorough. And by the end, we had made a company. A company of wonderful actors, singers, and "kind-of dancers" who would create those iconic characters. It is these actors' performances that have inspired and been imitated, not only in our original touring productions but also in thousands of productions worldwide.

MAXINE FOX (*Producer*): We auditioned two thousand actors in order to find the sixteen that would make up the original *Grease* cast.

JIM JACOBS: Auditions were endless. Like a machine, they just kept coming in. All of us were lined up, seated behind a long table in a rehearsal room on Broadway and Fifty-Third, above a car dealer's showroom.

I particularly felt sorry for the Chicago production kids who came in wanting to be in the show but were very clearly out of their league. It was sad. We had been watching people who have been in shows in New York who have great chops and can really sing, and then comes someone who's hitting a lot of clams, as they say, totally ill prepared for a professional show. Their reaction was the usual thing of, *Well, I created this role so how come I can't do it in New York?*

In the end, only two of the cast from our Kingston Mines production made it into the Broadway production. Jim Canning as Doody at the Eden and later Marilu Henner as Marty in the first national tour.

"Get a Job": The Auditions

DAN DEITCH (*Understudy*): On a sunny day in the fall of 1971, I am walking down a West Village sidewalk reciting Shakespeare to myself. "Thou, nature, art my goddess." After a year at the London Academy of Dramatic Arts trying to upstage John Lithgow, I'm thinking that I could handle anything.

"Hey, Dan, wake up and stop talking to yourself," someone yells behind me. It's Laurie Heineman, a friend from college. "We're heading to an open call across town. Everyone's going."

"What's it for?"

"A new '50s musical about greasers."

In high school I lived in deathly fear of those sleazy guys with the ducktail hair, drooping cigarettes, and pegged pants, like head greaser Mike Carbone.

"I loathe greasers. That's the last thing I'd audition for. I'm into legit theater, Laurie."

"OK, see you around," says she, taking off.

Then I think that Laurie is very cute and why not. Goodbye, Hamlet. Hello, Elvis.

BARRY BOSTWICK (*Zuko*): Given my recent past, I was ready for this '50s musical that seemed to hold promise. I had already been in two rock groups—I hesitate to call them bands. One of them, the Knowns, was a pop group put together like the Monkees, and we had one song, called "Lady Love," which hit the charts at thirty-eight with a bullet. Unfortunately the bullet was already going down. I was then part of a hippie-like group called the First National Nothing—which lived up to its name.

I tuned my guitar and learned "Be-Bop-a-Lula" as my audition song. Gene Vincent was the image of the street kid with the rockabilly sound that I wanted to capture. So I showed up at the audition as a cross between Gene Vincent,

Elvis Presley, and the overconfident, very cocky young actor that I was at the time.

I guess it worked because I got a callback.

KATHI MOSS (*Cha-Cha*): Tim Meyers, my dearest buddy from grad school, and my friends Jan and Taylor were also auditioning. Somehow we convinced the powers that be to let us audition as a group, giving us ten minutes rather than the two and a half we'd have had solo. The four of us came out and introduced ourselves à la the Mouseketeer roll call—"Hi, I'm Kathi" (Tim announced himself as "Annette")—and we sang "Jingle Bell Rock" together. My solo was Brenda Lee's "Rockin' Around the Christmas Tree." All this seasonal stuff was appropriate and, we thought, pretty clever because the auditions took place just before the holidays. We thought we did well enough, maybe better than that, but of course the smiling group in the front of the room didn't give much sign of anything.

KATIE HANLEY (*Marty*): The day of my first audition I was led into a small room with a long table of young, welcoming faces. A handsome, smiling guy, Tom Moore, introduced himself as the director and asked me to do a quick improvisation of a teen from the '50s. Immediately *American Bandstand* came to mind and I pretended to be on the show, and as Dick Clark held a microphone up to me, I looked at him, then turned my eyes to the camera and, just as I had seen so many times on TV, said, "Yeah, uh, I'd give that song a ten 'cuz I can dance to it." Everyone behind the table smiled, and I left the audition feeling affirmed by their enthusiasm and genuine kindness.

DAN DEITCH: What seems like a thousand aspirants are jammed into the open-call audition mandated by Equity [the Actors' Equity Association] to give all actors a shot, especially those sad ones without agents, like me. After waiting for hours, it's finally my turn.

I size up the jury. *Would Mike Carbone, the king of the greasers at my high school, even be fazed by this crew?* There was a Laurel and Hardy pair who seemed to be the writers (Warren Casey and Jim Jacobs). One had friendly eyes. The other looked a little like a crazed Medusa who had a run-in with a train. Comic relief came in the form of a long-haired guy, probably a musician, with an alliterative name involving one of the French King Louises (Louis St. Louis), and a gamine-like figure who was unquestionably the choreographer (Pat Birch). Last was a simpatico, snowball-in-hell fellow in charge (Tom Moore) to whom I thought I could relate.

"Why don't you sing something for us, Dan?" chirps the cheery leader-boy in charge.

What I sang and said have evaporated in the winds of time; I do remember telling them that I performed many diverse characters in plays from Sophocles to Congreve to Albee. Not surprisingly I'm out in five minutes.

WALTER BOBBIE (*Roger*): I sang "Sixteen Candles," the 1958 hit by the Crests featuring Johnny Maestro. I added some corny moves illustrating the number sixteen as a doo-wop visual. It killed. My baby-faced innocence, overwrought longing, and absurd choreography was funny.

ILENE KRISTEN (*Patty*): About three days before my audition for *Grease* I was called in for a replacement in *Godspell.* "Pick a parable," my agent had said. "A what?" My religious training consisted of lox and a bialy on Sundays. At the *Godspell* audition, the actor auditioning before me was so completely and scarily committed to his parable that a wee small voice in my head intoned, *Prepare ye the way of the Lord, get the hell out of here and work on your* Grease *audition.*

With that message from on high, how could I go wrong? I split, got home, and cobbled together a monologue and picked my song, "My Boy Lollipop."

The only snag in my audition preparation was my very successful but insecure boyfriend. The attention the world was now bestowing upon me was way too much for him, and somehow his fist collided with my face that night. The morning of the *Grease* audition my right eye was swollen, more than slightly black, and a not-so-lovely shade of purple. I could have hidden it with my hair but was sure a high ponytail was the key to a callback. My outfit was a cardigan sweater with pearl buttons turned backward (a '50s teen fad) and a pleated skirt.

I checked my eye, took a deep breath, and walked into the tiny audition space. I was greeted by smiling faces. The vibe was good. I broke into my monologue, so relaxed that I improvised most of it, giving it more of a '50s spin. They liked it! As for the black eye, in true '50s fashion I said, "I walked into a door."

Of course I didn't know at the time, but in the last scene of *Grease* Sandy slaps Patty and she tearfully wails, "*Oh my God, I think I'm going to get a black eye!*"

ADRIENNE BARBEAU (*Rizzo*): I discovered rock 'n' roll in 1957 and went from Johnny Mathis and Harry Belafonte to the Drifters, the Platters, and the Shirelles overnight. So when this young, blond, very Ivy League guy asked me my favorite groups from the '60s, I peppered him with Johnnie & Joe, Mickey & Sylvia, the Diamonds, the Ronettes; the list went on and on. We were sitting on the carpeted stairs of a theater and Tom Moore was asking me questions. Sort of a preaudition audition.

Years later, Tom told me he didn't know much about the groups singing '50s rock 'n' roll; he was just trying to get a sense of whether or not the actors he was interviewing were telling the truth.

ALAN PAUL (*Teen Angel / Johnny Casino*): At the time of my *Grease* audition I was in a deep slump because I felt my career was going nowhere. I had recently auditioned for *Jesus Christ Superstar*, soon opening on Broadway, and after *thirteen* callbacks I got nothing. I was very discouraged and thought about leaving the business. Then out of the blue I got a call from my manager telling me she had just arranged an audition for this new show called *Grease*. With *Zorba the Greek* having been a big hit a decade earlier, I thought the show was about Greece, the country. My agent quickly added that it was some kind of 1950s rock musical.

I sang "Only You" by the Platters, and after singing the song one time through, I thought I'd take a gamble and flirt a little with producer Maxine Fox. I walked over to the table and proceeded to speak the lyrics directly to her before my big finish. I got a smile from her and I thought I gave a good audition, but given my present state of mind, I didn't expect to hear anything back. In fact, after my experience with *Superstar* I didn't have any expectations at all.

MARYA SMALL (*Frenchy*): Ken Waissman and Maxine Fox, the producers of *Grease*, came way, way, way downtown to the Theater of the Lost Continent, where I was doing a play called *Boy on the Straight Back Chair*. They told me they were doing a new musical show about the '50s and I should come and audition. *Wow.* I thanked them with a big smile and said, "I'll be there. Thank you." Thinking to myself, *The '50s, yuck, the worst period of my life.*

My first audition was in the lounge of the Eden Theatre, where the creative team started laughing before they even saw me as I came down the stairs. They had heard me, and I guess I have a pretty unique voice. I got a callback.

KATHI MOSS: So I went home to New Orleans for Christmas, and it seems I *did* do well enough. My agent called me with a callback. Tim and Jan got one too. We abandoned our New Year's plans and hustled back to the city, where we were put through the reading/singing/dancing paces in multiple callbacks on multiple days. It's kind of a blur, actually, and at the end of each callback we still couldn't tell what those smiling people thought and if this was going to pay off.

MARYA SMALL: At the callbacks, a line of actors stretched around the block—dozens of actors of all types, all dressed in some semblance of '50s attire. Finally I got to the front of the line and stepped into the theater backstage, where I watched the other actors' auditions from the wings, a thrill. *Oh, my God!* They were really putting the actors through it and they were all good.

DAN DEITCH: After that ominously brief first audition, it's a bit of a blur, but I got the callback in California, where I had gone home for Christmas.

I go in, try to appear coordinated for the all-seeing eyes of Pat Birch, sweetly serenade Louis St. Louis, and do my best to reincarnate the greasers from Burlingame High.

CAROLE DEMAS (*Sandy*): After multiple callbacks, when would they decide? The music director, Louis St. Louis, privately asked me to "sing in my chest voice." He moved me vocally over three octaves of scales from basement to coloratura way above high C. Was he trying to help me get this part or trying to eliminate me?

MARYA SMALL: I stepped out on the big, gorgeous stage and my accompanist went straight to the piano with my music, Cole Porter's "In the Still of the Night," which I had mistakenly thought was the Five Satins' "In the Still of the Night" from the '50s. Undaunted, my accompanist played Cole Porter's 1937 song '50s style. I announced my name and then sang my heart out. When I finished, I thought I heard a few laughs, and I was asked to stay. *Whew!* I then had to read for most of the girls' parts. Cold reading is not too good for me either.

JIM CANNING (*Doody*): Jim Jacobs called me in Chicago. "Canning. They've got choices to cast the show, but they haven't found a Doody they like. Why'n'cha fly out and sing for 'em? It would be a gas!" So I went to New York and booked a room at the Hotel Beacon using about the last of my meager savings.

I was as green as a field in midsummer, salad behind each ear. I had never even auditioned in any formal way for anything other than the haphazard trolley-barn tryouts for the original show in Chicago the previous year. And yet here I was, on a Broadway stage of a darkened theater in the dead of winter. I was twenty-three years old.

I was green, but I had one ace: Warren Casey had sat me down at a crappy upright piano in the Kingston Mines Theatre basement during rehearsals the previous year and tapped out the chords for a new song he was working on, "Rock Progression" (later to become "Those Magic Changes" in New York), testing me to see how high I could sing and how much falsetto he could add. So the song was right in my range. And I knew it!

ILENE KRISTEN: I was told that the final callback would be an all-day affair. And it definitely was. I remember Mickey Leonard, the music orchestrator and supervisor, smiling at me after I did the song "Lipstick on Your Collar" and being bedazzled by Katie Hanley's velvet voice and mesmerized by Barry Bostwick's easy swagger and leather pants.

KATIE HANLEY: My friend Randee Heller and I had both made it through to this last audition. After our songs and readings we were thanked and asked to come back in the afternoon; I grabbed Randee and yanked her behind the curtain. I said, "OK, let's hide here until we hear someone read better than we did." After we heard several good auditions, Garn Stephens reading Jan really kicked it out of the park. Hearing her, I elbowed Randee, whispering, "OK, she won, let's get outta here and grab lunch at the deli."

ILENE KRISTEN: On the lunch break I went to the closest coffee shop, and Mickey Leonard came in. I could not live with myself if I did not tell him that his song "Why Did I Choose You?" from *The Yearling* was magnificent. He smiled and said he probably shouldn't tell me, but he was pretty sure I would be playing Patty. I went back to the audition glowing. I was going to get this.

JIM CANNING: Unlike everyone else there, my first audition and final callback were on the same day. I had to do a scene with the guys, the Burger Palace Boys, who had already been through several callbacks. The scene was Kenickie coming in with this beat-up jalopy Greased Lightning and the guys making fun of him and his crappy car. I was playing Doody, who was the odd kid out in the gang, the likable, loopy innocent who is always a step behind.

There's this line that Doody says while the guys are all mocking Kenickie: "Hey, Kenickie, neat dice!" These other actors, they all sort of took a beat as if to say, *Who the fuck is this kid from Chicago?*

And there was this audible laugh that came out of the darkness of the theater. I mean, it wasn't just like Jacobs laughed because he knew me and wanted me to get the part. No, it was a real laugh. Whoever was out there making their judgments and writing their notes, they're watching this scene that they have seen over and over and then this kid they don't know says a line that's not even a joke line or a punch line, and they all laugh. It was like a short chuckle that translated into language that seemed to say, *I think we may have found our Doody!*

ILENE KRISTEN: The main event of the day was being partnered up and dancing, because now Pat Birch was front and center. Tom Harris (Eugene), my partner, was at least a foot taller than me, so the funny factor flourished. I quietly commanded him to lift me high in the air and then slide me under his legs even though he was scared to death. I assured him, "I'm not going to break. Just do it. *Do it!*" And he did. Pat liked it. Pat didn't push her dance agenda so much as watch what you brought to the party and encourage your individuality.

MARYA SMALL: *Uh-oh, my turn for the dance auditions. Eek!* I was not a very good dancer. In fact, I flunked ballet. I had a lot of trouble getting all the steps and combinations right. Thank God for Pat Birch, who helped me turn my basic jumping up and down into dance.

When I first came to New York City, Pat was a bright star on Broadway, playing Anybodys in *West Side Story*. That was the first Broadway show I ever saw. Pat was incredible, thrilling, so good. Now she was helping me dance. *Wow, great!*

KATIE HANLEY: As the choreographer had shown us, the man I had just been partnered with was to lift me above his head during the jitterbug, then slide me down on the floor between his legs and quickly pull me back up again. When he lifted me up for the first time, he grimaced and let out a muffled groan, which fortunately only I could hear. Shaking his red face after we finished the dance, he looked at me as if he'd been forced to pick up a large farm animal.

WALTER BOBBIE: The final callback for the original cast of *Grease* was a daylong affair with what felt like hundreds of finalists being mixed and matched. Because it was impossible to clear the theater, we all watched each other's auditions with a spirit of collegial support and fierce competition.

Once more I did my now even more choreographed version of "Sixteen Candles," and once more it killed!

In some ways the group reactions to our individual auditions may have helped define who got cut as the day went on. We were each there to win the part, but winning over the crowd became part of how to win the game. Most of us were not trained dancers with Broadway technique. The choreography included specific steps that we were encouraged to "make your own," in Pat Birch's signature improvisational approach.

I recall a mob improv of the Stroll, a '50s dance where couples form a human corridor down which each couple sashays, exhibiting their personal styles: romantic, sexy, convulsive, slinky, comic, and sometimes pathetic. More personality is exposed in the Stroll than in a deep-dive psychological profile at a rehab. Showing off and humiliating yourself are offered equal opportunity.

Suffice to say I love the Stroll because I delight in both those options. Like most determined Broadway aspirants—this was all about me. The Stroll separated who wanted the job from those who would actually get the job.

CAROLE DEMAS: Down to the wire. Nervous? Very. I wanted this part.

Barry Bostwick and I were friends. What was called, years later, "friends with benefits." The choreographer, Pat Birch, put us together for a slow dance. Barry is a soaring six four. I was a tad over five three. Ever inventive, Barry whispered in my ear, "Stand on my feet and put your hands up around my neck." I gazed up into his amazing blue eyes and I'm guessing we were a very good picture! A mesmerizing moment for helplessly smitten me.

BARRY BOSTWICK: And now here I was onstage lined up with all these other poor desperate actors who were just hoping to not have to go to unemployment that week to pay the rent. We all stood on the stage while Tom and Pat tried putting every possible combination of Zuko and Sandy together. We all tried desperately to be enthusiastic (and to show it) for our immediate competition. Because there were so many of us, we were all in the theater at the same time. The cruelty of the process was unnerving.

But this is where the cocky and self-confident side of the young actor Barry Bostwick had to kick in. I'm sure there were other actors on that stage just as good as me, and maybe even better for the part, but I think I secured my fate during the drive-in movie scene. That's when, after multiple tries to get the ring off my finger to give to Sandy, I stopped, thought, and then rubbed my hand through my greasy hair, causing the ring to slip off easily while my elbow accidentally hit Sandy in the boob—well, I think in the boob—but that could have been a bit I added later. Whatever I did, I got a huge laugh. We left that day still not knowing who would be cast.

WALTER BOBBIE: That daylong *Grease* audition in late 1971 remains one of the most joyful, playful days of my theater life. So you can imagine my surprise, dismay, confusion, perhaps anger, when later that evening I was asked to come back for a fourth audition.

I asked the assistant with whom I signed in if I could speak to the director. A stage manager then came out of the audition room and asked what the problem was. I reiterated that I needed to speak to the director before I went in to my third callback, fourth audition. Where did I summon the nerve?

Tom Moore, bless him, actually came out of the audition room to speak to me. I briefly communicated that I didn't know what he/they were looking for; I didn't know what else I could do. Moore said the part was written for a fat guy, hence the character's nicknames Rump and Lard Ass, and that's what the guys were looking for. Tom asked if I would wear a fat suit. I said I would not. I said that fat didn't make the character of Roger funnier or more interesting, or make him sing any better. Nor did it give him a personality! I was unpersuadable and he knew it.

Tom Moore said, *OK, everyone likes you, so just come in and do what you've been doing.* Under the harsh fluorescent lights of a drab rehearsal studio, I delivered just what I had been doing, including "Sixteen Candles." I was not at all nervous. Most importantly, I was no longer confused.

Everyone watching seemed engaged and entertained, and Tom, bless him again, understood what casting me meant to both of us. Lard Ass would sing "Mooning" with a smaller ass.

ADRIENNE BARBEAU: I almost didn't get the job. Maxine Fox tells me they called me back to sing for them three times. And each time, I wore the same outfit—pedal pushers and a sweater. Maxine thought it was so I'd leave an indelible impression of me as a greaser. I suspect it was the only thing in my wardrobe that wasn't a wool dress with a wide belt and high-heeled knee-high boots. I really don't remember. What I do remember is leaving town right after my audition. My boyfriend and I flew to L.A. to spend the Christmas holidays with his family.

A few days after we'd arrived, I got a call from the producers asking if I could come back in and sing for them a final time.

Well, no, I couldn't. I was 2,800 miles away. I didn't want to leave my boyfriend at Christmas. And I couldn't afford to buy a new plane ticket. Watching my fledgling career go down the drain, I apologized and told them I wouldn't be coming in for a callback.

The day after Christmas, they called again. If they could wait to see me until New Year's Eve day, would I be able to fly back and audition then?

Well, Adrienne, I thought to myself, *if you don't want to be unemployed for the rest of your life, you'd better get on a plane and get back there.*

JOY RINALDI (*Understudy*): I was staying with my grandpa in Mount Gretna, Pennsylvania. When I came home to my apartment in New York City, my answering machine told me I had missed my final callback and to please come in immediately!

There was not a single soul in the waiting room when I arrived. It seems my final callback was just me. When I got into the audition room, they asked me to read Marty. I was then thanked and sent back to the waiting room. When I returned they asked me to read for Sandy . . . Rizzo . . . and Patty! I couldn't figure out why they were asking me to read *all* of those roles. Did they have no idea what they were looking for? But whatever they were doing, I definitely thought they were interested.

WALTER BOBBIE: I left after that *extra* audition thinking that if I don't get this job, there is no God. Later that day I was delighted to learn that God exists.

CAROLE DEMAS: Not your usual audition. Sweaty palms, hard to breathe—the whole thing. But I got it!

JIM CANNING: That night of the final auditions, the producer Maxine Fox called me at the Hotel Beacon. I got the part.

DAN DEITCH: Against all odds, I'm cast as the understudy for the male roles in *Grease*. This was great news for me but very bad news for my Hungarian, very conservative mother, who was highly suspicious of men without ties, not to mention with makeup. When I tried to assuage her with my good fortune that as an actor I could deduct everything, she said, "Deduct from vat?"

JOY RINALDI: I was in the apartment of my then boyfriend and said boyfriend casually handed me the phone: "It's for you." Whoever it was on the phone said, "Joy, we want you for the most important job of the entire cast." My instincts immediately told me that was a weird introduction. "We want you to understudy *all* eight female roles! Congratulations!"

The rest of the conversation was a blur because all I could think was, *OMG, can I do it? Am I even capable of learning eight roles at once? No, I don't think so.* And I started to say . . .

But what I said in that moment of disbelief was "Oh, thank you! Thank you so much. I am so excited! So, so happy!"

MARYA SMALL: Somehow I managed not to get 86'd, and I hooked the role of Frenchy.

ALAN PAUL: That night, to my amazement, my manager called and said that the *Grease* people wanted me for the dual roles of Johnny Casino and Teen Angel. Teen Angel has one of the great songs of the show—"Beauty School Dropout."

I thought I heard her wrong. "No callbacks?" She replied, "No callbacks, you got the job!" It had miraculously all happened in one day. Things were looking up.

KATHI MOSS: I was cast in the role of Cha-Cha DiGregorio. She was a troll character, a bit of a joke, and I didn't really have a song, but, come on—my first New York audition and I had my first job! Tim did even better, snagging the prominent role of Kenickie and one of the great songs of the show, "Greased Lightnin'." I was twenty-six years old, doing my first Broadway show from my first legit audition. Who in their right mind could complain about that?

ADRIENNE BARBEAU: Reluctantly, I left my boyfriend, left the upcoming New Year's Eve celebration, and flew back to JFK on a red-eye on December 30. Auditioned for Rizzo the next morning at eleven o'clock. They offered me the job that afternoon at four. It was New Year's Eve, 1971.

We started rehearsals two days later, and my life changed forever. Actually, I think all our lives changed forever, and how glorious is that!

5

"Whole Lotta Shakin' Goin' On"

Rehearsals

TOM MOORE (*Director*): After a few months working with the authors and honing the script at night while auditioning what seemed like every actor between eighteen and thirty in the city of New York, we were finally in rehearsals. They took place at the old Hotel Hudson on Seventy-Second Street, just off the Hudson River. The place had fallen on hard times, but the ballroom was large, cheap, and surprisingly warm and inviting. Good things could happen here.

WALTER BOBBIE (*Roger*): The first day of rehearsal was unsettling. The producers booked the top-floor ballroom of the derelict Level Club, and it was raining hard that day. The stage manager placed a bucket in the center of the room to collect the *drip drip drip* from the leaking roof.

After the meet and greet (shorthand for *Who the fuck are all these people?*), we read the script with the zest and abandon preapproved in our auditions. The cast was a natural fit, a spontaneous combustion of innocent swagger and hormonal awakening amped up by rock 'n' roll. Except for the guy playing Sonny, who looked just like you wanted Sonny to look. A hunk who made standing still look like sex. But he couldn't act. Not a lick. In truth, it was a heartbreaking moment. It had been a misfortune to cast him, and everyone could feel it. Rolling eyeballs made the *plop plop* of the leaking roof now seem charming.

By midafternoon it was clear the poor guy would be replaced (and, damn, it wasn't his fault). Tom Moore pulled me aside to ask if I knew anyone right for the role, as they would be auditioning immediately after rehearsal. I don't

Walter Bobbie (Roger), Jim Borrelli (Sonny), and James Canning (Doody).

think Tom wanted my opinion as much as he wanted us to know this was being handled immediately.

The next morning Jim Borrelli, who had never been within spitting distance of a musical, joined the cast as Sonny. Borrelli took one withering look at us guys and delivered his own master class in eye-rolling. Game on.

DAN DEITCH (*Understudy*): The cast was a friendly-looking group. However, from my extensive experience with fear at a very tough high school packed with sleazy, scary, greasy characters of every stripe, they didn't seem like real greasers. More like greaser victims. Like myself.

Greaser extraordinaire Mike Carbone from my high school had the heroic Sicilian aura of Michelangelo's *David.*

Watching Barry Bostwick as the alpha Danny Zuko, I couldn't help but notice something familiar.

"Where you from, Barry?"

"San Mateo, California."

"No kidding. I went to Burlingame High School next door."

Original cast, "We Go Together."

I didn't ask Barry if he knew Mike Carbone since it was obvious that he, like everyone else for miles around, had absorbed his well-known swagger and related mannerisms.

Seeing Barry play Danny Zuko, anyone from Burlingame High School would immediately recognize Carbone the Great. But they would also recognize that Carbone might no longer be king.

CAROLE DEMAS (*Sandy*): I'd had my Equity card for nine years and worked a lot, but that first day of rehearsal never gets easier. Kinda like the first day of school. New people. Everybody wanting to measure up. I brought my first-day curiosity, fear, and anticipation, and the showbiz scars so many of us have.

This time I would be playing the high school self I had actually been from 1953 to 1957. Maybe it would be more fun this time than it actually had been!

The chemistry, that potion we brewed, was there with the first read-through. Around me colorful, brash characters charismatically took the stage. I was in good company, my work cut out for me.

ILENE KRISTEN (*Patty*): After the first read-through I did not like my character, Patty, at all. I desperately wanted to be one of the Pink Ladies and not this ponytailed brat. I wanted to rehearse with a cigarette and bubble gum, not

Ilene Kristen (Patty), Barry Bostwick (Zuko), and Adrienne Barbeau (Rizzo).

pom-poms and a baton. I was so overly concerned that my fellow actors would think I was this Goody Two-Shoes that I could barely find my footing. *How do I play teacher's pet, be totally obnoxious, and yet be lovable and sexy?* I felt lost.

I know Tom thought that because I was the youngest member of the cast and rather hippie-ish, I didn't understand the '50s. Did I dare tell him that at eight years old I was well versed in all the risqué parts of *Rally Round the Flag, Boys!* and pored over the *True Confessions* that our cleaning lady hid in a secret drawer? Or that I never missed an *American Bandstand* and I could dance the Slop? Or should I have just told him I didn't want to play Patty?

JOY RINALDI (*Understudy*): There was no time for the understudies! With only three weeks of rehearsal before previews, I was completely on my own, madly taking notes with my eight colored pencils—one color assigned to each of the eight characters I was understudying—for blocking, choreography, harmonies, everything. Without my notes and those faithful colored pencils, I would have been lost. I wasn't nervous. I wasn't even questioning myself. I had much too much work to do.

OMG it was an exciting three weeks! I was in the company of enormous talent, crazy humor, and big personalities. With all the different things that were tried (and some of them failed), we would all be laughing until we cried.

Every time there was some new choreography, blocking, harmony, or character tics, out came the colored pencils and I'd make the changes immediately in my notes—even though it might all be changed again at the next rehearsal! As the *one* understudy covering all eight female roles, the task was massive. But I was young, excited, and didn't know any better . . . so I just did it. Everyone worked their butts off—but I worked *eight butts off!*

CAROLE DEMAS: The only person I knew was my friend Barry. We were close, but not "exclusive." Just recently, at the last audition, we had danced together, romantic, familiar, eyes meeting. I walked into the first rehearsal, said hello, and he looked at me as if he'd never seen me before in his life. It was tough and very high school. But I used it, as actors do. Damn! I knew how Sandy felt. I would make her shine.

ILENE KRISTEN: It was hard for me to conjure up this silly cheerleader Patty on demand. I had never even met one. Patty had to say things like "Goodness gracious!"—an expletive that no one ever uttered in the wilds of Brooklyn.

But Tom persevered. With his gentle guidance I slowly learned to start liking Patty and see the world through her eyes, and not the eyes of the cool

Ilene Kristen and Barry Bostwick.

kids who might not like her. She loved herself, and I had to learn to love her as well.

I did not want to make Patty sickening sweet or overly conniving but delightfully devious, and alluring enough to get Danny's attention. Barry Bostwick and I started spending lunchtimes together—and somewhat more. I have to thank him for unknowingly helping me find my way and feel like the popular cheerleader who ultimately got what she set her sights on. Once I got off book and the words got out of my self-conscious brain and down into my body, I finally stopped judging and started having a lot of fun—lots and lots of fun!

CAROLE DEMAS: Barry was perfection in the role, constantly coming up with new angles. Onstage with him, I was determined to hold my own. Sandy could just be a sweet little plot device, but I wanted her to have strength, charm, and just-budding sexuality under the genuine innocence. Something about Sandy disarms Danny, and I was going for that.

KATHI MOSS (*Cha-Cha*): The best part of the rehearsal period for me was the day someone decided my good singing voice was going to waste, so besides my role as Cha-Cha, I'd provide the offstage reverb voice for "It's Raining on Prom Night." People would get to hear me sing after all! Of course, only my parents would really know who was singing, but that was good enough for me.

I loved this cast and this creative team, and every day was a joy. I didn't have to go back to my day job, and I thought, *Who knows, this little '50s show might even run.* I was very happy!

ADRIENNE BARBEAU (*Rizzo*): We were days into rehearsal. I had the songs, I had the dances, but I couldn't unlock the character. I knew something wasn't working, but today I couldn't tell you how I knew—maybe I wasn't getting laughs, maybe Rizzo was too unlikable, maybe something else. I just don't remember that part. All I knew was Rizzo wasn't working. And then Tom saved my ass with his director's note. He told me to try laughing at myself after I delivered my lines. Evidently this was something I did when I wasn't playing a role, something I do to this day without really being aware of it. It worked. Laughing at herself was the key to Rizzo's character. Maybe she didn't take herself seriously, maybe it was a defense mechanism—again I don't remember what I built her on, except for that one clear vision of Tom standing below me in front of the stage and telling me to laugh at what I was saying. I did, and everything fell into place.

Adrienne Barbeau as Rizzo.

KATIE HANLEY (*Marty*): My castmates were only a couple of years older than me but already possessed a sophistication and seasoned professionalism that awed me. Adrienne introduced me to the business of show business. She had it down! Adrienne gave me the name of her accountant and encouraged me to get a little notebook to enter daily expenses for tax purposes.

And I quickly knew I was in good hands with those who steered and shaped me through the rehearsals; the reassuring direction and the inspiring choreography gave me wings, and the cherry on top was the delight-to-my-soul music direction. There was no monotony in this rehearsal room.

WALTER BOBBIE: With Louis St. Louis, pursed lips and an eye roll could substitute for the note of vocal correction. He was hilarious. And tough. Rehearsing with Louis was always welcome. Firstly because you got to sit down in a chair for an hour. Putting together the "Summer Nights" vocal backups was gut-busting funny and as exacting as being taught "the rain in Spain falls mainly on the plain." Developing the placement of "dah-doo ron ron," "shoo da bop-bop," "papa ooh mau-mau," or the inevitable "shoo-be-doo wop wop wop" was both precise and sublime. Once assigned and harmonized, Louis refined this nonsense with a gusto and diction worthy of Henry Higgins.

Katie Hanley (Marty) and Don
Billett (Vince Fontaine).

Louis taught you why so many guys stood on so many street corners trying to become one voice. Performing those backups with Louis was as much
sassy fun as being down center with a solo. Almost.

LIZ THOMPSON (*Assistant to Pat Birch*): Pat is a master at enabling actors
to dance and then making those non-dancers into a terrific dancing ensemble.
Their dance "mistakes" are often highlights of the finished performance.

Working with Tom, Pat created musical numbers filled with joy, adrenaline, and youth, but always focused and clear, and always advancing the sto-
rytelling. I was constantly amazed at this young cast and their openness and
willingness to try anything.

As a dancer/assistant I held movement memory while devising a way to
notate it. I'm proud to say Pat's entire *Grease* choreography is now notated
forever, right there on a special musical score of *Grease.*

MARYA SMALL (*Frenchy*): Early into rehearsals, I realized what a great
group this was. Tom was easy to work with—*and actually seemed to like actors.*
Warren and Jim were funny and fun. Louis St. Louis was so good, but I was

kind of scared of him. Thank God for Pat, who helped me turn my basic jumping up and down into a dance.

And the actors were thrilling. I was mesmerized as I watched them, worked with them, sang with them, and at least tried to do the dance steps with them. We'd only just begun and I was already falling in love with each and every one of them.

Original cast rehearsing the end of the second act: "Gee, the whole crowd's together again."

6

"Good Golly, Miss Molly"

Moving to the Eden

TOM MOORE (*Director*): Rehearsals had gone well, everyone got along—in fact, everyone loved each other. I don't remember ever not wanting to go to rehearsal or feeling my usual *What have I done?* which usually accompanied the beginning of every show. But it was the end of those halcyon weeks of rehearsal, and we soon moved into the Eden Theatre.

DOUG SCHMIDT (*Set Designer*): Designing the physical production for *Grease* was a fraught process. The schedule was unrealistically short, the budget unrealistically limited, and on top of all the usual practical considerations, the timing couldn't have been worse. The build period fell directly on the two-week Christmas/New Year's holiday. It was a nip-and-tuck race to make our load-in date.

CARRIE ROBBINS (*Costume Designer*): If you're the designer on the show, the compensation comes in the form of flattery. You're told how talented and clever you are, and that if anyone can pull it off, you can.

And so, sufficiently flattered, I set about trying to make it happen. I don't remember the budget I was given, but I did know that it would be totally impossible to custom-make *any costumes* on such a bare-bones budget. All the costumes would have to be existing clothes, most likely vintage '50s pieces which I could have a small shop alter to fit the actors and then reinforce significantly so that the outfits would have the strength to survive eight shows a week.

KATIE HANLEY (*Marty*): Shortly before our dress rehearsals and previews, a publicity photo shoot was set up to show the guys getting their long '70s locks cut and styled into '50s ducktails, turning them instantly into greasers.

WALTER BOBBIE (*Roger*): Unfortunately, the stylist was a nervous wreck, his scissors trembling in his hands. Camera shy doesn't begin to describe his panic. The more the cameras flashed, the more unnerved he became. He first cut Tim Meyers's hair. Badly. Very badly. And then he cut Timmy's ear. There was blood. And pain, even as Tim bravely cooperated with the stunt.

Before the barbering butcher could move on to me, I quickly told them I would get my own haircut. I wasn't about to sacrifice an ear to have my picture in the *New York Post*.

BARRY BOSTWICK (*Zuko*): On the day of the "big haircut," all of the Burger Palace Boys went from being flower children to Sha Na Na wannabes. The transformation was instantaneous. We were immediately and officially a gang! The photo op was apparently useful in creating some early buzz for the show. But I really missed my rock 'n' roll locks.

CAROLE DEMAS (*Sandy*): Samson's power, all the glamour, gone.

KATIE HANLEY: The girls' hair was a very different story. We were led into a room backstage that was lined up with chairs facing a wall of mirrors. A hairstylist appeared, asked us to take a seat, and since my chair just happened to be first in line, he started with me. He began brushing out my long hair and

LEFT: Walter Bobbie (Roger). RIGHT: Katie Hanley (Marty).

tied it into a ponytail. Then without warning, he pulled out an enormous pair of scissors and in an instant lopped off my hair at the nape of my neck. The other girls gasped. As I looked in the mirror, I was horrified at what had just happened and shocked to see him grinning as he held up my severed ponytail.

The other girls quickly rose up and moved away from their chairs. I grabbed my ponytail out of the sadist's hands and marched out onto the stage. Tom, Ken, and Maxine were seated in the audience and seemed stunned when I held out my hair. "Look what he just did to me!" Tom, genuinely appalled, was enraged and demanded to know how and why this had happened.

He later found out instructions had been given to cut our hair, and he tore into the guilty party with unmitigated fury.

After witnessing what had been done to me, the girls adamantly refused to have their hair cut, especially by this butcher. Wigs were soon ordered, and happily the stylist was never seen again.

DOUG SCHMIDT: To say the first production of *Grease* was a low-budget enterprise is a shocking understatement.

Barry Bostwick as Danny Zuko.

What was represented to us, the "creatives," as a 1950s nostalgic but edgy little off-Broadway musical may have been the first intention of the producers, but with the selection of the Eden Theatre that idea vanished.

A large, 1,100-seat Broadway-style house on Second Avenue, it was anything but what one thought of as an "off-Broadway" theater. To start with, there was the size of the stage: about forty feet across its proscenium. It presented a wide picture frame but was built as a presentation house at a time when scenery was mostly of a flat, painted nature. It was pretty shallow, with little offstage storage space. Once the Eden was designated as our home, everything changed. Everything, that is, except our budget and, directly related to the budget, the schedule. So Carrie Robbins, the costume designer; Karl Eigsti, our lighting designer; and I were tasked with designing a Broadway show on an off-Broadway budget—for an off-Broadway fee at that.

The Eden stage was backed by a brick wall that we planned to leave as bare brick painted white, with a basketball hoop and maybe some painted graphic signage meant to evoke a high school gymnasium. Our budget and the size and scale of this wall really precluded any other treatment options. Early on Tom had suggested a classic two-level platform arrangement with movable access stairs and flying flats covered with period-photo blowups to set our stage in specific locations, such as the Burger Palace exterior with images of an oozing triple-decker burger and a menu with 1950s prices. We found a classic photo of James Dean which, blown up, would dominate the set, and it became the central iconic image for the show.

The rest of the scene-setting chores—moving props and furniture—were to be performed by the actors.

Although the stage design allowed Tom and Pat to fluidly facilitate the staging of the show, to me it still lacked coherent visual impact.

Conceptually, Tom, Pat, Carrie, and I were treading a fine line, attempting to combine the zeitgeist of the 1950s and the high spirits of a goofy rock 'n' roll musical while maintaining the hard edge of the characters in an urban high school. We were still trying to find the balance between a gritty black-and-white documentary style and a colorful musical comedy.

7

"Slippin' and Slidin'"

Technical | Dress Rehearsals | Previews

KEN WAISSMAN (*Producer*): Once the take-in of the sets, lights, and sound equipment was completed, the technical rehearsals began.

TOM MOORE (*Director*): There were big problems with sound, for much of which I definitely take the blame. I thought the show should have the sound it would have had during the '50s: the original sound of '50s rock through the sound quality of '50s microphones.

Well, every year sound had become more and more sophisticated. The real '50s sound was now totally unacceptable to a '70s audience.

ILENE KRISTEN (*Patty*): The sound system, which echoed like a bad high school auditorium, was a disaster. At the eleventh hour, sound designer Bobby Minor was hired to salvage the situation for a show he had never even seen.

WALTER BOBBIE (*Roger*): The sound system had to be completely replaced. The result was endless rehearsals for the newly installed hand mics, mic stands, and miles of wire snaking across the original floor mics, which lined the stage edge like dead mice losing an acoustic war with the band. Being able to hear our performances moved to priority number one and benched a growing list of unfinished business. For the next days one might hear, *Mic 3 is caught on stand four and needs to be reset on table two for song seven. Also, there's an unmarked cable plug up my ass! Stop!*

TOM MOORE: After a major scramble, '50s music with '50s arrangements eventually soared through state-of-the-art '70s equipment.

ILENE KRISTEN: Our dress rehearsals were a little frantic. We really didn't have complicated sets, but there were photo flats flying in and out, the scene changes done by the actors were tricky, and the tricked-out golf cart Greased Lightning could create havoc if its entrance and departure went awry. The production had run out of money for costumes, so I brought in my mom's jacket and skirt for the opening alumni scene, which helped me play the more mature Mrs. Patty Simcox Honeywell. I felt jittery but raring to go.

CAROLE DEMAS (*Sandy*): Some of the dress rehearsal/preview costume pieces were actually my own clothes and my mother's from the '50s. Seventeen years later, there I was onstage, totally comfortable wearing my own sweetly modest white nylon blouse, which I had actually worn to a high school dance in 1955!

CARRIE ROBBINS (*Costumes*): I love vintage. Vintage clothes already have a lifetime of story in them; they look real because they are real.

GARN STEPHENS (*Jan*): For my character, Jan, Carrie came up with this plaid wool pleated skirt that I swear could have been found in my own closet just a few years earlier. That skirt was so well made and the fabric so indestructible that it is probably still floating around in some *Grease* production somewhere. Or maybe serving as a bulletproof vest for a soldier in combat.

KEN WAISSMAN: The dress rehearsals were quickly followed by an "invited dress," invariably made of up friends and freebies who are delighted to be there and are in a rooting mood. *Wow! That went well*, we all think.

TOM MOORE: The invited dress had gone better than expected, and we were ready for previews—or so we thought.

KEN WAISSMAN: First previews are always rough, no matter what. Unlike the invited dress, paying audiences are unforgiving.

TOM MOORE: Because the audience, with no hesitation and in no uncertain terms, lets you know exactly and immediately what they don't like.

KEN WAISSMAN: Our first preview was a disaster! Scenes weren't working, musical numbers didn't get off the ground, lead characters appeared superficial.

TOM MOORE: Subdued, the audience filed out of the Eden Theatre—some excited at what they had just seen, some confused, and some downright discouraged. As was I.

KEN WAISSMAN: After the show, a depressed mood hung over the theater. Ellen Neuwald, Tom Moore's agent, cornered me at the back of the theater and asked if I was going to fire Tom. "Why would I fire him?" I shot back, a bit flippantly, moving on before she could engage me further. It was a first preview, after all.

TOM MOORE: The producers wisely never told me any of this until months later!

KEN WAISSMAN: At that first preview, trouble had started shortly after the curtain went up. The stage shifts to the school cafeteria. The characters of Marty and Frenchy enter and sit at the cafeteria table—except there was no cafeteria table. The stagehands had forgotten to preset it. The choreography for the song "Summer Nights" depended on the table. From the back of the house, Tom started to run backstage. It wasn't necessary. Adrienne Barbeau as Rizzo made her entrance with a cafeteria tray in one hand and the *entire cafeteria table* under her other arm. She plunked it down where it belonged. This was an extremely heavy, authentic wooden high school cafeteria table. At intermission, the stagehands asked Adrienne to lift it again. She couldn't.

ADRIENNE BARBEAU (*Rizzo*): All I knew was that the table needed to be out there. I was ready to make my entrance. I had the cafeteria tray in one hand and saw the table sitting there in the wings. I picked it up with my free arm and carried it on.

TOM MOORE: Urgency and adrenaline! The scene continued.

ILENE KRISTEN: Considering all the screwy things that could go wrong on a first preview, it felt pretty smooth and . . . almost triumphant. I miraculously got through my song, "Yeucch," aided by the raunchy antics of the Burger Palace Boys and the Pink Ladies behind me. Everybody gave it their all, and I thought we put on quite a good show despite all the unforeseen complications.

KEN WAISSMAN: That first preview metaphorically could be compared to a cluttered teenage bedroom, so messy it's overwhelming. How does one begin? By picking up the first sock. For me that sock was the band. My overriding feeling was that the show looked small in the spacious, Broadway-sized Eden Theatre. I felt one of the culprits was the band playing on a platform above the stage behind a scrim photograph of James Dean. I walked over to Tom, who was sitting alone in a row of empty seats.

"The first thing we need to do," I said, "is move the band into the orchestra pit. It will increase the size of the show."

Tom was hesitant.

TOM MOORE: Having the band on an upper platform above the stage floor was visually very exciting and part of the show's style. They were quite dramatically part of the action.

JIM JACOBS (*Author/Composer*): I liked the band onstage up there on the platform. At the Kingston Mines the band was in an upstage corner, and you could see them all through the show and it was great. Pat Birch called it a Paramount Theater moment whenever someone picked up a mic to sing a song, because you saw the band and the singers, like in an Alan Freed rock 'n' roll stage show.

TOM MOORE: Although I fought moving the band for a couple of performances, I couldn't ignore the fact that the performers were having a hard time connecting with Louis and the band above and behind them. So with Ken's urging, I agreed to move them into the pit for one performance. If it worked, that's where they would stay. If not, it was back to the platform and we'd have to find another solution.

JIM JACOBS: When the band was moved into the orchestra pit, which in the Eden was out of sight, I thought, *Oh man, now the audience is going to think it's a recording.*

KEN WAISSMAN: Once the band was in the pit, *Grease* felt like an authentic Broadway musical. Tom never mentioned moving it back.

TOM MOORE: Well, it worked. Louis St. Louis, the music director, was ecstatic. The band stayed in the pit. Ken was right. And we were on to the next problem.

Marya Small arriving at the Eden stage door for rehearsals.

MARYA SMALL (*Frenchy*): On the morning after the first paid preview, I ran into Timmy, who played Kenickie, on our way into the theater. He handed me a joint and said, "I have a little surprise for you. Take a couple of hits."

I responded, "Just one, thank you." I took a hit. "Well, maybe two."

Timmy took another three or four; we laughed and headed into rehearsal. Only this was no normal rehearsal. Our beloved director Tom did not have just a few polishing notes. These were major changes, I mean lots and lots of changes—dumping whole numbers, adding new songs and new choreography. It seemed like we were redoing the whole show from top to bottom.

I'm sitting there trying to concentrate and take it all in—and completely freaking out. *Oh my God! What have I done? Freak out! Freak out!* My heart was pounding so hard I could barely hear Tom. Fear grabbed me deep. I looked at Adrienne (Rizzo), Garn (Jan), Katie (Marty), and the rest of the cast. They seemed fine and were all taking notes. I looked over at Timmy. He seemed to be fine too. But maybe this was normal for Tim. After all, he was from New Orleans.

Timmy was cruising; I was crashing. Tom's notes seemed to go on and on and on; it seemed like he'd never stop. Finally he said, "OK. Take five and we'll get started!"

Get started? Get started? I thought, *How? How am I going to get through this?* All these changes would have freaked me out even if I hadn't had that second hit! I downed five cups of black coffee, hoping they'd help me toward normal.

I never wanted to be so straight in my life. I was praying to be straight. Me, I'm not really the praying type, but I was praying now, seriously praying. Just the night before I had stood on the stage as Frenchy, saying the line "I wish I had one of them guardian angel things like in the Debbie Reynolds movie, somebody always there to tell you the right thing to do." *Help!*

I was so scared! *Please get all the pieces of my mind back together. I can't let everyone down. Please help!*

Well, I guess that guardian angel must have heard me because somehow, with help from Garn and Adrienne, one way or another I got through everything that day. But oh my God, you can bet your sweet apples I did *not* do that again!

KEN WAISSMAN: The day after the first horrendous preview, we cut a song titled "Yeucch," which the cheerleader Patty sings at the top of Act 1.

TOM MOORE: Pat had choreographed "Yeucch" very cleverly, but when it played with the audience that first night it stopped the show cold. Jim and Warren were very fond of it, but the song had long been doubted by the rest of the creative team, especially me. We all agreed: *it had to go.*

JIM JACOBS: It seemed like everyone was after Warren and me to cut the cheerleader's song, "Yeucch." So we get screwed out of one of the funniest songs in the show, defining the two camps: the collegiates and the greasers. Everyone but Warren and me wanted it out, so it was cut.

MAXINE FOX (*Producer*): It was most difficult for Ilene Kristen, who was playing Patty and after one performance lost her song.

TOM MOORE: It was her only solo in the show, and Ilene was young. Giving her the news would be on the edge of heartbreaking. But who had time for heartbreak? We had a broken show.

ILENE KRISTEN: The next day, when we got to the theater, we immediately assembled to hear Tom's notes on the previous night's out-of-body experience. I'm sure he made some sort of encouraging opening speech, but the first thing I remember hearing was "The show was moving along nicely until right after 'Summer Nights,' so the song 'Yeucch' is cut starting tonight."

Ilene Kristen (Patty), "Yeucch."

There was a lot going on that morning and a long list of changes, so Tom must have assumed that someone had already informed me. But they hadn't. I felt like ice water had been thrown on me.

As yucky as "Yeucch" was, it was my song—my only song—and I couldn't hold back the tears. I just wanted to disappear. It was a very long and hard day but, believe it or not, by the end of it I was actually relieved to be "Yeucch"-less. And I had to admit, without it the first act did move a lot better.

KEN WAISSMAN: I then brought up the idea of moving the song "Those Magic Changes" from the party scene in Act 2 to just after "Summer Nights" in Act 1. Doody tells Danny Zuko he's been studying the guitar and plays some '50s rock 'n' roll chords for him. This helps to establish his relationship to Zuko and sets us up for the musical style of the show. Tom agreed right away. I remember thinking, *Oh, that was easy!*

TOM MOORE: With "Yeucch" out of the way, "Magic Changes" was immediately moved up to become the second big number of the show. Sung by Jim Canning's Doody, it instantly added warmth to the show, not to mention the characters.

JIM JACOBS: When "Magic Changes" was pulled from Jan's basement scene in Act 2, it ended up in a scene out of nowhere, with the gang milling around, getting things in and out of their lockers on their first day back at Rydell High.

Warren and I didn't like "Magic Changes" being moved, because now we had a big hole—no music—in the party scene in Jan's basement. I went home and wrote "Rock 'n' Roll Party Queen" in one night. I wrote it in thirty minutes, man. I just did some basic Everly Brothers chords and changes and simple words. It was written for Doody and then somehow it became Doody and Roger and then it became Doody and Roger kicking off the opening scene of the party in Jan's basement. After a few performances it was frozen. That's the kind of stuff that happens in previews.

WALTER BOBBIE: A supporting actor would kill for two featured songs in a musical, especially when the second song is in the second act. Unless that song happens to be "Rock 'n' Roll Party Queen," which Jim Canning and I sang in a spotlight as the gang congregated in Jan's basement.

Setting our hair on fire could not distract from the upstage pantomime of plot-important gossip working its way through the party in that basement. No matter how well we sang—and we sang well—we were a musical hyphen while Kenickie crossed downstage to say, "Hey Rizzo, I hear you're knocked up."

In early previews, Canning and I were met with no applause and a WTF moment that offered nightly ball-busting opportunities to some in the cast who could purr hilariously withering assessments with the mastery of ventriloquists.

Future Rogers and Doodies knew what they were getting into, but at the launch "Rock 'n' Roll Party Queen" was a flat tire. At one performance before we sang the first words over Jim Canning's guitar intro, Jim whispered, "We're dying."

Like any survivor experience, "Rock 'n' Roll Party Queen" bonded Jim and me for life.

TOM MOORE: I would guess thirty percent of the show changed in that first twenty-four hours after the first preview.

ILENE KRISTEN: In the second preview, everything that could go wrong did go wrong and then some. To make it worse, my father was there on this legendary cursed second night. My crinoline slip fell down and got twisted

The unlamented "Bum Scene," cut during early previews.

around the heels of my pink prom shoes, which messed up nearly every step of "Shakin' at the High School Hop." There were a lot of cuts and changes that the cast and crew had not yet assimilated. We were on rocky terrain.

Backstage after the show my usually effusive dad's evasiveness spoke volumes. He didn't tell me until years later that he was concerned that if my first Broadway show, *Henry, Sweet Henry*, was considered a flop, *Grease* didn't have a shot in hell. I guess that is why, when the producers were looking to raise more capital for the show and I asked him to invest, he turned beet red and said he would talk to his accountant. We never mentioned it again until the day I told him the insane amount of money he could have made on the deal. Well over five hundred times his investment!

CAROLE DEMAS: There was an audience out there! We were on a trembling, raucous high. Scenes came and went. Entrances from left became from right and vice versa. We stuck little notes and clues to ourselves on the backstage walls, wrote them on our inner arms, made wild-eyed glances to each other—*Is this the right scene? Is this the lyric from yesterday? Is that line still in? I can't remember **anything**!*

JOY RINALDI (*Understudy*): During previews everyone was willing to try anything, then retry it, try it another way, discard it, and then try something else. And it was my job to learn and *relearn* all of it. *I did!*

WALTER BOBBIE: She's a sly one, that Pat Birch. She made us believe that any idea was worth trying. You never knew what she was up to, yet in the end every number in *Grease* was perfectly structured and storied within an inch of the bar.

We were a week into previews at the Eden Theatre and the beginning of "Greased Lightnin'" was really working, but it had not yet been fully staged. More serious issues were taking priority.

"Greased Lightnin'" was a solid lock with the extended first word "*Goooooo*," legs pumped, eyes gazing across outstretched arms smoothly tracking the horizon, left to right, then right to left, aggressive fist pumps punctuating the title of the song. Cool. Signature. But most of the number was still just us guys running around Tim Meyers and his soon-to-be Tony-nominated righteous snarl of delight.

One day we Burger Palace Boys rolled up the sleeves of our T-shirts and complained, "Hey, we don't know what we're doing in 'Greased Lightnin'.'" Pat Birch's actual response was "Fine. What do you want to do?"

"Greased Lightnin'": "'Then jump!' said she."

And that's how Pat began sculpting our mayhem. She transformed our chaos into safely organized chaos. Where lesser minds would have created a dance break, Pat encouraged a loudmouthed pantomime of teasing, topped by Zuko pulling Saran Wrap from Kenickie's car and rubbing it across his crotch, by which time we were all stuck on top of the car yelling, "What do we do now?"

Pat said, "What do you want to do?"

"Jump!" said we.

"Then jump!" said she.

And she nailed another showstopper—locked and loaded every night. The crowd went wild—each and every performance. It was thrilling!

KEN WAISSMAN: Still, compared to Act 2, Act 1 felt one-dimensional and lightweight. Something was missing. Tom saw the solution.

TOM MOORE: "Summer Nights" gives us the exposition of Danny's romance with Sandy earlier that summer. When they unexpectedly meet, he brushes her off. After their brief meeting we didn't see Danny and Sandy together again until the Act 2 drive-in movie scene, where surprisingly they are

Danny (Barry Bostwick)
and Sandy (Carole Demas).

on a date. We needed a Danny/Sandy scene in the first act to keep the boy-girl plot at the center of the show and to show the change in their relationship. The authors and I talked, and overnight they created the cheerleader scene on the track field where Sandy and Danny are interrupted by the baton-twirling Patty. It was a small scene, but it solved a big problem.

KEN WAISSMAN: I thought Sandy should wear a poodle skirt like the "good girls" back in high school, who wore these wide, gray felt skirts with pink poodles embroidered on the side, puffed out by what looked like dozens of crinolines.

CARRIE ROBBINS: Often doing my best thinking in my nightly shower, I was mulling over the problem of the poodle when I looked down and noticed that I had a small, pink, deeply tufted bath rug on my bathroom floor and a matching pink toilet-seat cover. Between the two there was just enough yardage for the poodle. Thanks to my pink bathroom accessories, the *Grease* poodle skirt was born.

KEN WAISSMAN: I was sure the poodle skirt would get a recognition laugh when Sandy made her entrance. However, Tom had staged Sandy's entrance upstage behind the cafeteria table. The audience didn't notice the

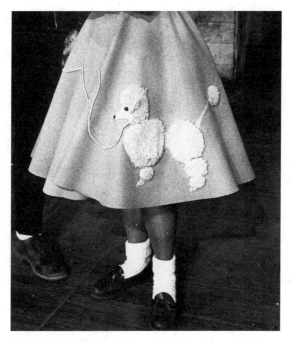

The poodle skirt.

poodle skirt. I asked Tom if he would bring her in down front. He answered that with the time pressure, he was focusing all his energy on the performances and on getting the scenes right. "I don't have time to restage a skirt," he declared.

The next day, when Tom called from rehearsal, I didn't take the call. In the afternoon the stage manager called asking me to OK an expense for an additional prop that Tom wanted.

"Tell Tom when I get my poodle skirt, I'll consider it," I told the stage manager.

That night the poodle skirt got a roar of recognition laughter. Tom came over to me in the back of the theater. "I should've done this sooner," he said with a sheepish grin.

CAROLE DEMAS: My gray felt skirt with the pink poodle was an entire era in a single perfect piece of costuming. Fifty years later I still see little Sandys running around in them on Halloween. That night it wasn't me making a star entrance, it was *the skirt*.

CARRIE ROBBINS: For Teen Angel's backup girls I had returned to my inner office—for my nightly shower—and what do you know? Staring through

Frenchy and her shower curtain backup.

my shower curtain, I began to see a beauty school smock and shower cap ensemble made out of shower curtains. I "borrowed" my curtain, which was sheer with white vertical stripes, folded it diagonally, cut in a neckline, and sent it off to Betty, my seamstress, to be duplicated. The Pink Ladies Backup Group was ready to go.

My husband, Richard, after following the saga of these garments for some time, queried mildly, "Would you mind *not* going shopping in our bathroom anymore? There's nothing much left except the porcelain."

GARN STEPHENS: For Jan to wear to the prom, Carrie found an aqua brocade cocktail dress. I loved it. After a preview one night, a lady came up to me. I don't remember her saying anything about the show. She was focused on my dress, which had been *her* dress, her prom dress no less, that she had worn to her high school prom in Fort Lee, New Jersey, years ago. I don't remember if the lady's reunion with her dress brought up any significant memories for her, but I had the impression that the brocade dress was definitely having a more glamorous life in its current incarnation. That dress provided the lady with a story for the rest of her life.

Danny's surprise at seeing Sandy at Rydell High.

MARYA SMALL: The *Grease* experience lifted up my life. A steady pay-check, at least for a moment, and new, amazing friends. But after the first couple of previews we were pretty discouraged and thought *Grease* might not make it, and that we would soon be looking for another job. Every night, over and over again, Jim Borrelli (Sonny) kept repeating, "This show's a turkey." Mostly in fun, I think, but we were all worried. At our five-minute call to showtime, we'd all come downstairs singing the Silhouettes' 1957 song "Get a Job."

ILENE KRISTEN: As previews continued I felt we had a good tailwind at our back. We were riding the first wave of '50s nostalgia, and I knew that Jim and Warren were definitely on to something. All the elements were getting better with each performance, so when I occasionally heard someone mutter "turkey" or "flop" it didn't faze me. We were an amazing ensemble and I had total faith—onward!

JOY RINALDI: Every performance I marveled at the show. I thought it was the funniest play with the funniest, most creative cast ever. The only thing missing up there was me. But in those early previews the audience did not always see it through my eyes. I saw quite a few people leave at intermission. My parents, a very kind and loving but conservative couple, thought it was a "filthy" show. Of all my friends who came to see it, not a single one of them thought it had any chance of survival. And some of them outright hated it!

It still gives me great pleasure to think how all of them had to eat their hats, or at least their words, when *Grease* became a huge hit, first at the Eden, then on Broadway.

TOM MOORE: Each audience told us new things. And sometimes a friend of the creative team told us very specific new things, which turned out to have huge gains for the show.

DOUG SCHMIDT (*Set Designer*): We were still trying to find the balance between a gritty, black-and-white documentary style and a colorful musical comedy.

MAXINE FOX: Several of the show's comic lines weren't getting laughs. We were all perplexed.

DOUG SCHMIDT: Enter the great John Houseman, protean producer, director, Academy Award–winning actor, and after a long, distinguished career, head of the Juilliard School Drama Division. I had been designing for John since 1968 and had a good collaborative relationship with him. Likewise, Pat Birch had worked with him on other projects. She invited him to see an early preview of our little "off-Broadway" musical.

While not the most adventuresome of directors, his gimlet eye was sure and accurate. He could put his finger on problems with performances and production better than anyone I ever met.

"My dear boy," he said when we met after the show, "it's all so grim. I understand the desire to ground the play in reality, but the documentary concept has its limitations. It's a comedy. It needs more color, more period reference, and above all, focus. The stage is very big and your resources are spread so thin, it looks quite meager. Try to pull it in and frame the performers so our eye doesn't wander off into the wings." A not unkind but brutally accurate critique.

KEN WAISSMAN: Houseman told us he thought the reason we weren't getting the laughs we expected was because we were playing against a "black hole." He was referring to the solid-black upstage wall of the set. "The dark background is swallowing the laughs."

DOUG SCHMIDT: Thus was born the photo collage of iconic advertising and cultural touchstones that replaced the sterile brick back wall.

Final *Grease* set design by Doug Schmidt.

Houseman's observations were convincing enough that Ken and Maxine sold their first-born whippets or somehow found resources to pay for these additions, and others, that not only lifted the spirit of the evening but in subtle ways helped focus and facilitate the narrative momentum.

TOM MOORE: When Doug created a giant photo montage of '50s photographs across the full back wall of the Eden stage, it pulled the entire set into a cohesive whole.

KEN WAISSMAN: Dick Clark came to one of the previews. He was complimentary but also mentioned that the show was bleeding out at the edges. He suggested a false proscenium inside the permanent one that would frame the show and better focus the audience.

TOM MOORE: Doug then added the portal of '50s black-and-white yearbook photos, and the space was complete!

TOM MOORE: At a later preview the writer Will Holt, a friend of Pat Birch, suggested that we were stopping our momentum every time a scene change happened. The cast was doing them efficiently, but why not have them do the scene changes in character and with the same verve and energy as the scenes? So in one two-hour rehearsal, Pat added musical staging and choreography (some from the discarded staging of "Yeucch"), and the scene changes instantly became energized and boisterous, almost as fun as the scenes themselves.

Garn Stephens (Jan) and Walter Bobbie (Roger), "Mooning."

WALTER BOBBIE: The original musical ending for "Mooning" was arranged to mimic '50s recording technology, when vocals faded away, growing softer and softer and softer, like someone disappearing down a long hallway. In our case, we weren't in a recording studio walking down an acoustic hallway. We were onstage at the Eden Theatre, and my fucking song (sorry, Garn, *our* fucking song!) was getting *no applause!* Nothing. Not even with family in the audience.

I was as angry and frustrated as any self-involved actor worthy of an Equity card. Yale University hadn't bothered to teach my sophisticated friend Tom Moore the crass tricks of "buttoning" a number (a last climactic chord that lets the audience know when to applaud). One afternoon in previews I begged Louis St. Louis, our genius music director and an ally, to hold the final chord at that evening's performance of "Mooning." I was going to vocally ad lib "There's a moon out tonight," after which he'd supply—*plunk!*—a button.

We did it. It worked.

Applause!

And the stylistic '50s pop studio recording technique was never, ever mentioned again.

Button!

"Summer Nights."

KATIE HANLEY (*Marty*): At the close of our dutiful singing of the "Alma Mater," the guitar gleefully erupts into our Greasers' irreverent intro to the parody, while the scrim rises to expose our unruly gang.

Some of our early audiences had been lukewarm; they seemed to recoil from the parody's crass opening lyrics. The '60s era of peace and love was still in the air, as well as passionate protesting for equality and an end to the Vietnam War.

In the first weeks of previews, it had taken these audiences a scene or two to loosen up and begin to enter into the fun.

But fortunately, as the show got better and better during previews, so did the audience. Maybe they now knew what to expect, because when I stood behind the scrim for the start of the show, I could now feel their excitement as they looked forward to joining us in our simple but joyous celebration of the '50s.

MARYA SMALL: One night during previews the producers came backstage to tell us that because of all the changes, they needed to raise more money. They wanted to know if any of us wanted to invest. *Invest what?* I thought. None of us had any money. Had we any idea what this show would become, we might (definitely would) have gone to some radical extremes to borrow money to invest—but who knew?

ADRIENNE BARBEAU: Barry and I talked about sharing a point—$500 each. But that was all I had in my emergency medical fund. Ever practical, I passed.

Katie Hanley sings "Freddy, My Love."

Garn Stephens, Marya Small, and Adrienne Barbeau.

BARRY BOSTWICK (*Zuko*): During previews, what our cast didn't do right was put our money where our mouths were. Close to our opening, Ken and Maxine needed some cash to buy sneakers, Zuko dance pants, and a few bigger things, and they approached us as a group to see if we could muster together $10,000 and split the points among us.

At the time we were poor young actors. We didn't have the money, and we couldn't find the money! Even from family, who reacted much like my dad. He came to the opening night performance. As we were stumbling up the stairs to my Bowery loft after the party, he said, "You'd better start looking for another job, Barry. This ain't gonna last!"

That $10,000 would now be worth about $1,200,000 and climbing. Who knew?

TOM MOORE: During the entire fraught preview period, Ken and Maxine remained confident and constantly encouraged the creative team to follow its instincts and just keep chipping away.

The changes we had been making in previews, however, were costing a lot more than the original bare-bones budget, but somehow Ken and Maxine kept finding ways to raise a little more cash and keep the show going. One of these ways, as I found out later, was giving a larger portion of the show to an associate producer who until then, despite his title, was basically just an investor. But give someone a little more ownership and they always want to take a little more control.

DOUG SCHMIDT: The early previews were rocky, but with conscientious rewriting and staging and scene work, the show was improving markedly from performance to performance, which the enthusiastic audience response increasingly confirmed.

At the final curtain of a preview, when the team is in some combination of exhilaration, exhaustion, and suicidal despair, the evening is just starting. In a preview period the producers, authors, director, choreographer, designers, and many of the management staff traditionally hold an after-show postmortem. Often running long after midnight, these meetings are my personal bêtes noires, but a necessary part of the job.

KEN WAISSMAN: Our associate producer Tony D'Amato, who was in from Chicago, asked if he could attend our production meeting that night. Despite associate producer billing, D'Amato was an investor, and I never let investors speak directly to the creative team. For some reason that still eludes, I went against my instincts and agreed to let him attend.

DOUG SCHMIDT: As the theater was being locked up for the night, we all headed out the stage door into the biting cold wind toward Ken Waissman's apartment a few blocks away. I was so bleary with lack of sleep and battle fatigue that I didn't even know where we were going. I just followed the herd. It was the hardest three flights I ever climbed. Upon late arrival we opened the door on a room so dense with cigarette smoke as to make one gag. In those days no one gave a thought to forgoing gassing their fellow collaborators for *hours.* Those who partook chain-smoked their anxieties into submission while the rest of us suffered secondhand asphyxiation. Between sleep deprivation and toxic fumes, you will understand if some details of that extraordinary evening went up in smoke.

There was a new face in the crowd that night, a businessman named Anthony D'Amato who, by virtue of collecting and bundling several investors' funds, became an associate producer. In the years to come he would be known by the sobriquet "Tony Tomato," but tonight it became evident he was also a man of strong opinions who had no compunction about venting them.

TOM MOORE: What happened that night is indelible because what D'Amato said and how he said it was not only destructive—it struck at the very confidence of all of us who had been working twenty hours a day to pull *Grease* into a tight-knit powerhouse of a show.

DOUG SCHMIDT: Warren Casey, the coauthor of the piece, had been up to this point a gentle, somewhat bemused presence around the theater. A soft-spoken, thoughtful, and quiet bear of a guy, it would have been difficult to pick him out of the crowd as one of the creators of this raunchy, profanely hard-edged musical. That night he was typically subdued—that is, until Mr. D'Amato took the floor.

Production meetings such as this are tedious and detail-oriented though seldom contentious affairs, but as Mr. D'Amato launched into a litany of disappointments and criticisms, a dark cloud passed over the room. *About as raunchy as Oklahoma!—where's the hard edge? This is not what I invested my money in* is perhaps not a verbatim quote, but it was very much his tenor and substance as he lambasted our production for being far inferior to the amateur Chicago version that preceded it. What we heard was *You've ruined this perfect play, you assholes.* Ironic, especially since the general opinion was that we were making good progress in the performances and in all departments.

TOM MOORE: As D'Amato attacked, we listened, appalled, and the energy and spirit slowly drained from the entire team. When his diatribe finally came to an end, the room was in total silence.

DOUG SCHMIDT: Totally exhausted and frayed at the end of a long week, Warren leapt to his feet, stood towering over D'Amato, shaking with rage, and screamed in his face, defending all of us and demanding he shut up or (and I do remember this) "I will throw you out that fucking window and there will be fucking blood running down fucking Second Avenue! What you need to do is get out of here so we can do what we need to do and finish the show."

TOM MOORE: We all sat there stunned. We had never heard or seen Warren do anything like this. We were in awe.

DOUG SCHMIDT: Sensing his status had changed from "angel" to persona non grata, the Tomato picked up his coat and charged out of the room. We all heard the apartment door slam on his exit. Tom quietly steered the meeting back on track as best he could given the trauma, and the postmortem continued as best it could.

TOM MOORE: We finished the note session and the next day got back to work and finished the show.

DOUG SCHMIDT: Though D'Amato's comments had caused considerable damage to our fragile confidence and enthusiasm, which took us some time to regain, Warren achieved heroic status and our admiration that night, proving gay bears aren't always as cuddly as they seem and tomatoes are easily crushed to paste.

TOM MOORE: Life not being fair, the sad thing is that this associate producer became very rich because of all the things we fixed in a show that became a financial colossus.

KEN WAISSMAN: With each new change during the preview weeks, the show worked a little better. But nearing the end of previews, there was still one problem that we hadn't been able to resolve. This was Rizzo's song "There Are Worse Things I Could Do." Each night Adrienne Barbeau sang her heart out, but the audience sat on their hands. Pat Birch tried restaging the number, which takes place at a party in Jan's basement when word gets around that Rizzo is pregnant, but the audience still didn't respond.

JIM JACOBS: In previews there was always talk about cutting "Worse Things." Even one of our biggest fans, Michael Feingold, wrote about it in his introduction to the Chicago Kingston Mines script printed by Winter House:

"Now hold on, what is this very serious song doing in the middle of a show that's all the fun and frolics of the fifties?" Then he quoted the line where Rizzo sings, "Even though the neighborhood thinks I'm trashy and no good."

The hairs went up on my arm. To these kids that neighborhood is their whole world.

KEN WAISSMAN: Jim and Warren told Tom and me they wouldn't argue if we wanted to cut it. It was slowing things down, and it took time to get the audience back. Tom didn't want to cut it. I didn't either. "Worse Things" was one of my favorite songs in the show. It was a bookend to the satirical "Look at Me, I'm Sandra Dee" in the first act. Both songs were about the double standard of the period. However, we also knew we couldn't keep a song that lost the audience every night.

The following night, Sylvia Herscher, the president of E. H. Morris & Co. Ltd., the music publishers who had just purchased the publishing rights to the *Grease* score, came to the performance. As we stood in the back watching the show, I mentioned the "Worse Things" dilemma. We watched the number together and, once again, the audience reaction was tepid.

"It's not the song," Sylvia said. "It's the scene leading into it. When word gets around the party that Rizzo is pregnant, no one reacts on her behalf, no one cares. Her defensiveness and nastiness just reinforces their lack of concern. So when she goes into the song, the audience doesn't care either."

After the show I joined the creative team for our nightly meeting where we discussed feedback and solutions. I reported what Sylvia had said.

Tom and the authors spoke, and that night Jim and Warren rewrote the scene leading into the song. In the rewrite, when word gets around the party that Rizzo's pregnant, Sonny runs over to her. "Hey, Rizz . . . if you ever need somebody to talk to," he says.

Roger follows, saying, "I'll help you out with some money if you need it." The other characters also express concern.

Tom put the new scene in the next day, and that night the applause at the end of the song was huge.

KATHI MOSS (*Cha-Cha*): Maybe it's because we were so far from mainstream Broadway, but when we started previews way downtown at the Eden Theatre, our audiences were far different from what I was used to. In our final previews, at several points during the show, people in the audience just got up and started dancing in the aisles. Who knew what it meant—maybe the show was drawing an audience that hadn't been represented on Broadway before? Whatever it was, they sure were having a good time. And there was a ton of enthusiasm.

KEN WAISSMAN: By the last preview performance, the hard work, dedication, and professionalism seemed to have paid off. Compared to the first preview, *Grease* felt like a whole new show.

At the Rydell Hop.

8 | *"Oh, What a Night"*

KEN WAISSMAN (*Producer*): Monday evening, February 14, 1972, *Grease* officially opened. We had selected that date as a good omen because it was Valentine's Day and we hoped the audience would be in a loving mood.

Opening nights are always a very tense time. The suspense about the upcoming reviews is unbearable. Yet as producers Maxine and I had to smile and look totally calm backstage as we visited each dressing room to say thank you for all your hard work and "Break a leg!" (good luck). We then went into the theater, maintaining that same calm smile as we greeted a full house of investors and friends.

KATHI MOSS (*Cha-Cha*): When opening night rolled around, Tim and I drove to the theater together. (Yes, I was a moron back in those days and had a car in New York City.) When he got in the car, Tim said, "You know, Kathi, this feels no different from all those times we were on our way for a performance at the University of New Orleans." But at the same moment we looked at one another and knew it was so much more. How much more we were soon to find out.

I don't think we said a whole lot more after that. We concentrated on the night ahead—which, it turned out, would change our lives. Although it didn't look like that for a while.

JOY RINALDI (*Understudy*): My most vivid memory of opening night is of our director, Tom Moore, pacing back and forth at the back of the Eden. He never sat down. He never even stopped moving, not for one moment. He looked like a tiger in a cage. And just like with a tiger, there was no way I would have approached him.

The producers were there. The authors were there. The choreographer was there. They would all come and go. But not Tom Moore. He just paced unrelentingly, back and forth, for the entire two hours and fifteen minutes, except for the intermission, when he ran to escape the audience.

While Tom paced, the cast was on fire that night. Everything that hadn't worked in rehearsals or previews worked perfectly that night. The scenery and costumes were perfect. The lighting and sound were perfect. It was amazing. In fact it was breathtaking! But Tom just kept on pacing.

TOM MOORE (*Director*): So there I was, standing at the back of the Eden Theatre on our opening night. The theater was packed, all 1,100 seats, and I was more than a bit nervous. I was just twenty-seven and three and a half years out of Yale Drama and this was my first big New York production. My entire future could be changed by the time the curtain came down.

Some directors can take a seat in the audience on opening night, but I never felt comfortable in the middle of all those possibly judgmental people who had nothing at stake but an evening of fun. As my budding career and life were on the line, I felt most comfortable guarding the gate by standing at the top of the left center aisle—which was convenient to the main doors of the theater should escape become necessary.

During previews we had made myriad changes to almost everything. In the excitement of opening, would the cast remember all those changes, which had continued right up to the last preview?

There are always one or two places where a play or musical hangs by a thread. For us it was the moment in the second act when the happy and always fun *Grease* took a turn to the serious. Kenickie finds out that his girlfriend, Rizzo, is pregnant. "Rizzo, I hear you're knocked up." Kenickie walks out. Rizzo, totally alone, sings the poignant "There Are Worse Things I Could Do," defiantly claiming her life and future.

It's essential in that moment of seriousness right before Rizzo pours her heart out that the audience be completely tuned in. If anything distracts them or makes them restless, the focus will be lost, not to mention "Worse Things" and the rest of the show.

So there we are in the second act. The first act had gone brilliantly; the audience was buzzing at intermission and the second act was humming along. The transition to the serious moment before "Worse Things" was working better than it ever had—even better than it deserved. I smiled . . .

But just at that moment when the orchestra began its intro for "Worse Things," a middle-aged woman rose from her seat in the front orchestra section, staggered up the aisle to the very place I was standing, and promptly collapsed at my feet.

Panic raced through my body and my head spun. *Help her? Help the show? Save her? Save the show?* My mind racing wildly as I tried to decide a course of action, I saw out of the corner of my eye ushers racing from both sides, converging upon us. I looked down and quickly checked. The lady was breathing and she wasn't in pain! I made the decision. To paraphrase the adage, *this show was going on!*

I turned to the ushers surrounding me and quietly but firmly said, *"No one is to move this lady until Adrienne has finished 'There Are Worse Things I Could Do'!"*

She did—and triumphantly. The audience burst into sustained applause, and the kind woman resting on the floor was helped to the ladies' room, where she quickly revived.

I held my breath as the show moved into its final scene, keeping the audience at full attention right through to the buoyant curtain call and an enthusiastic standing ovation. It seemed my career would not die that night, nor would the kind lady! Once revived, she had hurried back to the theater to see the last number, "All Choked Up," and she joyously joined in the applause.

I've thought often of that night and of that moment. I like to think I would have stopped the show for an undeniable emergency, but I've never been totally sure.

JOY RINALDI: Tom was *not* pacing when the audience burst into applause and then rose to a standing ovation.

KEN WAISSMAN: Following the performance, everyone headed uptown to Sardi's Restaurant for the opening-night party.

JOY RINALDI: We all piled in to wait for the reviews. It is the dream of every actor to be part of the theater tradition of celebrating at Sardi's, surrounded by all those sketches of famous people on the walls, anticipating the all-important review from the *New York Times.* We were all high with the excitement of the night and our accomplishment.

KEN WAISSMAN: Sardi's had a television mounted to the wall, so we could see the TV reviews as they came in. The first review was Stewart Klein on channel 5. It came on shortly after 10:00 PM and it was a pan. However, when Stewart Klein leads off with a negative review, for some unknown reason the other reviews often turn out to be good. So there was hope.

The next was the WNBC-TV review by Betty Rollin. It was a rave. "Run, don't walk to the Eden Theatre," she said.

Shortly thereafter our press agent, Betty Lee Hunt, as well as Maxine, Tom, Jacobs, Casey, and I, went across the street to the advertising agency Blaine Thompson. The agency had someone at the *Times*, a night watchman, who would call as soon as Clive Barnes submitted his review and read it over the phone. The actual print review wouldn't be on the newspaper stands until well after midnight.

We all listened on extension phones throughout the office as this fellow, with a less than perfect command of the English language, in a dry monotone *slowly* read us the review. It began with Barnes stating that all he could remember about 1959 was that it was a good year for Burgundy and ended with "If there is a place in New York for a modern 1950s rock parody musical, then *Grease* might well *slide* into it. The first-night audience seemed genuinely to enjoy it, so perhaps there is." Not a complete pan but definitely not a rave.

TOM MOORE: I was depressed, but Jim Jacobs was enraged. He threatened to find Clive Barnes and "punch him out."

KEN WAISSMAN: We felt devastated and returned to Sardi's. I can still remember getting off the elevator on the second floor, where the party was taking place, and revving up a smile as I faced everyone at the party. Spirits were still high from the Betty Rollin review.

A little after midnight someone went out to pick up the *New York Times*. When the paper arrived at the party and started getting passed around, a heavy, funereal weight descended. Nothing breaks up an opening-night party quicker than the moment the *Times* review arrives and it's mixed to negative.

JOY RINALDI: We were all crushed when the *New York Times*'s review came in from Clive Barnes. He was not a fan. "*Grease*, a joke that's bound to wear thin." Clive Barnes.

MARYA SMALL (*Frenchy*): One of the reviewers called us Greasers clearly a bunch of thirty-year-olds trying to play teenagers. Well, maybe one or two of us actually were thirty, like me.

BARRY BOSTWICK (*Zuko*): America—1972. I mean, who didn't love the '50s? Apparently one critic, who wrote, "The worst thing I ever saw opened at the Eden Theatre last night!" But I knew we were doing something right when a reviewer called my character, Danny Zuko, "the creep of her dreams."

KEN WAISSMAN: The next morning we gathered at Blaine Thompson to see the other reviews and decide what actions to take. The *Daily News* was a rave: "*Grease,* a lively and funny musical—the dancingest show in town!" Douglas Watt.

And the *Times* review didn't seem nearly as bad as it had sounded over the phone. Richard Watts, the critic for the *New York Post,* gave us a pan. Martin Gottfried from *Women's Wear Daily* also gave us a pan. Marilyn Stasio in *Cue* magazine gave us a favorable review, as did the Newark *Star-Ledger.* Walter Kerr would give us a very favorable review the following Sunday in the *New York Times,* but at this point that was unknown.

KATHI MOSS: In those days the *New York Times* alone could determine a show's fate. At some point I heard general manager Eddie Davis tell Ken and Maxine to "cut your losses, close the show." Well, so much for my Broadway debut.

I don't know what it was that made Ken and Maxine ignore this advice. Maybe it was because they were young and brave, but maybe they'd also noticed those people dancing in the aisles. For whatever reason they kept the show open. Which meant the world to me and to everyone in the cast and team, and eventually to the hundreds and then thousands of other performers and creative folk who followed.

Kathi Moss (Cha-Cha) and Barry Bostwick (Danny) winning the hand jive dance contest.

MARYA SMALL: Even after opening, Borrelli kept telling me I better be looking for another job. He never let up. He sent me notes: *It's over, get used to it. This dud is gonna fold any day now. Are you listening?*

"Yes," I said, "I'm listening." Jim, always a *tasty* thorn in my side. But I was thinking, *I am not missing out on enjoying this experience.* I did start looking at the *Backstage* job ads the next day though.

KEN WAISSMAN: Business had increased with each preview week, but we were still grossing under the weekly breakeven. With decidedly mixed notices and a less than favorable review from the *Times*, my general manager, Eddie Davis, and our attorney, Joel Arnold, recommended we put up a one-week closing notice. This would allow us to close the show at the end of the

Maxine Fox and Ken Waissman,
the intrepid *Grease* producers.

week without incurring further losses and debts. As a result of the preview losses, Maxine and I were already in debt for about $20,000. If business were to pick up as the week moved forward, we could take the notice down. However, once the notice goes up, all contracts are broken and actors are free to leave. Putting up the notice would also get around town in a flash, labeling the show a flop.

Maxine and I felt strongly that since the box office gross had increased for each of the preview weeks, the "pilot light" was burning, which meant that word of mouth appeared to be driving it. We told ourselves that since we didn't have the assets to cover the $20,000 debt we already had, we might as well not have the assets to cover a larger debt as well. We decided not to put up the notice.

Matthew Serino, our account executive at Blaine Thompson, started working on a quote ad.

At noon, we checked the theater box office. People were buying tickets, and in larger numbers than the week before.

Since the *Daily News* critic, Doug Watt, and the *New York Post* critic, Richard Watts, had names that sounded similar, I suggested we take the rave review by Doug Watt, lay it out to look exactly like a Richard Watts review, and buy advertising space on the *New York Post*'s theater page, reprinting the *Daily News* rave in the exact *New York Post* format. We made sure the repackaged Doug Watt review for the *Post* arrived exactly five minutes before the cutoff for the next day's ads. That way, we hoped, it would be too late for anyone to pick up on what we were doing and stop the ad.

The ad ran the next day, and it looked like the *New York Post* had given us a rave. The paper was furious when they realized what had happened and made bold threats to Blaine Thompson, but nothing ever came of it.

We broke even the week after the opening. The following week, we made a profit. It looked like we might beat the *Times* review!

New York magazine in those days listed "hot tickets." I told our general manager, whose office handled the house-seat requests, that they were to tell whoever called that all the house seats were sold out. After a month of "not having any house seats available," word reached the *New York* magazine editors, and they started listing *Grease* as a "hot ticket."

We were on our way!

The Greasers take the stage: Broadway's original Burger Palace Boys and Pink Ladies.

9 | *"Rock 'n' Roll Is Here to Stay"*

WALTER BOBBIE (*Roger*): *Grease* was a peculiar hit. Initially our bragging rights were slim and local. My mother had a hair salon in New Jersey. She proudly told one of her customers that her son was in *Grease*, to which her customer replied, "Greece. Has he sent you a postcard?" This is before the Internet, when it took longer for news to get to New Jersey.

MARYA SMALL (*Frenchy*): Our audiences were sparse in the beginning, but Ken, Maxine, and the press team had ideas about how to fill up the theater and make it look like we were a hit, like we were selling out, every seat in the house filled. Tom told me once, years later, "Fake it till you make it."

Well, that's exactly what they did. They brought in lots of high school students; the kids loved us. They filled those empty holes in the audience. A bonus: lots of our friends got to come for free, which was great.

It was a major team effort, and because the word of mouth was great, we were beginning to make it. In about two weeks there were crowds outside the stage door every night! Now we really did have a steady paycheck; I wouldn't have to find that job. Performing the show every night was always a thrill.

It was so fun becoming a hit. Being in a hit show—nothing like it! Every night I would stand in the wings when Adrienne sang "There Are Worse Things I Could Do," and every night she made me cry. Luckily I had socks in my bra to wipe away my drizzling mascara before going back on for the last scene.

BARRY BOSTWICK (*Zuko*): Before each performance the Burger Palace Boys would sing a few doo-wop songs in the wings, and Jim Borrelli would smash his fist into the back wall of the theater to get into character. I don't

Barry Bostwick, James Canning,
Timothy Meyers, and Jim Borrell.

ever remember anyone doing a vocal or physical warm-up before the show. We
would just light up another Lucky Strike and go out and pretend we were a gang
from Chicago and could beat the world with our prop chains and false teenage
bravado. Of course, we would all lose our voices every few months. Smoking
and singing falsetto don't really work together very well over a long run.

JIM CANNING (*Doody*): The show had been running for a few weeks,
and business was picking up. The producers needed to get a cast album out.
That's how we all ended up in a big-time MGM recording studio on our day
off, a Monday in March 1972. The cast had been told to show up at noon. It
would be a full day of recording all the songs in the show. We were going to
be paid $185 for the day. I have that in my journal.

There was an intense excitement surrounding the process of going into a
studio to record the songs we had been singing every night for a month or so.
Most of us in the original cast had never really been in a big-time recording
studio, but we knew our songs. We wanted to make them perfect. But in a

music studio the expertise seems to shift from the creative team and the actors to the sound engineers and technicians. The musicians would go first, putting down the tracks for our songs, and then we would go into our little cubicles and try to belt out our best rendition. I remember that I performed "Those Magic Changes" in one take. The engineers liked it and the writers liked it and the producers liked it and Louis St. Louis liked it. So that was that.

But not all the songs were that easy. There were all kinds of problems. Some were technical, but others were interpretation arguments. As the day wore on, tensions seemed to wax and wane. Singers can't really hear themselves as well as onstage, and the creative team was in a separate room. There were heated discussions in there. You could see them through the glass. The major emotion in that recording studio gradually became exhaustion. There are fifteen numbers in the show; they all had to have their due.

We worked through that entire day and into the night. The last "We Go Together" finished up around two in the morning.

After the recording session wrapped, we all stumbled over to Pat Birch's apartment on Seventy-Second Street. We had a few beers, and just about the time people were ready to leave, there was this commotion in the kitchen.

Recording the original Broadway cast album.

JIM JACOBS (*Author/Composer*): To this day I'm thankful for Jim Borrelli, not only because he was a great Sonny in the show but because one late night after a very long day recording the original cast album, I almost punched Ken Waissman in the mouth.

Something bad had happened during that day—something bad from the guy overseeing the cast recording. I was telling Ken and Maxine about it, and Maxine said, "Well, why didn't you go over and say something?" And I said, "No, that's your job. You're the producer. You never say anything. You always send someone else out to do the dirty work, you know."

KEN WAISSMAN (*Producer*): Jim, like everyone, was drained emotionally from the tension of the long-day-into-late-night recording session. He brought up his frustration with the guy who had overseen the cast-album recording. Actually I think Jim was having an attack of "flop sweat," as it was still hit or miss as to whether the show would make it or not. He started accusing me of being the reason we weren't a hit. He and I got into a heated argument.

JIM CANNING: Suddenly, like without warning, a fight breaks out between Jim Jacobs and Ken Waissman. I mean, like a real fight, with cursing and pushing. It was a quick escalation, moving from the kitchen into the living room. The writer/composer and the producer are ready to start beating the shit out of each other! Right there in Pat Birch's living room! We're all stunned and speechless except for Jim Borrelli, who grew up in a tough mill town north of Boston. He jumps up from the sofa and runs—I mean *runs*—across the room and gets between the two and pushes them apart. I remember that he looked like a referee in a boxing match who has to separate the two fighters and send them to their respective corners.

JIM JACOBS: And then Ken said something that really pissed me off, and I pulled back and threw a haymaker directly at his jaw, but all of a sudden my arm was grabbed from behind just as I was inches from his puss. Borrelli says, "You don't wanna do that, man." Then Warren grabs me and says, "Jim, come on, it's not worth it." And I walked away.

JIM CANNING: It was over that fast. There were some mumbled apologies and tepid goodbyes. I never knew what the fight was about, but it was pretty dramatic, especially for a green kid from Chicago in his first New York show!

JIM JACOBS: The next day I got called on the carpet by all the big honchos at our agency, ICM. *Now, Jim, this is not the streets of Chicago. You can't* *just go around punching people in the mouth because you don't like something about them.*

I'm going, *Yeah, OK. Sorry. Right. I need a break.*

JIM CANNING: The album turned out to be great, but the fight—man, that was unforgettable!

BARRY BOSTWICK: Performing in *Grease* was damn hard work, and the hardest work of all was performing "All Choked Up." I never liked that number and did everything I could to spice it up for myself—ripping my T-shirt to shreds, doing knee slides, eventually going halfway across the stage and singing more than my heart out.

I'm pretty sure I invented those knee slides—much to the detriment of the many Zukos to follow. There have been many damaged knees and lower-back issues for all of us elder Greasers. You're welcome!

There were many, many nights I would come offstage and not remember how the show went or even where I had been. It wasn't me out there—it was Zuko. And the others weren't just actors playing parts but members of a real gang.

ADRIENNE BARBEAU (*Rizzo*): The one scene from the show I really enjoyed had Rizzo and Kenickie making out on a bench, upstage center. Well, if it wasn't upstage center, it sure seems like that to me in my memory. I don't recall the entire scene; I have no idea what was going on around us. Zuko and Sandy could have been singing, Rump and Jan could have been flirting, Rydell High could have been on fire, I don't know. All I know is I was having a great time sucking face with Timothy Meyers.

And he was too, I think. At least if the predictable signs of physical pleasure were telling the tale. We just had a great time writhing around upstage. Timothy was a good-looking guy and a terrific actor—always a turn-on for me. I began to look forward to our scene on the bench much more than I should have. And I started thinking that maybe, just maybe, Tim and I might become something other than actors sharing the stage together.

Until he invited me to his apartment after the show one night. And introduced me to his boyfriend. Oh well. Didn't stop either of us from loving that scene—upstage center, on the bench.

ALAN PAUL (*Teen Angel / Johnny Casino*): In the summer of 1972, *Life* magazine, at that time the biggest publication in America, wanted to do a feature on the '50s revival sweeping America. They asked the just-opened

Grease to be a part of it. A photographer came by the theater and took photos of the whole cast onstage, but to my surprise the editor wanted to do a session with me alone. *Why me?* I thought they would want to shoot our star, Barry Bostwick, because he was the "leader of the pack," but I was told that they specifically wanted a Marlon Brando type, reminiscent of the biker he played in the film *The Wild One*, and they thought they could get that with me. Personally I think they chose me because out of all my fellow Greasers, I always won the award for best pompadour!

The photo wound up being the centerfold of that issue, and as Tom Moore recently said to me, "You became the face of *Grease*."

Alan Paul, the face of *Grease*.

Timothy Meyers (Kenickie) and Adrienne Barbeau (Rizzo) in rehearsal.

"Maybe Baby"

JOY RINALDI (*Understudy*): *Grease* had opened, but there were still very few rehearsals for the understudies during those first weeks. One day when I arrived at the theater a half hour before showtime, Katie Hanley (Marty) met me, limping across the stage and saying, "You're going to have to go on for me tonight. I hurt my foot!"

"Ha ha, Katie, very funny."

"I'm not joking, Joy!"

I could see by the look in her eyes that she *wasn't* kidding! At first, nerves set in and I wanted to run. But I didn't have time to panic; I had to get ready. *I was going to be performing in* Grease *for the first time in my life!*

It was magic! All those colored pencils and notes paid off, and I felt like I was born to be up there! Singing "Freddy, My Love" for the first time was amazing, and being part of the gang was fantastic. Everything went really well. When we exited on "We Go Together," I couldn't have been happier. When the curtain call was over, the cast hugged and congratulated me, and for a moment anyway I felt like I was part of the original cast!

DAN DEITCH (*Understudy*): During a rigorous rehearsal process, Joy Rinaldi and I carefully observe the characters emerge. But we have no rehearsals ourselves.

The week we open, Tim Meyers and Walter Bobbie get sick, so I have to perform both Kenickie and Roger with virtually no rehearsal.

Kenickie comes first. Going on as Kenickie was like being launched into outer space with no return ticket. Or being thrown into the Super Bowl without ever playing football. The blue spotlights blind me. Throbbing music beats fast and loud, rendering me deaf. And the cast transforms into mega-versions of the normal people I had watched in rehearsal.

Zuko, a nice guy from San Mateo, California, is now a hyper-energized, sneering version of Jumpin' Jack Flash, contorting his body into unreal postures. Roger morphs into a Macy's Thanksgiving Day Parade version of his prior self, hitting what seem to be ten high Cs. Marty is the incandescent platonic ideal of the girl next door. But the one who worries me the most is the new, amped-up Rizzo, eyes blazing in jilted fury. She is all muscle and pins me down so fiercely in one of Pat Birch's ingenious dance moves that I can barely breathe.

Greasers rush by at supersonic speed. If I get in the way, I'll be trampled to death. With a wild look in their eyes, the cast populates a crazy hallucination about the pleasure and pain of being a teenager at Rydell High. It is somewhat similar to my own bourgeois high school experience but with music, dancing, and lights. And roars of approval from the audience.

JOHN FENNESSY (*Understudy/Assistant Stage Manager*): The first time I ever went on for someone in *Grease* was as Kenickie. Very early on. I wasn't even officially an understudy yet. I knew the role well enough as I'd been watching the show for some time. I knew all the lines. I knew all the blocking. And I grew up with Kenickies.

Just before—and I mean *just* before—I went on at the top of the show, nervous as hell, ascending the steps backstage, feeling like Robespierre, Kathi Moss looked at me and with the sweetest smile said, "This is great, you're getting to do this. Really neat. It should be a great experience for you. But the thing I really want to say, and I mean this sincerely—it's straight from my heart—" And suddenly, in a nanosecond, her face twisted into an amalgam of Mrs. Hyde, Medusa, and Leona Helmsley, and she sneered into my face,

"Don't fuck up! You hear me? Do *not* fuck up! You fuck up, you're on your own, pal. I'm telling you, no one is going to help you out there. You fuck up anything tonight, it's your career. Remember that."

And as I stared at her stunned in absolute horror, Kathi threw her head back and with that wild Irish laugh of hers yelled, "We're on!"

JOY RINALDI: One night I was already onstage for Frenchy when Katie Hanley, who was playing Marty, for some reason could not continue for the second act. So, after some quick consultations with the stage manager, I continued in Act 2 as Frenchy but speaking both Frenchy's and Marty's lines. My mind was going a thousand miles an hour!

That night there were three people on that stage: Frenchy, Marty, and Joy, the actress, constantly trying to stay on top of the game. The coup de grâce was in Jan's basement when I walked across the stage to Kenickie and whispered that Rizzo was knocked up—not as the sexy, sassy Marty but as the sweet, bubbleheaded Frenchy. His reaction was unforgettable!

The Actors' Equity Association requires that an audience be informed when an understudy is performing, so the audience knew what was going on the whole time and at the curtain call rewarded me with a standing ovation.

I was in heaven!

"Bye Bye Love"

DAN DEITCH: We are a hit, and the show will eventually move to Broadway, but there is no way I'm going with it. No one knew, but after understudying all the male roles since the first rehearsal, I wasn't going to last much longer due to a required minor surgery, which took place at New York Hospital a month or so after we opened. It was done by the same doc that operated on the Shah of Iran. Jeff Conaway takes my place. It had been a wild and happy ride.

KATIE HANLEY (*Marty*): It was with great remorse and guilt that I chose to leave the show and this close group of gifted and dedicated friends, just as plans were excitedly being made to move from the Eden to Broadway.

I had a meeting with my agent, struggling to explain that something was changing in me. My twenty-two-year-old self couldn't yet grasp that the "something" was reuniting with my eighteen-month-old baby daughter, Jeanette.

My parents had encouraged me to pursue the acting career I'd worked for so hard at college, offering to care for my baby in Chicago so that I could try to secure a future for the two of us in New York. I had a fierce focus and drive to succeed when I went to New York, and some wonderful times, but I deeply missed Jeanette—seeing her take her first steps and celebrate her first birthday. After months apart, not long after *Grease*'s opening night, my mother flew my baby to New York to join me.

On performance nights when I couldn't find a sitter, little Jeanette and I would catch a bus to the Eden. She sat right next to me in the dressing room when I put on my makeup and costume, and the Pink Ladies and others in the cast would watch her during the moments I was onstage.

With each day that I was able to once again be the mother to my little girl, my heart melted, as did my drive and focus as an actress. I saw no other choice but to give my notice and leave the show.

It broke my heart when the two people I so adored, our director Tom Moore and beloved choreographer Pat Birch, pulled me aside to ask what was going on and why I had to leave. They tried everything they could to encourage me to stay. I didn't understand any of it myself, so it was impossible to explain it to them.

I'm profoundly proud to have such a fine daughter, but I'm also deeply proud to be able to say that I was Marty in the original New York company of *Grease*.

LEFT: Katie and Jeanette Hanley. RIGHT: Katie with the Pink Ladies.

10

"All I Have to Do Is Dream"

The Tony Awards

KEN WAISSMAN (*Producer*): The 1972 Tony Awards was scheduled to be broadcast live on April 23.

Although geographically located off-Broadway, we were in a 1,100-seat house, paying Broadway Equity scale to the actors and Broadway scale to the musicians. Our press agent, Betty Lee Hunt, and I decided that *Grease* should be considered Broadway and eligible for the Tony Awards.

I spoke to Alexander Cohen, who produced the annual Tony Awards show on behalf of the League of New York Theatres and Producers (now the Broadway League), the American Theatre Wing, and the ABC network. I was told that in order to qualify, a show must be in an official Broadway house located within the square blocks bound by Forty-First Street and Fifty-Fifth Street, from Ninth Avenue to Sixth Avenue.

We decided to file a lawsuit against the League, the Wing, and ABC. We prepared a press release to be distributed to the theatrical press corps. Before filing the suit, I hand-delivered a copy of the release along with a description of the lawsuit to Alexander Cohen. In the cover letter I said we were planning to file the suit and send out the press release that day at noon. Cohen called me in a fury.

"We don't air our dirty laundry in public," he stated. "We deal with it within the League."

"We tried that," I explained. "You refused."

"You'll never win this suit," he said angrily.

"That's not the point," I shot back. "If we were eligible, we might get some nominations and benefit from the national publicity. However, a lawsuit could perhaps get us even greater publicity."

Cohen asked if I would extend by two hours the time I was planning to send out the press release. I agreed. He would call ABC, and I felt certain they wouldn't want the negative stigma of a lawsuit. A little after noon, Cohen called. We would be eligible. He was not a happy camper and added that we'd probably not receive any nominations because, although the League and the Wing were agreeing, the nominating committee would still consider *Grease* off-Broadway and ignore us. They didn't. We got seven nominations!

They were for Best Musical (Maxine Fox and myself and the authors, Jim Jacobs and Warren Casey), Best Choreography (Patricia Birch), Best Performance by an Actor in a Leading Role in a Musical (Barry Bostwick), Best Performance by an Actress in a Featured Role in a Musical (Adrienne Barbeau), Best Performance by an Actor in a Featured Role in a Musical (Timothy Meyers), Best Book of a Musical (Jim Jacobs and Warren Casey), and Best Costume Design (Carrie Robbins).

Barry Bostwick, Adrienne Barbeau, and Timothy Meyers with their Tony nominations.

KATHI MOSS (*Cha-Cha*): 1972 was a different information world—no Internet, of course, and no multitude of cable stations covering every area of American life. The only way to find out a lot of things was to pick up a newspaper.

Which is what Tim Meyers did one evening in late spring 1972. He and his boyfriend were on their way to a movie in Brooklyn. Tim stopped at a newsstand for an early edition of the next day's *New York Times*. While they waited in line, he paged through the paper and discovered a list of the Tony nominations. He was happily surprised to see *Grease* on the list for best musical, but he was most startled to find his own name listed among the best supporting actors. He was stunned. He said it was an out-of-body experience—standing in a line of strangers, discovering his life had suddenly changed, that recognition of the sort he'd been imagining since childhood was suddenly his. He was more than a little overwhelmed.

ADRIENNE BARBEAU (*Rizzo*): I was on my knees in the bathroom, scrunched between the toilet and the tub with my head under the faucet, when the phone rang. This was long before cell phones or even portable handsets, so I ran into the bedroom, dripping shampoo, and raced back to the tub dragging the landline.

That's all I really remember about getting the call that I'd been nominated for a Tony. I haven't got a clue who called me—if it was a friend, one of the producers, or someone from the Tony Awards. All I remember was not understanding what they were saying. *The Tony Awards? A Tony nomination?* That didn't make any sense to me at all. We weren't even on Broadway! I'd never heard the Tony Awards mentioned; actually, I barely knew what they were.

But I knew I needed to dress up for them. I walked to SoHo, which in 1972 was a not-too-nice neighborhood south of Houston Street where a few new shops had opened, and I bought a pair of dark-green Yves Saint Laurent ankle-strap heels for thirty-four dollars—more money than I'd ever spent on a pair of shoes in my life. Then I went to the local yarn shop and bought skeins of this shiny gold Lurex yarn. I crocheted myself a huge, fancy evening shawl. At least, I thought it was fancy.

I've always been very proud that I was nominated for a Tony, but I don't remember anything about the awards night. I didn't win, I know that. Was there a party afterward? I don't know. If there was, I don't remember going.

All I remember are my oh-so-expensive ankle-strap heels and much-more-affordable homemade gold shawl. I still have them both.

KEN WAISSMAN: The majority of the Tony voters didn't respond to their invitations to come downtown to see the show, so we knew we wouldn't win any Tonys. However, we were able to publicize the nominations, and *Grease* was mentioned six times on the national broadcast.

With the Tony broadcast, *Grease* achieved full acceptance as an authentic Broadway musical. We had arrived. This paved the way for our transfer to a theater smack in the middle of the Broadway theater district.

The Phoney Awards

JOY RINALDI (*Understudy*): When *Grease* was nominated for seven Tony Awards, we were awarded none. We were the black sheep of Broadway.

The *Grease* creative team: Ken Waissman, Maxine Fox, Warren Casey, Pat Birch, Jim Jacobs, and Tom Moore.

Somewhere along the line, Ken and Maxine came up with the fun idea of having an ersatz annual event called the Phoney Awards to mimic the Tonys. The statues were gold-painted phone handsets (the old-fashioned *big* ones) attached to plastic stands. It was always party time as we all laughed with and sometimes at each other when the Phoneys were handed out.

Of course, I never expected anything because I was an understudy, but lo and behold, one year my name was announced. *Wow!* I thought, *maybe for "Joy Rinaldi, the Woman of a Thousand Faces!" or "Joy and Her Coat of Many Colors!"* But what I heard was "... and to Joy Rinaldi, a Phoney Award for Always a Bridesmaid, Never a Bride!"

Big laughter! I laughed too. But it hurt—a lot!

Being sentimental, I kept that ridiculous, ugly, gold-plated telephone until 2010, when my therapist in no uncertain terms told me to "throw it out or burn it—but whatever you do, get rid of it!"

Giving out the annual Phoneys at Sardi's, with Rebecca Gilchrist, Treat Williams, and Tom Moore.

11 | "Oh What a Dream"
The Broadhurst Theatre, June 7, 1972–November 19, 1972

MAXINE FOX (*Producer*): After the show had been running for about three months, our press agent Betty Lee Hunt brought up the idea of moving uptown. June was approaching and she worried that tourists, the dominant ticket buyers during the summer, wouldn't be willing to find their way downtown.

Ken was hesitant. Moving would double our weekly overhead, and he was nervous that the uptown Broadway audiences wouldn't embrace *Grease*.

Betty Lee took a yellow legal pad, drew a line down the middle, and marked one side PRO and one side CON. We began making a list. There was no doubt. The PRO column had it! We decided to move.

Bernie Jacobs, the head of the Shubert Organization, offered us the Broadhurst Theatre on West Forty-Fifth Street until November. At that point we'd have to move to another theater because Neil Simon's new play *The Sunshine Boys* was moving in. Bernie said if we couldn't agree on another Shubert theater and the Nederlanders or the Jujamcyns had one available, he would let us out of our contract. The move was on.

TOM MOORE (*Director*): When the decision was made to move uptown, it was met within our company by almost universal excitement. But not everyone was so sure our little show would survive the journey, and I was one of those in doubt. However, despite my fears of an early closing, I was pretty quickly seduced by the idea of having my first show on Broadway.

After the Broadhurst load-in, while we were in the middle of our tech rehearsals, I kept looking around at the carefully restored detail of this historic, classic Broadway theater. It was mesmerizingly beautiful.

91

As we kept working, I began to have a mystical feeling. I knew I had been in this theater before. Then it hit me. The perspective had been different because my friends and I had been in the balcony, but this was the same theater in which I had seen my very first Broadway show on my first visit to New York while in my first year at Yale.

The show was the musical *Half a Sixpence,* starring the legendary song-and-dance man Tommy Steele, and here I was only five years later with my own song-and-dance show. The serendipity of the connection seemed transcendent, and from then on I had no doubts whatsoever. Everything was as it should be. I just knew we would be successful and run. Of course, just how far and how long we would run, no one—especially this one—could have possibly imagined.

KATHI MOSS (*Cha-Cha*): It was clear early on that Ken and Maxine's decision not to close the show was the right one. Despite the mixed reviews we soon started selling out, and by June we'd moved uptown to the Broadhurst,

a real live Broadway house. I was just twenty-six years old, only a few months away from being a file clerk, and now I was appearing in a genuine, Tony-nominated hit *on Broadway!* It was as if a door I'd been pushing against suddenly swung wide open to let me through.

JOY RINALDI (*Understudy*): *Grease* was moving from the Eden Theatre downtown to the Broadhurst Theatre uptown on Broadway. Katie Hanley, who was the original Marty, had just left the show and a replacement had not yet been found. I had been playing Marty since Katie left, and that continued during the move to Broadway. The show was rereviewed by Emory Lewis of the *New York Times*: "There was an exciting newcomer named Joy Rinaldi in last night's cast, and she was splendid. With her big voice and a glowing stage presence, she turns 'Freddy My Love' into a showstopper. It is a most promising Broadway debut."

I was thrilled!

With such a glowing review I was floating on a cloud, but I was back as understudy a few weeks later when a new Marty joined the cast. No way around this—I was devastated.

MEG BENNETT (*Marty*): I joined the Broadway cast of *Grease* in June, just as the show was moving uptown to the Broadhurst Theatre. Because of the move, rehearsing me into the show was less than simple. The cast was busy transitioning to their new digs. I never even met most of them until my one rehearsal the afternoon I opened.

I basically learned the role of Marty by watching the show from the audience, and from Tommy Smith, our most amazing stage manager, who taught me all the blocking. But it was Adrienne Barbeau who really saved me. She was the designated "dance captain," which meant she was assigned to teach me all the musical numbers. However, she'd just been tapped by Norman Lear to move to Los Angeles to play Bea Arthur's daughter in *Maude* and was leaving in two weeks. But in that short time she managed to whip me into shape, transforming me into something resembling a rough-and-rowdy greaser. The best part was we also became friends—a friendship that has lasted to this day.

However, the Burger Palace Boys thought I was too sweet to be a true greaser. They decided I definitely needed some on-the-job training. So a few nights before I opened in the show, a crew led by Jim Borrelli along with some of the stagehands took me to a seedy strip club on Forty-Second Street to give me a little seasoning.

Meg Bennett, too sweet to be a Greaser?

I've blocked most of it from my memory, though I do have a vague recollection of slipping a five-dollar bill into the panties of one of the exotic dancers. I guess it did the trick since the guys never complained about my Marty again.

JIM WESTON (*Vince Fontaine*): My entry into *Grease* was unexpected and sudden. I was cast when Don Billet, the actor playing Vince Fontaine, left the show. It was a really easy part, although ironic for me as a singer—no song.

That weekend the stage manager walked me into the show so I had the opportunity to see how all the moving parts fit. Tuesday the cast came in an hour before half hour to do my put-in rehearsal of the Rydell prom scene and dances—and that was it. It was half hour.

I had the first act to anticipate, since my one big scene was at the top of Act 2, but I was as confident as Vince himself when I joined the cast for the big dance.

When my cue came to give the rules for the hand jive dance contest, I left Marty, who I had been flirting with as only the second-rate disc jockey Vince could do, bounded up the stairs to the upper platform to join Miss Lynch and Johnny Casino, and grabbed the mic. I opened my mouth to begin my fast-talking spiel—and *went completely blank*. Every word of my well-rehearsed patter

Jim Weston (Vince Fontaine).

was nowhere to be found. I continued to grin out at my captive audience, and the only words that came out were "Hey, hey, hey," which echoed across the stage.

The Rydell kids in their prom finest, totally in character and with no idea that their idol disc jockey had forgotten his lines, all yelled back in unison, "Hey, hey, hey!" It snapped me right back, and I was in! Everything came back, and my Vince glibly prattled away, winning those teenagers' hearts and maybe even the respect of the actors playing them.

By the way, when I had seen the show that weekend, the character that made the biggest impression on me was Kenickie, played by Tim Meyers. It was obvious that he had been cast straight from Rikers Island prison. Imagine my surprise when I joined the cast and found out he was not only a very fine actor but the gentlest, kindest man on the stage.

ADRIENNE BARBEAU (*Rizzo*): Timmy was so brilliant as Kenickie that the William Morris Agency immediately wanted to sign him. When he went in for his interview, the agent insisted on leaving his office door open. Halfway through the interview he got up and closed it. Then he apologized to Timmy, explaining he'd left the door open in case his secretary needed to call security. He'd truly believed Tim was the juvenile delinquent he'd seen onstage.

Timothy Meyers, the gentlest man onstage.

BARRY BOSTWICK (*Zuko*): One of the major differences between our cast and all the others to follow was that the original cast was older and grew up during the end of the actual '50s. We had firsthand knowledge, and we remembered a lot.

Thanks to Adrienne Barbeau's Rizzo, I got to cop my first onstage feel during the park scene! And when it didn't get cut in previews, I got to repeat it in every single performance.

I loved props and didn't stop adding them after we previewed and opened. I thought they were "inventive additions." Our director Tom Moore called them "improvements," and he was quick to remove one if it wasn't integral to the scene.

Later in the run we were out of control. The cast was pretty bored with the same old same old, and being the creative creatures we were, we got more creative. Every note session with Tom began this way, "Barry . . . no more walking on with scuba-diving flippers, masks, and snorkels . . . or a paddle-ball set . . . or a Hula-Hoop . . . or a set of jacks, or a . . ." Well, you see what I mean? What was a creative guy to do? Tom would laugh—and then he would cut it. He was relentless.

The original *Grease* gang.

ADRIENNE BARBEAU: I loved singing "Worse Things." I especially loved the moment of silence right after the music finished, before the audience started clapping, when if I'd done my job right, I'd hear sniffles from the people I'd touched.

On the night of my final performance, as I stood in the stage-left wings preparing to sing "Worse Things" for the last time and hoping I'd be able to get through it without weeping, I looked across the stage to the stage-right wings, and there in all their bare-assed glory were five naked Burger Palace Boy butts staring me in the face.

Still didn't keep me from crying when I finished the song.

The Burger Palace Boys and the Pink Ladies.

12

"Roll Over Beethoven"

The Royale Theatre, November 21, 1972–January 27, 1980

KEN WAISSMAN (*Producer*): The Labor Day issue of the Sunday *New York Times* was traditionally filled with large Broadway ads announcing new shows coming that season. Maxine and I had taken out a full-page ad for *Grease*. Our headline was SEE GREASE! JUST FOR THE FUN OF IT! I took an advance copy of the *Times* with me when Maxine and I met with Bernie Jacobs to discuss which theaters would be available in November when we had to leave the previously booked Broadhurst.

I spread the full-page ad on Bernie's desk. He said that unfortunately the only theater that would be available in late November would be the Ambassador Theatre on West Forty-Ninth Street. The Ambassador was known as a jinx house—a theater that seemed to attract flops. And it was too far uptown for easy walk-in trade.

Jimmy Nederlander had called earlier to say that if Jacobs and Maxine and I couldn't agree on a theater, he would offer us the Palace. I wanted to go to the soon-to-be-vacant Royale Theatre on Forty-Fifth Street. Bernie said legendary producer David Merrick wanted the Royale for his upcoming production of *Out Cry*. I reminded Bernie of his promise that we could go to another theater owner and mentioned that Jimmy Nederlander had offered us the Palace.

"You'd put *Grease* into that barn?" he asked.

"We don't want to," I answered. "But better there than the Ambassador."

He gave me a long, intense look and glanced again at the full-page advance copy of our Labor Day ad sitting on his desk. Then he abruptly got up from his chair and left the room.

After what seemed like an eternity, he returned. He walked behind his huge oak desk and pounded his fists so hard on the desktop I thought it would crack. "All right," he said. "You can have the Royale."

I found out later what happened when Bernie left the room during our meeting. He went to another office and called the box office treasurer of the Broadhurst. He told her his predicament and that Jimmy Nederlander had offered us the Palace. She told him he'd be crazy to let *Grease* go.

MARYA SMALL (*Frenchy*): When *Grease* moved to Forty-Fifth Street, I had the luxury of being able to walk to the Royale from my Hell's Kitchen sixth-floor walk-up. One of my fondest memories was hearing beautiful voices blending together in sweet harmonies lightly floating through the air as I approached the theater. It was Alan Paul (Teen Angel) rehearsing with his friends, Tim, Janis, and Laurel, in the alley that connects the Royale, Majestic, and Golden Theatres. A cappella in the stage door alley—wow, truly gorgeous. You just never knew what treasure you might find in that alley! I used to leave early just to hang out and listen.

WALTER BOBBIE (*Roger*): Many Broadway performers began doing club acts in the early '70s. More often than not, the acts were little more than personal

Garn Stephens (Jan), Marya Small (Frenchy), Joy Garrett (Rizzo), and Meg Bennett (Marty), "Freddy, My Love."

stories sandwiched between proven audition material for a two-drink minimum. But they were fun. Especially late night after a Broadway show.

Alan Paul began inviting us repeatedly to shell out two-drink minimums to hear his new vocal quartet. And we went repeatedly because they were not just fun, they were jaw-dropping. The sound was fresh, witty, retro, tight, sophisticated, and thrilling—and would soon cost way more than a two-drink minimum. Not only did Alan Paul have the best hair in the cast of *Grease* (damn him), he was on his way to becoming one-fourth of the Grammy-winning phenomenon Manhattan Transfer, and it was fantastic to witness them at the very beginning of their meteoric rise to international fame.

BARRY BOSTWICK (*Zuko*): Being part of "The First Family" of *Grease* has given me bragging rights for my whole life and career, and I have taken happy advantage of it. With my first Tony nomination for *Grease*, I had become a real part of the New York theater community. And I loved it. I had also become the pseudo–rock star that I always yearned to be. I especially loved being a Broadway lothario. The cast would all fall into Charlie's, Joe Allen's, or Sardi's after the show and continue strutting our stuff though many beers and female admirers. Who wouldn't have loved that?

A particularly high point was when they did a satiric drawing of me to be added to the collection of celebrities on the Sardi's Restaurant walls. As an actor in New York, when that happened, you had truly made it. It's still there, but maybe not so prominently displayed—for all the diners not to notice.

Barry Bostwick and his caricature at Sardi's.

MARYA SMALL: One night Kathi Moss asked if I wanted to go for a ride. She had a car in New York City—*Wow!*—because she had driven with Timmy (the future Kenickie) all the way from New Orleans to New York to break into show business.

She picked us up at the stage door. I hopped in and slid across the red leather seats to the middle, and Timmy hopped in and closed the door. We looked at each other, big smiles on our faces. We looked at the *Grease* marquee, we looked at the crowd at the stage door—mostly kids but every age, every kind of person you can imagine. Wow, we had fans, a lot of fans. Usually we'd hang out with them, signing autographs. People actually wanted our autographs!

But tonight Kathi was taking us for a ride. With her steady but delicate hands on the candy-apple-red leather steering wheel, she looked over her shoulder and slowly pulled out into moving traffic. Kathi was calm and gorgeous as she drove her cream-colored Cadillac convertible slowly up Broadway, just the three of us under all those Broadway lights with the sweet scent of warm pretzels in the air.

Then it happened. One of those real-life Nirvana experiences. I looked into Tim's green eyes that always sparkled, and it was as if we could see through time together. I looked into Kathi's eyes, so deep, so soft. We looked at each other. We laughed and looked again to see if we each experienced what we thought we did.

There was no time, just the three of us together. And just like that, in a moment, we were one. We were one, one for all time. I think about that moment now, and I begin to cry.

The next day we checked in with each other. *Was that really real? Yes, yes it was.* And it lives in me today nearly fifty years later.

WALTER BOBBIE: What I know is this: a good story needs conflict. And *Grease* had more than just conflict—it had crisis. Crisis in spades. Solved, scarred, healed, we emerged defiantly entertaining by opening night.

Our troubles now seem too tedious to taint our memories. What we remember is that nothing could stop the magic happening in the rehearsal room, onstage, and finally in the audience.

Magic is not knowing how the trick is done, not wanting to know. Magic is innocent. A blinding moment, when something impossible looks real. Not a trick but a wonder. That's what we had. We didn't really know how we did it.

Creative freedom, mutual respect, and celebrating everyone's uniqueness created fire in our rehearsal room so that when something wasn't working, it was a gut punch. We all wanted this, and we wanted it for each other as well!

When good fortune enters your life, you pray it comes again. Sometimes it does. At the very least there is joy recalling a time when it did. I believe in joy undeterred. Profound joy. That is what happened with the original company of *Grease*, and that DNA has passed along to generations of Greasers.

Marya Small, Ilene Kristen, Joy Garrett, Carole Demas, Meg Bennett, Garn Stephens, Barry Bostwick, Timothy Meyers, Jim Borrelli, James Canning, and Walter Bobbie, "All Choked Up."

13 | "Take Good Care of My Baby"

TOM MOORE (*Director*): One of the most common questions I'm asked regarding *Grease* on Broadway and on tour is "How long did you stay with the show?"

And the answer is this: When you create a show, you're forever its director, as long as your production runs. None of your work can ever be copied or duplicated in any form without credit and/or compensation.

A director comes back from time to time to check up on a show, to do touch-up rehearsals and to choose replacements. In the case of *Grease*, with its eight-year run on Broadway, its eight tours, and two London engagements, that's a lot of returns to the scene of the crime. It behooves a director to keep his show in opening-night shape for its entire run. Your name is on the showboard and in the program; it is your responsibility and your reputation. But a director moves on to other projects, and the care of a show is left in the trusted hands of the stage management team.

Grease and I were very fortunate to have a number of talented, terrific stage managers: a production stage manager, a stage manager, and sometimes an assistant who doubled as an understudy in each of our productions of *Grease*.

Although I don't want to slight anyone, as many fine professionals came our way, there are six who stand out for their importance in our *Grease* history: Tommy Smith, Steve Beckler, Lynne Guerra, Michael Martorella, John Fennessy, and John Everson. Legends all.

Tommy Smith, a gentle, stylish man who cared deeply, kept me so well informed that during my weekly telephone call from him, while I listened I

104

could eat dinner, organize the next day's work, get ready for bed, and brush my teeth, at which time I would thank him and gently bring the call to an end. His affection for actors and the show was unending, and he helped many replacement actors find their way to the heart of the show.

Steve Beckler, a man who was always at least one step ahead of you, made sure everything you needed was in place, sometimes before you ever even thought of it. A wonderful sounding board, always honest in his observations but encouraging. A great collaborator and a great friend.

Lynne Guerra was a formidable, totally accessible woman who became a den mother to all who came within her happy stage family. Always with an easy laugh and great sense of humor, and always on top of it all, Lynne became an institution at *Grease*. Everyone adored her.

Michael Martorella was a masterful stage manager, ready for anything, with a droll sense of humor and a great sense of the wonder of it all, making everyone comfortable but very clear on what was expected and how things were going to be. Michael made touring and Broadway seem easy. The cast and crew loved and respected him, as did I.

John Fennessy: With the show from the early days, John was also an understudy for many of the roles, and he juggled them all with talent, skill, and humor. When you were in a pinch, you called for John. And we did—many, many times.

John Everson: As assistant stage manager and understudy, John is one of those people who quietly becomes indispensable, a stalwart in a company, someone you can always count on, always.

These stage managers and their compatriots kept me always secure that *Grease* was in great hands. I am forever grateful to all these unsung heroes who I knew would keep *Grease* in that opening-night condition. The energy, the spirit, the finesse, and the consistency that audiences saw all those years owe a great deal to their careful watch.

14

"Let the Good Times Roll"

The First National Tour, December 1972–December 1974

A national tour of a Broadway hit is the way the United States discovers a show. The tour plays long runs in major cities, always in their showpiece theaters; the advance sales are terrific, the press attention is enormous, and the casts are feted in the cities they play. A national tour is the first-class way to go. "Broadway adjacent."

—TOM MOORE

The Auditions

TOM MOORE (*Director*): Once *Grease* became a Broadway hit, every young actor between the ages of eighteen and forty auditioned. There were thousands of auditions across the country—L.A., Chicago, San Francisco, and of course New York. *Grease* was now industrial strength—a big business—and we needed help. It was our good fortune to find the casting teams of Otto & Windsor (Linda and Geri) for the first years and then Johnson-Liff (Geoffrey and Vinnie). Vinnie was often the first face of *Grease* a scared young actor saw; Vinnie loved them all and they loved him. Through agent submissions and massive open calls, the search never stopped. There was a constant need for new actors on the tours and on Broadway.

JERRY ZAKS (*Kenickie*): I can't even begin to tell you how badly I wanted to be in *Grease*.

I came to New York in the fall of 1969 to be an actor. I had grown up as a kid in Paterson, New Jersey, passionately singing '50s rock 'n' roll songs to myself in the mirror over the bar of my parents' semifinished basement, so when *Grease* was announced I knew I was so right for it. I had to make it happen.

But I didn't have an agent, so I couldn't get an audition. Instead I went down to the open call, where a nice casting associate took my picture and résumé and said she'd be in touch. She never got in touch.

A year later, after the show had become a big hit, casting for the first national tour was announced. By then I'd found an agent (Jeff Lowenthal). He got me the audition, so I went to work as though my life depended on it. I came up with an arrangement of "Sixteen Candles" (by the Crests) that let me sing all the parts. I would follow that with a song called "Rockin' Robin." But the smartest thing I did was see the show the night before the audition. I bought an SRO ticket, stood in the back, and watched. I was looking for clues to Kenickie's character. The late Timothy Meyers was brilliant and so vivid: shamelessly, comically, unselfconsciously ferocious. His performance helped me understand what the creative team wanted.

I remember stepping out onto the stage of the Royale, my first footsteps on a Broadway stage. I was so nervous and so determined. I handed my sheet music to the piano player, Phyllis Grandy, and sang my songs.

A voice from the dark asked if I knew "Hound Dog." I said sure. I looked at Phyllis, she gave me a two-bar intro, and my inner Elvis erupted.

I read Kenickie's first scene. "Hey, where you at!"

Tom Moore asked if I could make the character a little more ferocious. So I did the scene again, only this time I gave them my best Timmy Meyers. I could hear the folks in the dark react. I finished the scene.

"Thank you. That's all we need today."

I started offstage, not quite sure how it went. I heard someone, maybe Tom, say, "See you again." That meant a callback!

Before I could say thank you, someone else, probably Jim Jacobs, stood up and said very emphatically, "Yeah, real soon!" That meant more than a callback. I floated out of the theater, beyond exhilarated.

After a couple more auditions, my agent called. "You got it!"—the greatest words an actor could hear. And so began two of the best years of my life.

MICHAEL LEMBECK (*Sonny*): The thing about auditions I remember most is that there were a *lot* of them, and they were held both in New York and all over Southern California. There were a few of us I saw at almost all of them in L.A., which was the same group that gathered at the Greek Theatre for the final. It was me, John Travolta, Judy Kaye, and Mike Clifford. The lasting memory for me at that final audition is how many times Louis St. Louis made me sing my audition song—each time a half step higher. It was easy for me, and I thought, *The guy I'm being considered for must have a great song.* When he finally stopped the singing audition, Louis said to me, "Just wanted you to know you can do it."

Unlike virtually everyone auditioning, I had never seen the show, never heard the score, and didn't know anything about it. I figured I had played a character like Sonny so many times before, I'd just do what I know and see what happens. So when I finally got the part, what I did not know in my own naïveté, chutzpah, and lack of intelligent curiosity, was that Sonny was the *only* Burger Palace Boy without a song. *WTF!* I thought. All that went away once we started rehearsals. Singing with my guys was a blast, and ultimately it didn't matter that I didn't have a song. It really became about the show, the relationships, and the journey of fun that was a year on the road.

JOHN TRAVOLTA (*Doody*): In the summer of '72 I had just moved from New York to Los Angeles. At that time there was a famous L.A. casting director by the name of Lynn Stalmaster; he tried hard and almost succeeded at casting me in a movie called *The Last Detail* with Jack Nicholson. The competition was between me and another young actor named Randy Quaid. Randy won the role and the following year received an Academy Award nomination. I was devastated.

But because I was eighteen, I was resilient and proceeded to book two small parts on two different TV shows that summer: *Owen Marshall, Counselor at Law*, a legal drama, and *Emergency!*, a medical drama.

My manager, Bob LeMond, called to tell me they were casting the first national tour of the Broadway production of *Grease*, and they would like me to audition for Danny. I had seen *Grease* when it opened at the Eden Theatre in New York in 1972, and it affected me deeply for all the same reasons it has affected millions over the years. Its power is inexplicable. I have stopped trying to figure out why, because art is an interpretive form and different for each of us who experiences it.

So of course I wanted to audition for Danny Zuko!

I commuted through L.A. to the audition on a tiny Honda motorcycle (more like a scooter). Having seen the show a couple times and knowing exactly what I should look like and how to behave, I had gone to a vintage store and purchased a worn-out black motorcycle jacket to wear with an iconic white T-shirt. I slicked back my very thick head of dark hair into a '50s pompadour and, with my tight jeans and scooter, found my way to the Greek Theatre, where the auditions were being held.

I sang Carole King's "I Feel the Earth Move." Louis St. Louis, the music director, who looked like a later-day beatnik, seemed very impressed with my voice; and Tom Moore, who appeared to be my age but looked totally collegiate, welcomed me warmly and seemed impressed with my abilities. There was also a dance audition later that included the Stroll and the hand jive. Pat Birch, the choreographer, thought I moved pretty well. All I remember is being exceptionally happy to be dressed up as Danny Zuko, having the opportunity to hopefully be in this terrific musical.

I was excited when I got the offer to do the show, but to my disappointment the offer was to play Doody, not Danny, because apparently the creative team thought I was "just too young."

I thought I had an advantage because I was the actual age of a high school senior and I would be perfect casting, or at least more accurate. But since everyone else was being cast older to play younger, I had to accept the situation. Resigned to the reality, I accepted Doody, which was an endearing, lovely part and included the songs "Those Magic Changes" and "Rock 'n' Roll Party Queen," which would be fun to sing.

The irony is that Lynn Stalmaster, the casting director who almost got me in *The Last Detail*, begged my manager Bob LeMond not to let me do the stage production of *Grease* because it would take me off the movie market for a year. Bob told me he might have to agree with Lynn because he felt we had established momentum in Hollywood. He also said that if I were playing the lead role of Danny, it would be a great career move, but that playing Doody, though I'd be great, would be more of a job for experience and employment.

So I had two powerful people in my life asking me not to do *Grease* because it wasn't Danny Zuko, but being a strongheaded young man who always made his own decisions, I opted to disagree and take the role because I had such affection for the show.

ANN TRAVOLTA (*Understudy*): In December of 1972 my agent submitted me for an audition for *Grease*'s first national tour. My mind was whirling with excitement, apprehension, and anxiety, and of course I was chanting the normal young Catholic mantra, "Please, God, help me get this part."

Up to this time in my acting career, I had only worked in dinner theater, summer stock, and children's theater, where I got my Equity card. But never had my aspirations flown so high that I could imagine being offered an opportunity to be in the already legendary *Grease*.

After I sang "Losing My Mind" from *Follies*, Louis St. Louis, the music director, said he thought I looked like I just came out of a Fellini movie. And here I thought I was just paying homage to Dorothy Collins and her torch songs.

After reading several other parts for director Tom Moore and being put through all the dance moves by choreographer Pat Birch, I knew I had made an impression. When they told me that they wanted me to be the understudy for five different roles, I think they thought I would be disappointed not to be cast in one of the signature parts, but I couldn't believe my good fortune.

Imagine making $300 a week just for learning and performing all those fun character roles—and with a year's contract! At this point I felt I had died and gone to heaven. It was a best dream come true.

JOHN TRAVOLTA: Another bonus of the tour was that, unbeknownst to me, on the other side of the country my older sister Annie had auditioned and was cast as an understudy for five different roles in my tour, and would join me on the road. My manager told me that the director thought this was a bonus for everyone because I was so much younger than the rest of the cast and she could keep an eye on me.

I remember being pretty insulted because at eighteen I felt independent and mature enough to take care of myself. After all, I had already been in Hollywood alone for six months, so why did I need a babysitter? *Don't they all know that?*

My defensiveness wore off after a month or so, and Annie and I ended up having a wonderful time together on the road.

ANN TRAVOLTA: What could be better than crossing America with my loving, adoring brother, who made me laugh every time we were together and was also my biggest fan. *Grease* was a game changer that gave me confidence and strength and the humor and wisdom to survive the years ahead. And a whole lot of fun!

REBECCA GILCHRIST (*Patty/Jan*): In the fall of 1972 I was an actress-in-waiting—and waiting tables in a dreadful restaurant in the Bowery. I was absolutely miserable, wondering if I'd ever get cast in anything. When I got an audition for *Grease*, I was thrilled. I sang "It's My Party" and "To Know Him Is to Love Him." The director then asked if I could do a cheer for them. Fortunately high school at that point was only a few years past: "Dynamo, let's go! Dynamite, let's fight! Dynamo, dynamite, let's *F-I-G-H-T*"! They seemed to like it.

One night while I was hopefully waiting for a callback, most of the *Grease* cast came into the restaurant where I worked. Barry Bostwick, who played Danny Zuko, was legendary for his tight leather pants, and he and they did not disappoint. I thought I'd go into a dead faint when they all sat in my station. I wanted desperately to be a part of that happy company of successful actors.

There were two more nerve-racking auditions, and as I was leaving, following my third, thinking, *I'm done—there's nothing more I can show them*, the director, Tom Moore, came out of the room to tell me that they were offering me the role of the cheerleader, Patty Simcox. Truly that was one of the happiest moments of my life. I floated three feet above the sidewalk back to my waitressing job to tell the manager that I would not be in the following day or ever again.

RAY DEMATTIS (*Roger*): I had just lost one hundred pounds, and *Grease* was the first audition I was sent on by my first New York agent; I was very excited. I sang the Platters' "The Great Pretender" and Gary Puckett's "Lady Willpower." After my audition I exited into the wings and Leslie Nichol, our future Miss Lynch, gushed and said, "You're going to get this!"

However, the final callback was unlike anything I had ever experienced. It was a friggin' marathon, a full-day affair, something like eight hours long! First there was acting, then acting improvs, then singing, then singing improvs, then dancing, then dancing improvs. I left exhausted, thinking, *If this is any indication of what rehearsals will be like . . . the hell with it!*

JUDITH SULLIVAN (*Cha-Cha*): First off I had to sing. I have no idea what I sang, but I got through it and was then asked to dance for Pat Birch. She scared me to death! The first thing I said to her was "I don't know how to dance! Honestly!" I weighed 240 pounds, and dancing wasn't something I did much of.

Pat ignored me and just started teaching me the hand jive and the cha-cha-cha. And then teaching and teaching and teaching. I have never worked harder on anything in my life. But it paid off. I was cast as Cha-Cha DiGregorio in the first national tour.

My thanks to Pat for not paying attention to anything I said that first day.

JOHN LANSING (*Understudy*): It was 1972 and Richard Nixon was in the White House. I was twenty-three years old, weighed in at 135 pounds, and had a middle-class hippie ponytail. I went from the exhilaration of touring Paris with Chicago's Free Street Theater to the reality of a stack of bills in my fourth-floor Manhattan walk-up. Rent was due, and the only job I could get was playing Santa Claus at the Kings Plaza Shopping Center in Brooklyn. They were desperate and so was I. My biggest fear at the time was that I would be forced to wear a rabbit costume come Easter.

I checked my phone service after a day of wailing children, and there was a message from a talent manager. He asked if I'd consider going on the road again. I said yes, yes, and yes.

I suffered all the insecurities that plague actors but led with bravado that day of the audition. I sang Leon Russell's "A Song for You" on a bare stage in the Royale Theatre. It was my lucky song, and I knew I'd killed it. I was asked if I'd be willing to cut my hair. I told them not only would I cut it, I'd turn it into a D.A., a '50s hairstyle known as a "duck's ass." That elicited a few laughs, and I walked out pumped and filled with youthful adrenaline and optimism. Little did I know that the job I booked that day would change the trajectory of my life.

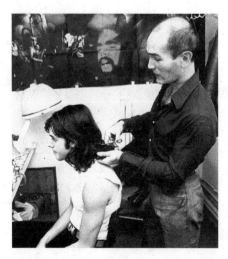 

LEFT: Stylist John Delaat turns John Lansing into a Greaser. RIGHT: A future Zuko!

MARILU HENNER (*Marty*): In March 1972 I had taken a trip to New York to see Jim Jacobs and the new production of *Grease*. It was awe-inspiring. Tom Moore had worked with Jim and Warren to give the show structure, pace, story—and real production value. Now it was like the real Broadway shows I grew up with. I went home torturing myself over the decision I had made months earlier not to audition for the Broadway cast. I had thought at the time, *This show is too Chicago. It will never be a hit. Stay in school!*

Nine months later Jim Jacobs called to tell me that rehearsals for the first national company of *Grease* were starting on Tuesday, and they couldn't find a Marty. "I'm trying to keep the part open for you, but you have to fly in and audition. You'll be kicking yourself in the ass *again* if you don't come!"

"*Jim!* I'm in college, remember? I'm also in a show, in a relationship, I have two papers due, and I'm on the way to the library right now! Thank you for thinking of me!"

I walked to the library and realized I had parked my car in front of it the night before, which never happened. Strange coincidence? Sign from God? I looked at my car, looked at the library, looked at my car, looked at the library, threw my books in the car, and raced to O'Hare.

I auditioned for Marty, and Tom Moore asked if I could come back in two hours to audition for Pat Birch. *No problem.*

"You're fabulous and we want you for the part," producer Maxine Fox told me. Then she asked in a lower voice, "But we'd like you to lose some weight. Do you think you could do that?"

"No problem!"

"Then be at the first rehearsal tomorrow."

"I Got a Feeling"

JERRY ZAKS: It was the most significant job I'd gotten since I'd arrived in NYC in the fall of 1969.

I had to tell someone. I had to tell everyone. I would've told the doorman, if I'd had a doorman. Of course I told my parents. My mother said, "That's nice," and my father made a sound. They were not impressed. To make matters worse, rehearsals were still several weeks away, and I just wanted to get to work. What to do?

I know: I'll just go see the show again—the show I was going to be in! I got on the subway and headed down to Times Square. All the way to the theater I hoped I'd run into someone I knew to tell them the good news: *I'm gonna be in* Grease! *I'm gonna be in* Grease! But no luck.

I went to the stage door and asked for the stage manager. (When the doorman asked who I was, I told him I was going to be in the show on the road. *Yes!*) The stage manager (I think it might've been Tommy Smith) walked me in, and I stood in back. The crowd, full of anticipation and expectation, buzzed with excitement and cheered as the lights went down. It was like playoff baseball, and I was right there with them. The show had barely begun and it was already a home run.

After the Rydell alma mater, the school bell rang and the scrim flew. I thought I would explode. There was Kenickie (Timothy Meyers) in all his glory, and there was me in disbelief that I would be part of this—that I had made the team.

When the curtain came down for intermission, I was vibrating. I had to tell someone, so I turned to the guy next to me and here's what I said:

ME: Great show, right?

HIM: Yeah, great show!

ME: I'm gonna be in it!

HIM: Me too!

His name was John Travolta. He was eighteen years old and had just gotten the part of Doody. We grinned from ear to ear and celebrated our great good fortune.

Soon rehearsals would begin, and I'd meet the rest of the company. We'd get to work together and fall in love with each other. And that's what we did.

Jeff Conaway (Danny Zuko) and the first national company.

15 | "Got My Mojo Working"
Rehearsals

MARILU HENNER (*Marty*): As rehearsals began the day after my audition, there was no time to fly back to Chicago. I slept on Jacobs's couch and showed up for rehearsal in the only clothes I had with me—suitable for the library but cute enough to meet my future? Hardly.

When I saw the roomful of talented up-and-comers, I almost died. Jeff Conaway, Jerry Zaks, Michael Lembeck, John Travolta, Judy Kaye, Ellen March—and Richard Gere, who was the new understudy for Zuko on Broadway.

I had an immediate crush on Jerry Zaks, who was not only talented and sexy but also analytical, insightful, and very funny. He became the resident therapist-confidant of the group. Jerry had gone to Dartmouth, so every time he used a multisyllabic word like *specificity* to explain some '50s greaser thing, the cast would bust him: "Whoa, 'spe-ci-fi-ci-ty'?" And he'd say, "Hey, I fuckin' went ta college." That became one of our great lines on the road. Whenever someone busted you for saying or doing something a bit lofty, you'd say, "Hey, I fuckin' went ta college!"

Johnny and I were the two youngest cast members, with a lot in common. Once we started talking, we never stopped laughing.

NANCY ROBBINS (*Assistant to the Director*): The rehearsals for the first national were in a run-down hotel ballroom complete with a mirror ball hanging from the ceiling—very decrepit and very seedy. Right off the ballroom was the former bar, and that's where the lone phone was located. While using the phone, I would pound nonchalantly on the bar with my fist to smash hordes of baby cockroaches.

Jerry Zaks, Vivian Fineman, Michael Lembeck,
Ray DeMattis, Marilu Henner, and John Travolta.

In the first few days, I was mainly running around finding rehearsal props. On the Friday of my first week, I showed stage manager Tommy Smith the list of props that I had found and the ones that I still needed to hunt down. I said that I would be able to get the rest on Monday. He looked at me quizzically and said, "No, tomorrow." That was when I found out that theater folks worked six days a week. Quite a shock since I had already been bemoaning that I was being paid only seventy-five dollars a week—and I thought that was for a five-day week! I thought, *Wow, what on earth have I gotten myself into?*

REBECCA GILCHRIST (*Patty/Jan*): When rehearsals started shortly after Thanksgiving, because I was cast as cheerleader Patty Simcox, I dressed the part on the first day, with a short, pleated skirt, a sweet little sweater, and a ponytail with a big bow. I was absolutely in heaven at rehearsals but also frightened to death! *My first big show!* It was a highly charged atmosphere, with an energy that was nearly palpable. We were young and acutely aware of this being a special time. And we all wanted to prove that we had a right to be there.

For me, an unsophisticated hillbilly from West Virginia, it doesn't get much better, or more painful, than those early rehearsals. *Am I going to be good enough? Will people like me?* But I was happy, except for one little problem. Patty is a Goody Two-Shoes, and I would much rather have been a bad girl and part of the fabulous Pink Ladies. Patty is definitely not a part of the cool club. As Patty I was on the outside, looking in at all the fun. I was too insecure in real life to be happy that way onstage.

Then on the third day of rehearsals, when the role of Jan had still not been cast, a peculiar thing happened. I was pulled out of rehearsals to read yet again for the full creative team! *What's going on?* I thought nervously. *Am I about to get fired?*

I was handed a script and asked to read for the role of Jan. After reading the scene and singing a little of "Mooning," Pat said, "Rebecca, lose the bow in the hair." And when I did she said, "There, now you're Jan." Tom confirmed it with a smile.

I was stunned and thrilled all at the same time. Three days in and I had gone from goody-good girl to bad girl. Insecure Rebecca Gilchrist would now be part of the cool gang.

Rebecca Gilchrist (Jan) and Ray DeMattis (Roger), first national company.

RAY DEMATTIS (*Roger*): By the end of rehearsals, the national tour Burger Palace Boys had become a tight-knit unit for life. One evening, as though we hadn't had enough *Grease* in our rehearsals, we thought we'd head over to see the Broadway show again before going on the road. We were, of course, a great audience and the cast's biggest fans.

After the show, feeling complete ownership, one with the team and cocky as hell, we sauntered down to the area in front of the stage and waited for the cast to congratulate them. The laughter had continued, as had our fanboy enthusiasm, when out of the blue and apropos of nothing, our sweet and goofy eighteen-year-old Doody, without fanfare but with complete conviction, said, "I'm gonna play Danny Zuko one day."

We looked at Travolta and there was a silent beat of *Uh, huh?* and then we all picked up right where we left off. It was never mentioned again.

Ray DeMattis and John Travolta, "Rock 'n' Roll Party Queen."

"Big Girls Don't Cry": Previews and Opening

MARILU HENNER: Before the first preview in Boston, we were setting up our dressing rooms when all of a sudden there was a bloodcurdling scream coming from Judy Kaye's dressing room! In setting up her room, she had confused her contact lens solution with *astringent!* Thank God one of our crew guys had been a fireman and knew enough to throw Judy on the ground, break open the fire hose, and basically waterboard her eye. When sufficiently hosed, Judy was immediately rushed to the hospital, where they gave her an eye patch and told her to rest for a few days. Annie Travolta went on until Judy was back to normal, in time for opening night.

ANN TRAVOLTA (*Understudy*): It was a true emergency, and while everyone was rushing to her aid, the only thing I could think about was that I would be playing Rizzo that night. When I joined the company after rehearsals had started, Tom had advised me to focus on Rizzo first, so I knew my lines and "Worse Things," but I also had to remember all the props, the blocking, the many entrances and exits, and of course all the songs.

What kept me from panicking was knowing all "the kids" would be right there for me and cheering me on. How could I fail? That old adage "The show must go on" never felt more real to me than it did that night.

Pamela Adams (Sandy)
and Judy Kaye (Rizzo).

ELLEN MARCH (*Frenchy*): Marilu and I hadn't hung out much during rehearsals in New York, but when we hit Boston for our first preview, we found ourselves sharing a dressing room.

Marilu's family had sent her a sweet bouquet of flowers, and to have a little fun, we turned the card over and wrote:

> *To Our Two Stars,*
> *Without you, Grease wouldn't have been possible*
> *Keep up the good work*
> *Love*
> *Ken and Maxine*

Like two devilish schoolgirls, we called over to Judy Kaye and Rebecca Gilchrist's dressing room next door to come see our flowers from the producers. When they looked surprised, we shamelessly said, "Oh, you didn't get them too?"

I can't remember when we decided to tell them the truth—if ever. It was the beginning of a great tour and an even greater friendship.

JOHN TRAVOLTA (*Doody*): Opening night in Boston was exciting, but I was feeling under the weather because we had worked really hard during the eight-hours-a-day rehearsals in New York and then the twelve-hours-a-day dress rehearsals in Boston. Every day was at full throttle.

Ray DeMattis, Judy Kaye, and John Travolta, "Sandra Dee."

On our opening night, however, Carol Demas (who was the girlfriend of Jeff Conaway at the time and played the original Sandy in New York) came backstage and told me I had a gorgeous voice and my performance was her favorite part of the show. And Tom Moore told my manager that onstage I appeared less like Doody and more like a French movie star! With those two compliments, I started to feel a whole lot better—and Doody and I became great friends.

REBECCA GILCHRIST: We opened on December 23 with a matinee on Christmas Eve and no performance on Christmas Day. This was my first Christmas away from my family in West Virginia, and I remember sitting in the bar across the street from the theater on Christmas Eve with those of us who were staying in town, trying not to cry from feeling so homesick. I had a huge crush on one of the stagehands, who introduced me to tequila sunrises at that bar. Ultimately I don't think that was a good idea—the stagehand or the tequila sunrises.

JUDITH SULLIVAN (*Cha-Cha*): My parents came to the premiere just after Christmas. They *loved* it and flew back to Illinois.

In the second week of the Boston run, when I made an entrance as usual running down the staircase, I took the first step down and caught my heel in the hem of my costume. My run down the stairs turned into a series of terrifying somersaults. When I landed, I saw bones coming out of my ankle! At that same moment, Kenickie was making his entrance in Greased Lightning. Fortunately, just as the lights were coming up, he saw me and slammed on the brakes, stopping just shy of my head. Two stagehands ran out, put me in a chair, and carried me offstage.

When the ambulance arrived at Mass General, I was still in costume—a big yellow dress on a stretcher. The doctor walked in. He thought I was from Greece—the country, not the show—and kept asking me about my heritage. Finally he stopped talking and admitted me.

Happily I was able to eventually rejoin the company a few months later, but I never did another performance without first checking that the hem in my dress was sewn tight, tight, tight!

REBECCA GILCHRIST: During the scene change into Jan's basement, there was a flash of yellow as Judith came rolling down the steps, ass over teakettle. All the stagehands rushed onstage to take care of her, so no one was left on the pin rail to fly in the scenic flat for Jan's basement wall. We went on with the scene as if nothing was amiss until John Travolta (Doody) couldn't help himself and blurted out, "Hey, Jan, didn't your basement used to have paneling?"

Despite the trauma of Judith's broken leg, it was all we could do to get through the rest of the scene without breaking up in gales of laughter.

VIVIAN FINEMAN (*Understudy*): On January 3, 1973, long after my last audition callback and rejection, I got an unexpected call from casting asking if I would be available to assume the role of Cha-Cha while Judith recovered.

My replacement rehearsals were with Tommy Smith, the New York stage manager, who was very kind and supportive. One evening he sent me to see the Broadway show. There were no available seats, so I stood at the back of the theater, near the concessions bar. Standing next to me was the handsome young understudy covering Zuko. I thought that he was very attractive, with his dark eyes and warm smile.

Because of my height (five feet one), I was having trouble seeing the performance. He suggested he lift me onto the refreshment counter so that I could see over the crowd. I thought he was very gallant since I was definitely no lightweight at the time. I thought that he must be in really good shape to be able to hoist me up the way that he did.

My suspicion was confirmed some years later when I saw his level of fitness in the movie *American Gigolo*. Did I mention that the young actor was Richard Gere?

I loved being in the show—a highlight of my life.

Ooh, Richard! Richard Gere, "All Choked Up."

16

"We're Gonna Rock Around the Clock Tonight"

The First National Hits the Road

MICHAEL LEMBECK (*Sonny*): The tour was a remarkable experience for me. Every night I knew we were going to walk out onstage and hear the palpable excitement of the audience behind the first-act scrim, the wonderful noise that is a visceral shared anticipation from a sold-out house. And when we slammed into the opening number, if you allowed yourself a quick, unprofessional peek at the faces nearest you down front, you saw an ecstatic response that drove you the rest of the show.

We were a wildly tight bunch that really liked each other, so being together in any kind of group was fun. Almost all of us were in the twenty-five-years-old range, and Travolta was eighteen, the baby of the group. The boys all joined the YMCA, and most of us went to the Y every day to work out and run and play basketball—even Ray DeMattis. The boys hung out together, ate together, and formed an amazing bond. We were there for one another.

In my experience in the theater, this lifeboat was different in that we were all basically enjoying our first big job and really did love and support one another. There was no ego. And the laughs . . . there is no way to quantify how hard we laughed all the time, onstage and off.

JOHN TRAVOLTA (*Doody*): Our cast was a wonderful group of people. To save money, Michael and I were roommates for two or three cities, and my sister and I roomed for one. And then we were all on our own. For whatever reasons, we all seemed to connect.

MICHAEL LEMBECK: Johnny T. was my roommate on the road, and of all the whimsical habits he formed while we were traveling, my favorite

Jeff Conaway (Zuko) wins the dance contest.

Michael Lembeck (Sonny), Barry Bostwick (Zuko), and Jerry Zaks (Kenickie).

was that in each city, the day we got in, he would go to the local Walgreens or whatever and purchase huge bags of candy, like the ones you get to dump into the bowl at Halloween. It was nutty. I still don't know why he did that, but it doesn't matter. Sharing in the goodies was fantastic, and he probably left an aggregate of one ton of uneaten Milky Ways, Mars bars, Tootsie Rolls, and M&M's across the lower forty-eight.

There was another very personal joy in touring across America: my dad, besides being my dad, was a well-known character actor, and one of the special pleasures of the road was playing theaters he had played on his own national tours all those years ago. It was an amazing generational thing, and even at twenty-five I became emotional whenever I walked on those stages. I will have our first national tour as a beacon in my life forever. I had no idea when I got picked for *Grease* that a one-year tour across America could provide me with such happiness for the rest of my life.

RAY DEMATTIS (*Roger*): I had done tours before, but riding the '70s nostalgia for the '50s and introducing rock 'n' roll and our *Grease* teenagers to road audiences was truly a phenomenon. And in an era of *No, No, Nanette*, it was a musical "for guys"! Our entire cast was in top form, and the pressure for us each to hold our own was immense.

A personal tour highlight was our stop in New Haven—my hometown. The publicity gang decided that "local boy makes good" might help boost ticket sales, and Bernie Carragher, an arts columnist for the *New Haven Register*, was sent to interview me and my "supporting cast" in Philadelphia. This was a very exciting first in my life! My interview with Bernie was supposed to last an hour, but he was so besotted with us that he stayed for three hours! He wrote a wonderful, effusive article headlined SING FOR THE HOMEFOLKS, RAY.

I was floored and felt like king of the mountain, or at least New Haven! My mother was beside herself. To celebrate she insisted on cooking lasagna for the company. We hosted actors, staff, and crew at the Italian American Independent Club of New Haven. It became folklore in my family, and for years after, my Uncle Tony talked about that cute Marilu Henner sitting on his knee! To top things off, on opening night I received a congratulatory telegram from the governor of Connecticut, Thomas Meskill!

MICHAEL LEMBECK: CINCINNATI, OHIO: We were told prior to a matinee there that we were not allowed to use the specific language that permeates the text and lyrics of *Grease*.

Slow dancing at the Rydell prom.

We were totally pissed off as a group, so we had a contest company-wide to see who could come up with the worst replacement for an expletive. "Used rubbers" became "wet balloons," "fuckin' A" became "darn right," and so on. It was a real wake-up call that we don't all live in the same kind of culture.

COLUMBUS, OHIO: When we arrived a bunch of us decided to go over to the theater and check out the space. There was a filled-to-the-rafters revival meeting going on in there! This was not a good sign for our slightly profane show. Armed with the knowledge that Columbus might not be a great city for *Grease*, we played the show a *lot* faster that week. *A lot!*

INDIANAPOLIS, INDIANA: When our bus finally arrived after a very long and very tiring trip, the city streets leading to our hotel had US military hardware lining every block for some sort of patriotic celebration. Steve Van Benschoten (Eugene) leaned out the bus window and yelled, "Hey, when did America declare war on Indianapolis?"

TORONTO, CANADA: After making this same move for at least one hundred performances, it was in a beautiful theater in Toronto where I jumped off the bench upstage at the end of the first act—and broke my ankle upon landing. As I hit the ground and crumbled, I knew I had done something bad. The crystal-clear memory of that moment is not so much my own personal pain or knowledge that I had to get up and get offstage as it is looking up and out into the audience and seeing our understudy Tommy Oliver already hurrying down the aisle, ready to take over in Act 2.

MARILU HENNER (*Marty*): One of the best things about being on the road with a bunch of talented actors is you'll also get to meet the other endlessly entertaining characters lurking inside of them and just dying to come out! When given the right prompt, Ellen March and Annie Travolta could launch into all sorts of voices, mannerisms, and wacky personas that could have landed them on *Saturday Night Live*, but it didn't exist at the time. And Johnny had what he called his "bag of characters" at the ready. He'd pick up an envelope and say, "Let's see . . . who's in here?" and you just never knew who would come out and play! The big favorite was a long and limber stud named Stretch who was always trying to seduce the imaginary camera that followed him around. Once Johnny had a nickname, it was only right the other guys were appropriately named for their lovable quirks. With his lightning-fast insights and quick thinking, Jerry was called Flash Zaks. Wiry, sportsy Michael became Lank Lembeck. And cuddly, adorable Ray, who was always pitching something, was suitably named Sluggo DeMattis!

MICHAEL LEMBECK: Ray DeMattis (Roger) had serious problems with his antenna. One night he ran onstage swinging his antenna pre-rumble and accidentally swiped Zaks right across the forehead. Jerry walked off a bloody mess, and Travolta and Ray and I just improvised the rest of the scene.

On another night he charged out from the wings, wildly swinging the antenna like he always did, but this time it broke, and a piece of the antenna went flying into the second balcony. An audience member came backstage to return the missing piece, kind of like a fan returning a foul ball in the hopes of getting an autograph.

And on another night, he arrived brandishing the antenna with a substantial piece of tissue hanging from his chin. I'm talking at least three inches in length. He could neither see it nor apparently feel it. When Jerry, John, and I saw the tissue blowing in the breeze, we lost it—I mean bent-over hysterical laughter. Ray had no idea why we were all laughing, and it infuriated him. The more we laughed, the more perturbed and angry he got, and the more

Doin' the hand jive.

we lost control. I don't know if we got out a word of the subsequent scene or song. I have never laughed that hard onstage in my life.

And then there was the matinee when Ray forgot the dialogue prior to "Greased Lightnin'." Instead of saying, "Nice color, what is it, candy apple primer?" he came up with "Nice color, what is it . . . (*long pause*) . . . beige?" And another hysterical loss of discipline.

And on we went, every stop another wonderful adventure.

"When Will I Be Loved": Standing By

JOHN LANSING (*Understudy*): I wasn't a very good understudy. The job description was covering Zuko and four other characters, but I was all about Danny Zuko. New to the cast, I gave less thought to those other four characters—especially Teen Angel.

Tom always emphasized that pacing was everything. No dramatic pauses. Keep it moving!

Fifties music was already being piped throughout the theater when I was notified by the frantic stage manager that Teen Angel had come down with a terrible case of laryngitis and I was up. *What?* My first performance as an understudy and I had a half hour to prepare. I was terrified. I'd learned all of Zuko's songs but felt totally ill prepared to play Teen Angel.

The character had a showy entrance, and I steeled myself for the performance. On cue I swung in on a rope, landing on a platform, dressed in pure white with an even whiter spotlight, and started singing "Beauty School Dropout." The Pink Ladies on the stage below, dressed in beauty school smocks and shower caps, began singing and executing Pat Birch's perfectly timed choreography.

Everything came together, and I started getting into the groove. I got lost in the moment and took the dreaded dramatic pause. The music director furiously waved me on with his baton. I glanced below to see one of the Pink Ladies, who had been balancing on one leg, fall out of the line, and then a second almost hit the ground before recovering. My recovery wasn't quite as immediate. I finished the song, nailed the final falsetto high note, and walked offstage knowing I'd blown it big time.

I received well-deserved cold shoulders from those very talented actresses for the next few weeks. I learned my lesson.

Vivian Fineman, John Lansing, and Ann Travolta.

BARRY PEARL (*Understudy/Sonny*): As I was finishing my senior year at Carnegie Mellon University, my friend John Lansing came through Pittsburgh with the first national tour of *Grease*. He thought I'd be perfect for future companies. When I went to see the show, lo and behold, my doppelgänger Michael Lembeck stepped out onstage as Sonny. It was like watching myself.

Within weeks, with my urging, my agents arranged for me to fly to New York for an audition. A week after that, I was asked to a callback because Michael Lembeck had broken his ankle during "We Go Together," and they needed a replacement ASAP. So I flew in again and landed the gig.

Then after working as the understudy for only a short time, on Saturday morning, May 19, 1973, I got a call from the stage manager telling me that I was going on that night as Sonny! I only played the part while Michael was recuperating, but then when Michael left the show after L.A., I took over in Chicago. The fun fact is that four years from the day I first performed Sonny in Detroit, May 19, 1977, I was cast as Doody in the *Grease* film.

17

"Don't Let the Stars Get in Your Eyes"

The Shubert Theatre, Los Angeles, June 1, 1973–September 9, 1973

RAY DEMATTIS (*Roger*): After our long tour across the country, opening in L.A. was surreal! Broadway's Zuko, Barry Bostwick, switched places with our Zuko, Jeff Conaway, and instantly became a great and generous colleague who brought out the best in all of us. Our energy and focus were through the roof, and we were flying high. Everyone, including Barry, knew that major career moves could and would happen from this run, and we were stoked!

On opening night the L.A. audience went crazy for us! Cars from the '50s were parked in front of the theater, people arrived dressed in '50s outfits, and during the show some even tried to come up onstage for the prom.

Throughout the run TV stars of the '50s showed up nightly. I definitely saved my autographed note from Annette Funicello. Every performance was a new celebration.

MICHAEL LEMBECK (*Sonny*): Like all L.A. events, particularly where it pertains to show business, openings are an opportunity to see and be seen. *Grease* was highly anticipated, and our opening-night audience was filled with celebrities. And yes, we as a cast spent much time peeking through the scrim prior to the first act to try and find all the famous people.

The celeb that garnered the most attention that night was Ann-Margaret, especially as far as Bostwick was concerned. Once Barry spotted her, the entire show's blocking moved down right, where she sat. I mean the whole show—at least when Bostwick was on. It was hysterical. And *shameless!* And so much fun competing for space to see Ann-Margaret while onstage. We definitely overacted just a little to try and gain her personal attention. And as it turned out, she enjoyed the show as much as we enjoyed performing it for her.

132

Carol Culver, Judy Kaye, Pamela Adams, Marilu Henner, Rebecca Gilchrist, and Ellen March, "All Choked Up."

ELLEN MARCH (*Frenchy*): For a group of young actors, babies really, traveling and performing *Grease* on the road to unbelievably enthusiastic audiences in every major city in America had been a wild and incredible time. Every day had been an adventure and every night was—well, romance and musical beds. It was the '70s!

I was the first actor to leave the first national to make the move to Broadway. Marya Small was from L.A. and very much wanted to play the show in her hometown, and I very much looked forward to going home. After opening the show in L.A., I flew back to New York to play it on Broadway. Incredibly exciting! I was thrilled.

Of course, I didn't realize until I was packing up how hard it was going to be to leave my *Grease* family—all now great friends. My darling Marilu drove me to the airport, and we cried the whole way to LAX.

MARYA SMALL (*Frenchy*): It was hard leaving my beloved Broadway *Grease* family to go to a new *Grease* family in Los Angeles, my hometown, but I had been in New York for eleven years. The new work was in the West.

The first national company welcomed me with open hearts, open arms, like a new family member; they were kind, helpful, and fun. Playing Frenchy opposite Johnny Travolta's Doody was a complete delight. He always sparkled, long, long, long before he became famous. I think he was born sparkling.

We became good pals that summer. Johnny and I were each in a time of searching—searching for something, something that would help us be more stable within. Inside ourselves, not show business, just something. Some kind of knowing we were all right.

Johnny was fun and kind. One of the things he did with the Burger Palace Boys was serenade all the Pink Ladies at the doorway of our dressing room every night before the show, each night with a different '50s hit song. One night "Little Darlin'," the next night "Don't Be Cruel," next the Coasters' "Searchin'," right on through the week: "In the Still of the Night," "I Only Have Eyes for You." Every day we'd get a different great '50s song. They were so cute, so funny, so loving. Those bad boys won our hearts.

STEVE VAN BENSCHOTEN (*Eugene*): Everyone in the company was keen to capitalize on our arrival in L.A., the great talent pool of filmdom and TV, and secure an agent who would no doubt propel us to even greater heights. (And get us off the bus!)

Walter Charles and Steve Van
Benschoten at the Twinkle, Twinkle,
Little Star Talent Agency.

Being of a cynical bent, Walter Charles and I concocted a mockery of the whole system and created an ersatz agency, calling it the Twinkle, Twinkle, Little Star Talent Agency, Inc. We put up a big sign outside the dressing room we shared and worked hard to make it look as cheap, shoddy, and phony as possible. The sign included our mottoes No Waiting, Habla Español, and No Job Too Small. When we had time away from the stage, we would attempt to recruit the cast as clients. We decided our around-the-bend agents were heavy drinkers, and Walter affected a bit of delirium tremens as he pulled a fake bottle of cheap whiskey from a drawer during the interviews. To enhance the joke, we asked the cast to give us their worst-ever eight-by-ten photos to adorn the walls of our dressing room. We of course asked for résumés and insisted that everyone sign their photos with endearments to their fabulous agents, like "Dear Walter and Steve, without you there would be no me." Cooperation was enthusiastic, and we eventually developed quite an impressive client list.

FRANK PIEGARO (*Understudy/Zuko*): I auditioned on a Tuesday in mid-August of 1973 for an understudy opening in the first national tour, and two days later I was in Los Angeles. I had just turned twenty-one. Whirlwind!

Although I would eventually inherit Danny on Broadway, one of the first times I went on in that role was at the Shubert in Los Angeles.

Rebecca Gilchrist, Candy Earley, Barry Bostwick, and Judy Kaye.

I was ready, but it was still a blur. But one thing was very clear: Candice Earley was my Sandy, and I can tell you without reservation that "All Choked Up" *smoked!* Candy was one of the best vocalists I ever worked with. What a set of pipes. God bless her.

And then it was back to being an understudy. I loved to perform. But as a guy on the sidelines, there is no satisfaction. I wouldn't want anyone to be ill or anything to give me a shot, but that's what an understudy is there for. To wait. And to prepare. The incredible thing is that despite their skill, understudies often aren't taken seriously for their ability to suddenly take over a part in a show. Sometimes it's better for a company to have an actor who can fill in for many parts than a performer who can only fit one. You become valuable because of your diversity. But I was patient, willing to wait.

JOHN TRAVOLTA (*Doody*): Although I had been excited and disappointed at the same time when I was cast as Doody, it turned out to be a very big gift, because in the next couple years I got to observe three to five different Zukos and could see exactly what worked and what didn't, and think about what would work better. The role of Danny Zuko was still an unrequited love.

As I observed the Dannys in action, I also found myself thinking, *I may be too young to play Danny now, but by the time they make the movie, I will be the perfect age to play Zuko!* (Spoiler: it turned out I was right.)

Barry Bostwick was the original Broadway Danny Zuko. The first time I saw the show, Jeff Conaway, his understudy, was on for him, and later Jeff became the Zuko for our first national company, so all my first impressions were of Jeff's performance.

But when our national tour was going to L.A., Barry left Broadway to lead our show, and Jeff took over on Broadway. When I finally saw Barry's Danny Zuko in our L.A. production, I quickly realized that all the Zukos were inspired by Barry's original ideas—including, as it turned out later, me!

My only gripe in that whole year of touring was that being such an aviation geek, I wanted to fly to every city, but we always ended up taking the bus. If I remember correctly, out of ten cities, we were only scheduled to fly three times. I spent most of my paycheck buying airplane tickets for the other seven so I could be on an airplane instead of a bus.

After my eleven months on the road with the first national touring company, I was asked to go to New York to replace Jim Canning on Broadway, where I played for only a month before being cast as Misfit in Ken, Maxine,

Barry Bostwick (Zuko) and John Travolta (Doody), "Those Magic Changes."

Pat, and Tom's new Broadway musical, *Over Here!*, with the Andrews Sisters. Doody and Misfit were supporting roles, but I was on my way.

BARRY BOSTWICK (*Zuko*): "I created the part that Travolta played in the movie." I can't tell you how many times in the past fifty years those words have sprung from my mouth.

I met John when we did the first national tour together. He was right out of high school and incredibly charming and talented. He played Doody in our production and sang "Those Magic Changes" with innocence and guile.

We had the same manager, Bob LeMond, who ended up managing many of the Zukos over the years: Patrick Swayze, Jeff Conaway, Treat Williams, Adrian Zmed, among many others. By the time the film came along, John had grown up and built a great career in TV and film. He became a name with *Welcome Back, Kotter*, and *Saturday Night Fever* was a real star maker. He was perfect for the part, with his sexy grin and terrific singing and dancing.

"And he stole his entire performance from me!" he says, only half meaning it, with an obvious twinkle in his eye. That "he," by the way, is me.

REBECCA GILCHRIST (*Patty/Jan*): One night during our three-and-a-half-month run in L.A., Barry was very excited because his brother was going to see the show. They hadn't been together for a long time, and they had a great reunion, staying up, talking late into the night in Barry's dressing room.

The night after Barry's brother saw the show, he was killed in an automobile accident. Barry was devastated, and we were all heartbroken for him. Each of us experienced the feeling of loss—for Barry, of course, but also for ourselves. We were all very young, and death was an unlikely visitor. That night doing the show, I felt empty and vulnerable, and I was always close to tears. It was the only time in the nearly one thousand performances that I did of *Grease* that I went up on my lines.

We all did our best to give the audience the show they deserved. It was an uphill battle and not entirely successful. We were just too sad. When all of us went back to our hotels that night, we each called our families and the people we loved most—and tried to hold them just a little bit closer.

BARRY BOSTWICK: There have been many sad losses to our original company of *Grease*. The deaths of Warren Casey, Tim Meyers, and our wonderful stage manager Tommy Smith (being three of the first AIDS victims).

My contest-winning prom-dancing partner Kathi Moss, who finally lost her long fight with a rare illness.

Jeff Conaway's tragic passing after a long struggle. Jeff and I had gone to NYU together before *Grease*. He was my understudy in the beginning before he led the first national tour, and we remained close during his short but troubled life.

But there was one that was especially hard on me personally. When we were doing the West Coast premiere in L.A., the stage managers got a call from my father before the curtain went up, telling them that my brother, who had only recently seen us perform, had been killed that day in an automobile accident in Northern California. My dad told them not to tell me until after the show was over. And they didn't.

My parents had always acted like *Grease* grandparents. In New York they would often cook a whole Thanksgiving dinner for the cast, and in California when they visited, they would host get-togethers in their hotel room. So it was no surprise that they didn't want to interrupt the performance, knowing everyone like they did and always wanting us to do well.

I left to catch a flight home immediately after curtain.

18 Meanwhile . . .

Playing on Broadway, 1972–1973

GREG EVIGAN (*Zuko*): The now long-running, very successful *Grease* was looking for its very first Danny Zuko replacement—a daunting search as the original was the great Barry Bostwick. I had just come off two years on the road and one year on Broadway with *Jesus Christ Superstar* at the Mark Hellinger.

I don't remember much about my audition, but I definitely remember being cast. Even before my first rehearsal, I became part of the *Grease* publicity machine. I had long rock hair from doing *Superstar*, and the *New York Times* did a before-and-after article with back-to-back photos of me in my long, flowing hair as Jesus Christ and the slicked-back greaser hair of Danny Zuko. Quite a leap. The article talked about Greg Evigan, the new Zuko coming in to replace Barry Bostwick.

I had just two weeks to learn the entire show, replacing one of the most talented people I'd ever seen on a stage: Barry Bostwick! I couldn't believe this guy—he was like the old kid in high school that didn't graduate until he was twenty-one. From his first entrance he owned the show, and I had to replace him. I was scared to death!

In my first performance, everything I learned disappeared as soon as the lights went up. But like it usually did, instinct kicked in and saved me. I wasn't bad, but I definitely wasn't yet up to the best Zuko *Grease* had ever known.

ALAN PAUL (*Teen Angel / Johnny Casino*): "You're nuts to leave *Grease* to be a part of some singing group!" "Don't do it! You're in a hit Broadway show!" "You're throwing away your career and making a huge mistake!"

139

Ilene Kristen (Patty), Tom Harris (Eugene),
and Dorothy Leon (Miss Lynch).

That is what everyone kept telling me when I decided to leave the show to join the Manhattan Transfer. When Tim Hauser, Janis Siegel, Laurel Massé, and I put the group together in October of '72, there definitely wasn't any conflict with being in the show, but by May of '73, offers started coming in for us to perform, and the conflict grew. I knew it was time to leave the show and dedicate myself full-time to the group. It was a very sad and difficult decision to make; it felt like I was leaving my family. All of us from the original cast had a unique and special bond that none of us wanted to sever. To this day that love and friendship still endure.

It seems to have been the right move at the right time. The Manhattan Transfer went on to become one of the world's most successful and innovative vocal groups of all time.

CAROLE DEMAS (*Sandy*): I didn't want to leave. Ever! It was a sad, painful decision. My father was quite ill and facing surgery, and I longed to be with my family. I loved the show, loved playing Sandy, and wanted to continue in the Broadway company. *Grease* friendships were at the center of my life. But if I wanted this family time, I would have to leave the show. No time for agonizing. Tearfully, I did. That's showbiz.

JOHN FENNESSY (*Assistant Stage Manager/Understudy*): For Carole Demas's final performance as Sandy, our sound man, Jimmy Limberg, hooked up Sandy's bedroom phone to be live for a two-way conversation. He and Borrelli had concocted this fiendish plan.

Carole Demas (Sandy), "It's Raining on Prom Night."

CAROLE DEMAS: When I picked it up to call Frenchy, there was a drooling, hoarse, disgusting (and hysterically funny) breather on the other end. Pretty much everyone was in on it, and they all watched to see if I'd survive.

JOHN FENNESSY: Carole was greeted with "I'd like to dip you in a vat of hot chocolate," and it got raunchier from there. But no matter how inventively disgusting Borrelli's call became, Carole showed not a glimmer of a reaction. Carole was a pro!

CAROLE DEMAS: It was so clever, crude, unexpected, and fall-on-the-floor hilarious that it took every bit of my control to remember what I was supposed to be saying and to hit the next musical cue. I was overwhelmed by my love for the show, for my friends in the cast, and it hurt deeply to be leaving them. I went home and cried.

ILENE GRAFF (*Sandy*): When word went out that the brilliant Carole Demas was leaving the show, Louis St. Louis suggested that I audition and then made it happen. Although I can't remember what I read or sang, I remember in great detail the dance audition. Dance is not what I do well. Pat Birch divided us into couples, and I was terrified that she would ask me to do the hand jive. But it was my lucky day; all Pat asked us to do was the Stroll!

Hey, I grew up Strolling away every afternoon while watching *American Bandstand*. I was ecstatic. I had this. When it was our turn, my "date" and I Strolled onto the stage and I just kept on happily Strolling—Strolling my little heart out.

Ilene Graff (Sandy), "It's Raining on Prom Night."

I joined the Broadway cast in December and embarked on one of the great life-changing experiences of my career. I'm still a lousy dancer, but I can still Stroll.

GREG EVIGAN: On Broadway it didn't take long before my young confidence kicked in, and after playing Zuko at the Royale for a few months, I was becoming a darn good Danny and having a great time. I just loved this show.

Then the Rydell High principal (well, it felt like that) called me up to the office. I was thinking, *This can't be great. What could this be about?* So the producers say, "Greg, look, we love what you've been doing on the stage. We think you've been doing a great job, *but . . .*"

Oh crap, here we go, I'm thinking. *I'm barely in, and I'm out!*

They continued on with "we had always promised Broadway to Jeff Conaway. He's coming in from playing Zuko in the first national tour, now in Chicago. So you have a choice: you can either be Jeff's understudy and a swing"—the most thankless job on Broadway—"here in New York, or we can offer you the Chicago company, where, of course, you would be playing Danny Zuko every night."

Well, that was an easy decision because there's no way I wanted to be an understudy, and having played Zuko at every performance, I didn't want to cover and hardly ever get to go on! So I took the Chicago company.

19

The National Tour Goes Home

The Blackstone Theatre, Chicago, *September 12, 1973–December 16, 1973*

GREG EVIGAN (*Zuko*): During the last week of my four-month Broadway run, and shortly before I left for Chicago to trade places with Jeff Conaway in the first national tour, my uncle Ernie came in with some friends from New Jersey to see me in the show. My uncle Ernie (think *The Godfather*) wasn't really my uncle, but he had been like an uncle to me growing up. After the show he comes backstage and says, "Greg, you were great, really, unbelievable! I'm takin' everybody out tonight and we're gonna celebrate." He puts his big arm around me—"I'm so proud of this guy!"—gives me a couple of knuckle head rubs, and we're all off to a dinner party celebrating my last performance on Broadway before Jeff took over.

So we're having a great time at the restaurant, drinking it up pretty good, and Uncle Ernie comes over to me and says, "So, Greg, you like this part, huh?" And I said, "Yeah, Ernie, I mean . . . it's such a great role, I get to act, sing, and dance. Everything I love. Yeah, I really love the part. It's the best!"

Ernie says, "You want the part?" I said, "Well, yeah, Ernie, I mean I got the part." Then he drops his voice a little: "I mean you want the part all the time?" A little confused, I said, "Well yeah, I want the part all the time." So he gives me a nod, pats me on the back, and says, "OK, OK." Then he walks away.

As he walks away my Jersey instincts start kicking in big time, and I'm thinking, *What the hell's he talkin' about?* And then it hits me. *Oh, crap! I got to fix this. Now!*

Nervously I wait for the right time to approach Ernie alone. When it comes I ask, "Hey, Ernie, when you said, 'Do you want the part all the time,' what exactly did you mean?" Ernie says, "Don't worry, Greg. I'm not talkin' about killin' the guy. Knees, Greg. Just knees, that's all."

Panicking a little, I said, "Ernie, listen, hey, this guy's a really good friend of mine"—of course I hadn't even met Jeff yet—"I love this guy, a truly great, great guy. I would never ever want anything to happen to him! I mean seriously, Ernie, I'm really very happy to be going to Chicago. I'll get a chance to see a new town, have some new adventures. And I'll get to do the show every single night. I'll be doing the part *all* the time—*all* the time!"

Ernie gives me the look. "You sure?" "Yes, Ernie, really sure!" He looks at me a little disappointed: "Well, if that's the way you want it." "Yeah, Ernie, that's the way I want it. Yeah, no, yeah, yeah!"

And shaking his head, Uncle Ernie walked slowly away.

So, Jeff Conaway, God rest your beautiful soul. Back in 1973 I saved your kneecaps.

Greg Evigan and the first national company, Chicago.

"Chicago, Chicago, That Toddlin' Town"

JIM CANNING (*Doody*): It was great to be back where the original version of *Grease* had premiered. I was from Chicago, grew up on the West Side, went to school there, and had my first romance there. It was my town. So I asked the producers if I could trade places with the actor playing Doody in the national tour when it played Chicago. That actor, by the way, was John Travolta, and he gladly accepted the chance to be on Broadway. I was soon off to Chicago—that kid who left town a nobody and was coming back a star. At least it seemed that way to me. I mean, I was young, you know.

Now the city of Chicago also felt a certain amount of pride in the fact that a little homegrown community theater piece had become a big Broadway hit, so the city fathers arranged a big welcome for the cast. On the day of the first performance, the entire cast was to assemble for a lunchtime concert in Daley Plaza, the big park in the center of downtown. In olden times it would have been the place where noble heroes would march and give speeches. And here I was, a local hero, returning in glory. Well, actually it wasn't all that; we had to hang around the plaza for a few hours and then only sang two numbers from the show. But for me, definitely, it was LOCAL HERO RETURNS IN TRIUMPH.

STEVE VAN BENSCHOTEN (*Eugene*): On the first national's arrival in Chicago we were to perform a number from *Grease* on an outdoor plaza somewhere near city hall. It was a rather elaborate celebration, and city officials had pulled out all the stops.

Triumphant James Canning with Judy Kaye.

Only one thing went amiss. To hype the crowd for our dynamic appearance, some clueless individual was regaling the audience with a preshow entertainment of Greek bouzouki music, as in *Zorba*. Somewhere, indeed, there seemed to have been a failure to communicate.

CAROL CULVER (*Patty*): The first national tour was going to be in Chicago for eight months, so Frank Piegaro (understudy for Zuko), Jeff Baron (our sax player), and I rented a three-bedroom coach house in Old Town.

One night as I was getting ready for bed, I heard someone break a window in the basement. I let out a terrifying scream, waking my two housemates, who came running, Frank with a baseball bat and Jeff with his saxophone, ready to pound anyone who might be breaking in. My bloodcurdling scream must have scared whoever broke that window as much as it scared my housemates, because no one was ever found.

But it turned out that I had hemorrhaged a vocal cord with that scream, and it rendered me unable to perform for several weeks. Susan Pomerantz went on for me until I recovered, and one night Shannon Fanning had to go on for Rizzo. When Shannon jumped off the bench in "We Go Together," she broke her leg! There were no understudies left, so Shannon did the entire second act with a broken leg.

I couldn't talk, I couldn't do the show, and boy did I have a lot of guilty feelings about both.

MARYA SMALL (*Frenchy*): Jim Canning had asked to play the national tour's stop in Chicago, where we got to play *Grease* together again at the magnificent Blackstone Theatre for a whole amazing, glorious month—a treasured time. I always loved Jim singing "Those Magic Changes." He was so handsome, with a beautiful voice and shining spirit.

My time playing Frenchy came to an end in Chicago, and looking up at Jim singing "Magic Changes" that last night made me sad. That was the end of my glorious *Grease* experience, the end of an incredible, magical time. I hung up my Frenchy costumes for the last time, said goodnight, goodbye, and thanked each cast and crew member for the great fun of being able to be with them—hugs all around, precious hugs.

Jim and I stepped out of the beautiful Blackstone Theatre together for the last time, into the cold night air, extra chilly as the wind from Lake Michigan swept us down the street.

20 | *Broadway*
1973–1974

TREAT WILLIAMS (*Understudy/Zuko*): When I started auditioning in New York, I was singing all these ballads from all the big old-school musicals; Stephen Sondheim's "Being Alive" was my go-to audition song. After a month or two of working with accompanist Phyllis Grandy, out of the blue she asked if I sang rock 'n' roll.

"Yeah, that's all I did in college. I had a band."

She said, "Well why didn't you tell me?"

"I don't know, you never asked."

"Oh, Treat, I'm taking you over to the Royale to audition for *Grease.*"

Phyllis was the first one who brought me to the *Grease* team's attention, and she knew exactly what they were looking for. I owe her a lot. When I auditioned I came with my guitar and sang "Breaking Up Is Hard to Do." After I finished, the music director asked me to sing it again, a third higher. And then he asked me to sing it another third higher. And then a third higher than that. When I got up into the falsetto range, Louis finally stopped me with "OK, you're gonna be fine. Come back next week, but don't bring your guitar."

I think they just wanted to see if I could move and sing at the same time. And apparently I could, because I was cast. But not for the road company. The team decided to keep me in New York as the understudy for a number of the male roles, including Danny Zuko.

JIM WESTON (*Vince Fontaine*): *Grease* had its share of repeaters and would-be groupies, but the most dear and the most special was the daughter of restaurateur Vincent Sardi. Jennifer adopted us. She loved the show and loved the cast, and we loved her.

MEG BENNETT (*Marty*): Ten-year-old Jennifer was a passionate *Grease* fan. She'd come daily and stand outside the stage door to get a glimpse of us all. She was irresistible, and we ended up taking her under our wing and inviting her backstage. She soon became a regular fixture at the show. Vincent Sardi was so touched at the attention his daughter was getting, he gave the entire cast their own charge accounts at Sardi's. It became our regular hangout, and a group of us would go there nightly and spend our paychecks at the upstairs bar.

JIM WESTON: Not needing a second invitation, our shabbily dressed Greasers started going over to Sardi's between shows on matinee days and after the show on others. We were a pretty rowdy group, and after a few visits the maître d' politely but firmly asked us if we wouldn't be more comfortable in the upstairs dining room and bar, where they even had an "actor's menu." Many happy nights we could be found there, having a few beers and talking about the show. It was our own private club.

Jeff Conaway as Zuko, with James Canning (Doody),
Walter Bobbie (Roger), and Timothy Meyers (Kenickie).

Pippin might dispute this, but *Grease* won
the Broadway League bowling trophy.

When the show had moved a block over to the Royale, we added Charlie's—just across the street—as another of our main hangouts. We were stars
at Charlie's, and most nights we were offered the big round table at the back.
At Charlie's we could make all the noise we wanted—and sometimes we did.

BOB GARRETT (*Teen Angel / Johnny Casino*): Early in my career I had
learned that you do everything and anything you can to keep your performance
fresh and each moment spontaneous, like it is happening for the first time. I
was committed. I was also a big ham.

Dorothy Leon, the original Miss Lynch, was perfect casting, and I got a kick
out of her portrayal in every performance while standing next to her as Johnny
Casino at the Rydell prom. One night I spontaneously put rabbit ears behind
Miss Lynch's head while she was making her big prom speech. A high school
kid, especially Johnny Casino, would do things like that, so to me it seemed
perfectly appropriate and funny. The cast loved it and so did the audience.

Fortunately Dorothy thought the laugh came from her line. I was more than happy to let her go on thinking that. I continued those rabbit ears for weeks without Dorothy ever catching on. But one night she finally saw what I was doing and went nuts when we got offstage.

The next day, furious, she called the director in California and kvetched about me and my behavior. Tom assured her he would address the situation. When he called the stage manager, the stage manager told him that I was getting big laughs, the audience loved it, and it seemed integral to the show. Tom then called Dorothy back and, in his inimitable manner, calmed her down and even convinced her to let it go, assuring her that it only made the audience love her Miss Lynch all the more. The gesture became a permanent part of the show.

Dorothy never spoke to me again.

TREAT WILLIAMS: Being an understudy is a mixed and often confusing journey. I was thrown into *Grease* two weeks out of college. I didn't have the skills of being in a long-running show or the discipline of doing eight shows a week. And bottom line? I didn't really know how to act. It was to be trial by fire.

Kathi Moss, who played Cha-Cha, was the dance captain. It fell to her to teach me the show. As dance captain, she knew every single role by heart. It was a lotta repetition, a lotta laughs, and a lotta screwing up, but Kathi was never annoyed and always patient. Kathi became my *Grease* mentor, in terms of learning not only the show but also how to fit into the show.

Within a month of joining the cast, for my *Grease* debut I was put in for Walter Bobbie (Roger). Walter had an extraordinary energy, and he was spectacularly good.

What I learned in those first few months was that onstage there was no such thing as an understudy. This cast had been doing this show for a *very* long time. Their main concern was not that you were good but that you did exactly what the actor you were covering did, so that you didn't mess up any of their bits of business and laughs. Instantly and throughout my time as an understudy, I felt like a square peg in a round hole.

Jim Borrelli (Sonny) scared me to death when I went on as Zuko. Zuko enters with all his bravado and swagger to greet the guys for the first time since summer vacation. At some point Sonny is facing upstage and Zuko is facing out when there's a blackout as the girls sing their version of "Summer Nights." In the blackout Jim Borrelli looked me in the eye and with no humor or empathy whatsoever said, "Don't fuck up!" When the lights came up for the guys' verse of "Summer Nights," I was done for the evening. I could barely drag myself through "Summer Nights," much less the rest of the show.

It was a tough night, and not surprisingly I was quite awful. I got better as I played the part more often, but I never had the time, the rehearsal, or the confidence to make Zuko my own.

21

"Reelin' and Rockin'"
Life in the Orchestra Pit

ILENE GRAFF (*Sandy*): *Grease* was unique in that the band and the cast were all friends—there was no hierarchy or separation between the two. As *Grease's* first music director and conductor, the brilliant Louis St. Louis set the style and a high bar for all who followed.

BEN LANZARONE (*Music Director/Conductor*): In one of those lucky moments of one's career, I met Louis St. Louis when he was the artist performing "Mammy Blue" in a recording session for which I was the arranger. He and I hit it off, and I guess he liked my work because he soon asked if I would like to be the alternate conductor for the show when it moved from the Eden downtown to the Broadhurst uptown.

I usually played *Grease* twice a week, and Louis would do the rest. I loved playing that music. I grew up in the '50s and was even in a doo-wop group, so I definitely knew the style. It was also a joy playing with some of the best musicians in the city.

I played and conducted the show from 1972 to 1978. I will always be grateful for the lifelong friendships that came from our years with the show, and for my wife, Ilene Graff, who played Sandy, and for our daughter, Nikka, who wouldn't even exist if not for *Grease*.

JOHN TRIVERS (*Bass Player*): Twenty-five years old and very excited, I walked into the dark, cramped orchestra pit of the Eden Theatre and took my place as a bass player between guitarist Bob Rose, a first-call studio regular, and Buddy Saltzman, drummer—forty-five years old and already a legend! Buddy played on "The Sound of Silence" by Simon & Garfunkel, "I'm a Believer" with the Monkees, "Dawn (Go Away)" with the Four Seasons, "If I Had a Hammer" with Peter, Paul and Mary, and of course, "My Way" with Frank Sinatra.

The music director, Louis St. Louis, was a brilliant musician and performer in his own right. Louis had hired me a year earlier to do a Broadway show called *Soon*, featuring unknown actors Richard Gere and Barry Bostwick. *Soon* lived up to its name and closed very soon—after one show! With *Grease*, I was hoping for a longer run.

BEN LANZARONE: When *Grease* moved to the Royale, the basement became the home of the longest-running poker game on Broadway. Musicians, stagehands, and actors would congregate before the show, during intermissions, between shows on matinee days, and even between musical numbers. The band usually left the pit during the long break between the opening number and "Summer Nights," some just to relax but most to join the game. Although we always made it back in time for the downbeat of "Summer Nights," sometimes it was a close call, making the actors and stage management just a little bit nervous as we hurried back into the pit at the very last moment.

BERNARD GROBMAN (*Guitarist*): When I was growing up in East New York, Manhattan and Broadway were a very long subway ride away, but as early as I can remember, I knew that's where I wanted to be.

When I was twenty-two I scored my first gig on Broadway, subbing at *Grease*. I couldn't have been more excited. On that first day, when I went through the stage door of the Royale, it was as if I had stepped into a movie. Smiling, I headed downstairs and ducked into the orchestra pit, where I took my place next to the guitar player to "watch the book." When I looked up I could see the Royale's painted ceiling and hear the '50s top hits playing over the chattering audience as they began to fill the theater. It was thrilling.

In the next few weeks, Louis St. Louis let me play on a few songs, and eventually I got the opportunity to play my first full show. I was nervous as hell, but I was also well prepared. After the curtain calls, as the audience was leaving, we each got a chance to play a solo. After my solo Louis turned around and smilingly shouted something. I couldn't hear what he said, but I knew by the smile that I was going to be a regular. Happy doesn't quite describe it.

When *Grease* had its giant celebration to mark becoming the longest-running Broadway show in history—one of the most magical theater nights of my life—I couldn't help but think that this was a far cry from East New York and Brooklyn.

I played *Grease* for the next five years, all the way till closing night at the Majestic Theatre.

JEREMY STONE (*Music Director/Conductor*): I was a twenty-six-year-old newbie when I had the amazingly good fortune to succeed Louis St. Louis as the music director and conductor of the Broadway company of *Grease*. I was well aware that although I had assumed a position of responsibility over the musical performance of both band and cast, I was junior to just about every one of them in both age and experience.

One night I received a complaint about the tempo or energy of "Mooning" at the previous show. I needed to figure out a way to get more energy from my drummer.

The drummer happened to be Buddy Saltzman, a venerated star of the recording studio who had played on a lot of the big hits of the '50s. It wasn't going to work to try to tell Buddy that his playing was tired, and certainly not if I told him that the complaint had come from the stage. Instead (and I hope Buddy, wherever he is, and any cast members reading this will forgive me) I approached him before the next show about "Mooning."

"Buddy, I'm sick and tired of watching these actors be all over the place with the rhythm. They couldn't find the beat if you handed it to them on a plate. Will you do me a favor? I recognize this is unmusical as hell, but would you just really slam the backbeats so loud that they can't possibly miss them?"

Buddy came through. "Mooning" regained its energy and enthusiasm, I knew the cast would be happy, and I gave Buddy a smug thumbs-up like *We really showed 'em.*

Who says doing *Grease* wasn't preparation for a later career as a psychologist?

STEVE SINGER (*Drummer*): Funny thing about musicians. You have to hire them first, and then you have one rehearsal or performance to decide if you want to keep them. The *Grease* test was to play with the Broadway orchestra during a performance. That tryout started right at the top of the show with the opening number.

Although at twenty-one I was a seasoned musician, I was pretty nervous. The show is basic '50s rock, and I knew I could handle that, but it was with a new group, with no rehearsal, and not only was it New York, it was Broadway!

When I first entered the Royale orchestra pit, I was instantly struck with how high it was. The audience could actually see us! They could see me! My confidence began to fade. Just as my nerves were about to get the best of me, we were off. The houselights went down, the stage lights came up, and behind the scrim the cast began to sing the Rydell High "Alma Mater" song.

My heart was beating way too fast. My mouth went dry and beads of sweat were forming on my forehead and upper lip. I felt the sweat starting to run down my back, and I was just praying I didn't pass out. All the while I was desperately trying to keep my hands still until I needed them.

Too late for that! On a word cue, Jeremy, the conductor, counts off: "One, two, three, four." I hit the snare and the floor tom on the next "one"! *I was in!*

It was a simple, basic '50s rock song, and in three minutes it was all over. But to me it was Carnegie Hall. That night I was OK'd to join the tour then playing in Ontario, Canada.

LIZ MYERS (*Music Director*): My inspiration at *Grease* was the stage manager, Lynne Guerra, who was the only other female production crew member at the show. She was ballsy, tough, skinny, and no-nonsense. I respected her and was a little afraid of her. I didn't know then that we were both breaking ground for women's equality, being the first female stage manager and music director for *Grease* on Broadway at the time.

Lynne, the cast, crew, and musicians, and I were tasked with making sure the show went well and the audience got their money's worth. Long-running shows are like that. It feels like someone hands you the Olympic torch and you have to run, and run hard. *Grease* was a perfect show. Sixteen Equity-scale actors, great musical numbers, rapid-fire dialogue and lyrics, brilliant staging, and a tried-and-true story: boy meets girl, boy loses girl, and, well . . . girl comes back changed. If you looked deeper into the show, you might get lost trying to figure out why Rizzo sang of a futuristic morality about sex without guilt, and how the group could fat-shame Cha-Cha like they did when she was the best dancer in the show. But you didn't think about that very much because the audience was having such a good time. We musicians were out there closest to the audience and incredibly aware of how the show was going. If Kenickie's first line brought great guffaws of laughter, then you knew it was going to be a great night.

"Eat me!" Simple and shocking. Worked night after night.

And we set the beat. The music is the driver for a show like *Grease*, and the tempo you set in "Summer Nights" becomes the launching pad for the story of the show.

I feel today and I felt back then that we have a righteous obligation to the writers and producers of the original show to perform the show exactly as it was created. Our job is to play with enthusiasm and passion every note and nuance that made the original performances great. You get on the train that is *the show* at the first station, and you ride that success all the way to the end of the line. In *Grease*, when that cast comes down to the front of the stage in the last musical number and sings "We Go Together," as a conductor you look up, and the cast and audience are one. It's a contagious high. You've done your job, and the audience loves it. The exhilaration is euphoric.

22

The First Bus and Truck Tour

October 1973–November 1974

> *Bus and truck tours are just what the name implies. The scenery and the crew travel by truck overnight, while the cast mostly travels by bus during what is called a "travel day." A bus and truck tour usually plays the smaller cities and towns; the stops are often very short and more often than not, one-night stands. The schedule can be grueling. It's one of the reasons we cast younger and younger as the tours went on.*
>
> **—TOM MOORE**

"Let It Be Me": The Auditions

DANNY JACOBSON (*Kenickie*): I was working as a garbageman in upstate New York. I did it for half a dozen summers throughout high school and college, and it was the best job I'd ever had. This was before the garbage trucks picked up the garbage. This was when men picked it up. Broken men, to be frank. Men whose lives had not gone according to Hoyle. Most of them were war veterans, whose reward for saving their country was a lifetime of collecting its garbage.

It was the early 1970s, and the '50s were echoing back. Even on the trucks. Three of the other guys and I started singing doo-wop just like they did on the street corners back in the day, but we were singing on garbage trucks.

Then one night that summer, a girlfriend of mine took me to see *Grease*. As soon as the scrim rose up, they had me. *Wow!* (Of course, back then I didn't know *scrim*.) A curtain went up.

157

By midsummer I was belting out "Beauty School Dropout" into beer bottles. Or saltshakers. One night I was serenading a four-time Jewish American Princess Award winner in her parents' lavish Scarsdale kitchen when her mom, in *midverse*, said, "Not with my good saltshaker!" and literally handed me another, clearly more generic saltshaker. Midverse! Well, I slept with her daughter but never sang for her again. But that same girl, Amy Buchman, would later give me a notice from something called *Backstage* that said "*Grease* Replacements—Open Call." She had to explain what an open call was. I had never been in a play, unless you count life. But Amy pressed me to go, so I said I would. She said I wouldn't. And Amy Buchman was right. I had no intention of humiliating myself on a Broadway stage.

A year or so earlier, I had been invited to another tryout. This one was for the Mets at Shea Stadium. I hardly thought the Mets were looking for a five-foot-nine Jewish infielder, but it was a chance to play on *that field*. Something I could tell my grandkids, or other people's grandkids . . . and so I thought about it. Maybe I could tell those same grandkids that I got to sing on a Broadway stage. That was really the kicker, and also the ceiling of my expectation. Get to sing on a Broadway stage.

The open call was on a muggy Sunday in August 1974 at the Royale Theatre. The Hotel Piccadilly coffee shop was across the street and pretty packed at 10:30 in the morning. I could not believe how many great-looking girls there were. And great-looking guys who seemed less than interested in these great-looking girls. Who were these people? I soon realized I was not the only one in the coffee shop with sheet music for *Grease*.

As the group of them, en masse, headed to the alley, I followed and eventually was greeted by the production stage manager, Steve Beckler, who asked me for a picture and a résumé. *A picture and résumé of what?* Not even in the building and already unprepared. I was sent to the basement. Banished, I felt, for sure. But banished to heaven. A room full of young women in tights and leotards, stretching and vocalizing—and in tights and leotards. *When my grandkids hear this . . .*

It wasn't too much longer before I'd make some very clear eye contact with one lady—Phyllis Grandy, the accompanist in the pit. As I handed my sheet music to her, I said, "'Beauty School Dropout,'" and she rolled her eyes. Raised by Jews, I knew what an eye roll was. Still, something in me knew I was up. This was my time. So I stepped back and took in the moment. Me, on a

Broadway stage. I recall taking in the view and even that very specific Royale smell. Phyllis played the opening chords, and I got as far as "Your story's sad to tell" when a career-saving voice cut me off: "Danny, do you know 'Greased Lightnin'"?" I really didn't, but somehow I knew enough to say I did!

PS: As an homage to my (still) dear friend Amy Buchman, I named Helen Hunt's character in *Mad About You* Jamie Buchman.

CHICK VENNERA (*Sonny*): It was February of 1973. I had recently finished working as a backup performer on the Raquel Welch show in Las Vegas when I got an audition for the first bus and truck company of *Grease*.

It went really well, but I didn't hear anything until August, after I'd come back to L.A., when they contacted me to let me know I had been cast in the role of Sonny. Because the creative team was in L.A. to brush up the first national company—then performing at the Shubert—the meeting of the first bus and truck company was held on the stage of the theater before an evening performance. Although I had met most of the creative team at the auditions, I had never met the authors.

So I'm at the Shubert, and as I'm walking onstage from the back of the theater, I hear "Francis Vennera, what are you doing here?" I turned around, saw who it was, and replied, "Oh hey, Mr. Casey, what are you doing here?"

To which he replied, "I wrote this." Warren Casey was my high school freshman-year homeroom teacher. I had no idea he and Jim Jacobs were the authors of the megahit *Grease*. What a cool surprise. Thank you, Mr. Casey!

COSIE COSTA (*Doody*): I was living in Los Angeles in 1973 when my buddy from college, Chick Vennera, called to tell me he had just been cast in the touring company of *Grease*. He was having lunch with one of the authors, Warren Casey, and invited me to tag along, as he thought I was very right for the show.

We went to a very fancy restaurant in Century City. Warren asked why I hadn't auditioned in L.A. I told him (I'm sure with a bit of an attitude) that holding casting sessions for L.A. actors was bullshit, because they were really looking for New York actors living in L.A. He smiled and asked if I could do a falsetto. "Sure," I said. "Let me hear it," he said. I belted out a nice falsetto run, not to the delight of everyone in the restaurant. Warren liked it though, and asked if I would travel to San Francisco to audition. For the first time in my young acting career, I realized that I had a real shot at my first professional acting job.

I flew to San Francisco, excited yet apprehensive, asking myself if I really had what it took to get this job. I was the last actor in that day's auditions. As I was leaving the theater, Tom Moore and Pat Birch were getting in a cab. Tom yelled something to me like *Nice audition, you'll be hearing from us soon.* And I did!

And that show has made all the difference. Because I'd had to drop out of the acting program at the Pasadena Playhouse when I was called up to serve four years in the air force during the Vietnam War, I felt I'd never have a chance to do what I wanted more than anything in the world, and that was to be an actor. Warren gave me that chance, and I am forever grateful.

CYNTHIA DARLOW (*Jan*): I had sunk to a new low: passing out pamphlets in Times Square for four dollars an hour dressed as a gorilla. I saw an advertisement in *Backstage* for a cattle call (all actors welcome) for the *Grease* B&T. I had always wanted to sing but had always been told that my voice was too husky, and that there was no future for me in musical theater. But why not give it a chance?

The morning of the audition, I thought I was being so clever by getting there really early, 7:30, but when I arrived the line was already around the block, and my number was somewhere in the two hundreds.

It was a *looong* day, 10:00 AM to 6:00 PM. People had dropped like flies all during the day; I was starving and I was scared—no, I was terrified! Suddenly my name was called. Shaking from head to toe, I found myself on the stage of this cavernous Broadway theater singing "Breaking Up Is Hard to Do" and "Where the Boys Are."

"Best audition I've seen all day! Come back Friday to dance."

Dance? I didn't even have dance shoes. Luckily the choreographer and the director were looking for actors first, singers second, and actors who moved well third.

The Friday dance marathon went by in a flash, and somehow, miraculously I came out of it with the part of Jan. I was ecstatic. I was going to be on Broadway!

It wasn't until I signed my contract that I found out "*Grease* B&T" stood for "*Grease* bus and truck tour." My gas and electricity had already been shut off, and I had just gotten an eviction notice. Touring was just fine with me.

DENISE NETTLETON (*Marty*): It's hard to believe, but I knew nothing about *Grease* when I arrived at the Shubert for the audition, woefully unprepared.

Filled with my usual self-doubts, my hands were shaking as I walked out on the big stage and saw that huge, empty theater. I thought my knees were going to buckle under with fear. The whole creative team was there, except for the coauthor/lyricist Jim Jacobs.

Whether I was shaky or not, they all seemed to like my audition, because I was asked to see the show before a callback. I took my dad, and we both *loved* it! It seemed impossible to believe I might be in a show that was this cool!!

After two callbacks, my agent called to say it had come down to me and another girl for the role of Marty, and the other girl got it. A short time later, however, my agent called again and said they had made a mistake! They'd gotten my photo and bio mixed up with the other girl. I felt truly sad for the other girl, but I was *thrilled* to be cast as Marty.

LLOYD ALAN (*Understudy*): My mom loved going to Broadway shows and came home excited one day and said, "I just saw this wonderful musical, and you would be perfect for the leading role. You should go see it."

So what could I do? My mom told me to. I went to see *Grease*. From that moment on, I became obsessed with playing Danny Zuko. It was all I could think about.

My memories of the auditions and callbacks are a bit hazy, but I was cast in not Broadway but the bus and truck company. And not as Danny but as an understudy. Always the bridesmaid, never the bride. My dream of playing Danny on Broadway was still a long way off.

JOHN LANSING (*Zuko*): I was finally offered the role of a lifetime. The *Grease* team offered me Danny Zuko in the first *Grease* bus and truck tour. I'd made the grade, the difficult transition from understudy to headlining. I was in heaven. The hard work was finally paying off. But at twenty-three I was still an actor without an agent and needed to negotiate my own contract.

Eddie Davis, the company's general manager, who had a reputation for being a hard-ass, called me in Los Angeles. He said it was time to negotiate. I could almost feel him smiling on the other end of the phone line while my stomach was doing a flip-flop. We went back and forth on a few deal points, and then at eight o'clock that night, Eddie said he had an urgent call to make and would ring me right back. He told me to sit by the phone until our deal was struck. I was a nervous wreck and fell asleep on the couch, my head inches from the phone.

It rang—at seven the next morning. "Are you asleep?" Eddie asked, a swagger in his voice. "Yeah," I croaked. "Good," he said. "Let's negotiate."

23 | *"Movin' 'n' Groovin'"*
Traveling Across America by Bus

JOHN LANSING (*Zuko*): The rehearsals in NYC had been as rigorous as boot camp, and then our cast was deployed. Ninety cities in nine months. Every night was opening night. We started the tour in Kalamazoo and crisscrossed the country. It was a heady experience. We were young actors earning a paycheck, playing across America in a hit Broadway show. Life was sweet.

DENISE NETTLETON (*Marty*): Mostly one-night stands in ninety-nine cities, thirty-three states, and two Canadian provinces—places like Wichita, Oklahoma City, and Memphis. Although I might be able to tell you about the dressing rooms, I can't tell you anything specific about those cities at all. My salary was $325 a week. Out of that my agent took 10 percent, and we had to pay for our own hotels and food.

Although it seemed like it would be exciting to be on the road, I soon learned that it was less than glamorous: getting up at the crack of dawn to ride on a bus all day, stopping at truck stops for lunch, and then hours on the bus to our next destination.

I felt particularly bad for Ruth Russell, our Miss Lynch, who was probably in her early seventies. It seemed she should have had some kind of seniority. But she had to schlep her own luggage on and off the bus just like the rest of us.

Some people could sleep; I could *never* sleep on the bus. Some of the more experienced people had it in their contract to get a double seat. I did not. In fact I *hated* being on that bus!

DEREK KUCSAK (*Understudy*): This was my first time away from friends, family, and home. I lost so much weight the first week, I guess from nerves, that my belt was tightened to the last notch.

John Lansing as Zuko, "All Choked Up."

Denise Nettleton, Kathy Levin, Ruth Nerkin, and Karren Dille.

It got lonely at times, even with a busload of people. Thanksgiving was the worst. I don't know what happened. We were in Roanoke, Virginia, at a great hotel, and everyone from the company just vaporized. Home for the holidays. Not only that, there were no guests in the hotel, only a few staff. Worst holiday ever!

DENISE NETTLETON: Late one night after the show in Albuquerque, Joene Lewis, Jerry Barkoff, Jane Marion, and I got the munchies and decided to go down to the snack machine in the basement of our hotel. We all still had our stage makeup on. As we were headed back up to our rooms, a man with a long black leather coat slipped into the elevator and pushed the top-floor button. Seeing our stage makeup, the man asked if we were in the circus or something. Before we could answer, he said, "You know what I do for a living? I'm a stick-up man," and pulled out a gun—which he pointed directly at me! All I could think of was the phone call my mom and dad would soon be getting telling them their daughter was lying dead on an elevator floor in Albuquerque.

Jerry actually ended up saving the day, and maybe our lives, by suddenly sticking his foot out and keeping the elevator door open. Down in the lobby the night watchman noticed that the elevator had been stuck on our floor for a long time, so he ran up the stairwell to see what was causing the problem. When the gunman heard the watchman coming up the stairs, he pushed open the door and quickly hightailed it out of the building. We definitely didn't sleep much that night.

Denise Nettleton as Marty.

Derek Kucsak.

DEREK KUCSAK: After the holidays passed, things went back to normal. Kind of. We were in Cincinnati, Ohio. The curtain had just come down on a really great show for a sold-out audience of screaming teenage girls when the police came running backstage, telling us, "Leave now—don't look back and just keep going. The girls are storming the stage!"

Laughing, we all left the theater. I walked back to the hotel with Kenny Blye, the bass guitar player, and we got halfway to our hotel when suddenly not one but two carloads of girls dressed like they were going to a prom pulled alongside us. The window rolled down, and one girl screamed out, "Oh my God! They're with the show!" They all started screaming like we were the Beatles or something. For about two seconds we thought, *How cool!* Then we were afraid they might start pulling our hair out and who knows what else. We started running and ducked up an alley, where we knew they couldn't follow us. Funny what a bass guitar and a *Grease* T-shirt will do.

DENISE NETTLETON: Vince Otero (Roger) was a best friend from day one. He was a real Jersey guy, nineteen years old, and I was a seasoned California girl of twenty-five, but we just clicked. He made me laugh all the time, and I loved his sarcastic humor. He'd often tell me I reminded him of his "muhthuh."

Vince was a genius at puzzles and games. We did crossword puzzles on the bus, and we were a perfect fit since he turned out to be a leftie. I *adored* Vince!

When we left for our Christmas break, Vince handed me a note to read on my plane ride back to L.A. It said he really liked me, and if I felt the same way, after the break all I had to do was sit down next to him when I got back on the bus.

Well, I didn't sit with him when we got back on the bus. Unbeknownst to anyone on the tour, Jim Jacobs and I had started our long-distance romance in New Orleans. One night after the show, a few of us were hanging out in my hotel room, and Jerry blurted out to Vince, "All the other Rogers are gay. How about you?" Vince looked startled and then became very angry; he didn't talk to Jerry for quite some time. Eventually Vince came out, around the end of the tour. Of course, we remained BFFs always.

We were both living in L.A. when Vince called to tell me he had AIDS. I was devastated and wanted to help him in any way I could. I visited him in Hollywood once a week and brought him home-cooked meals, usually enough for a few nights' dinners.

People didn't know much about AIDS at the time and were frightened to be around Vince, but when I sent a letter to his friends asking for support, it was amazing how the *Grease* community stepped up to the plate. He was very, very touched.

We lost Vince on October 3, 1986. I miss him.

Cynthia Darlow and Vince Otero.

Kenny Morse with Danny Jacobson and Frank Piegaro.

Trials of an Understudy

KENNY MORSE (*Understudy*): In St. Louis I learned the roles of Sonny and Roger, and then we left for Cleveland. Cleveland is . . . well . . . Cleveland. It turns out there is a newspaper strike in Cleveland and a blinding snowstorm, and *no one knows* that *Grease* is playing at the Hanna Theatre—*no one!*

On a Saturday Danny Jacobson (Kenickie) announced that his back had gone out, and he would not be performing.

"You've got to be kidding me. No!" Not good. I hadn't had the time to rehearse Kenickie yet. I begged Danny: "Don't do this to me!"

And in his inimitable style, my friend Danny J. replied, "You've been begging to go on—you're *on!*" And on I went . . . for three ladies of a certain age in the orchestra of the Hanna Theatre who made up the entire audience. I hoped the three lucky ladies would enjoy the show.

And then I gave what I consider perhaps the *worst performance* by an actor in a musical ever on an American stage. When my Kenickie sang "Greased Lightnin'," I was so flummoxed as to when to step left and right, or even on- or offstage, that I called Rizzo (Kenickie's girlfriend) Zuko. Oh, dear god! I was so horrible it seemed indisputable that I would be fired, but Mike Martorella (production stage manager) and Carol Culver (dance captain) saved my bacon.

Philadelphia was the closest the tour was going to get to my home in NYC, and I desperately wanted my dad to see me in the show. So against all the rules, I offered Vince Otero a bribe to let me do *one* performance and sing Rump's big number, "Mooning." I think he knew how important it was for me to perform for my dad. And when I did, I loved it. And my dad loved it. And I may have even redeemed my disastrous performance in Cleveland. But most importantly, my dad got to see me onstage for the very first time—a lifetime memory.

PS: I never did get to Broadway, but I finally did have an NYC debut when I was asked to play Teen Angel in a special performance by the Broadway cast for the prisoners at Rikers Island. The prisoners were thrilled. I was thrilled. Though not quite an official Broadway debut, it meant a lot to me, and kind of brought the whole *Grease* dream full circle. Teen Angel was the role I had auditioned for in the first place.

DENISE NETTLETON: My understudy came up to me one day and said, "You know, when Louis St. Louis tells you your song is wonderful, it's really not! He's just being lazy—because he doesn't want to take the time to work on it."

She continued, insisting "Freddy" needed *a lot* of work and she'd be happy to work with me on our days off. Michael Rose, our music director, overheard our one-sided conversation, and when the news got around, everyone in the cast started calling her Eve Harrington, like in *All About Eve.*

When I was sick one night in Ottawa, my understudy had to go on for me. After the show Kathy Levin (Jan) came to my room, made a mean fist in my face, and told me, "You'd better not be sick again, and be back in the show by tomorrow night, or else!"

I was still down with laryngitis the next day, so I was out again. But I was so curious to see what Kathy was talking about that I bundled up and snuck into the theater to watch the show. During the scene change before the park scene, Rizzo and Marty were staged to each push one half of the park flat onto the stage and lock it. The lights came up on half a park flat and "Eve," sitting on the park bench wearing her gold bedroom slippers from the pajama party! I could see Karen (Rizzo) frantically whispering to her.

Eve suddenly ran off the stage and pushed on her half of the park-scene flat—*backward*—with the instructions "*GREASE* Park Scene Flat—Stage-Right" *facing the audience!* The cast was having a hard time holding it together. Eve was completely oblivious to the problem and to the angered cast.

I was back in the show by the next performance, sore throat and all!

The next time Eve went on, it was as Rizzo, and she forgot *a lot* of lines. The rest of the cast's parts expanded a lot that night as we had to fill in the holes. During Jan's basement scene, Eve whispered in my ear, "How's my rouge?" I hissed, "Who cares about your rouge, how about your lines?"

About six months into her contract, poor Eve got fired. As I recall, the movie *All About Eve* didn't end well either.

Kathy Levin (Jan), Denise Nettleton (Marty), Marcia McLain (Sandy), Susan McAneny (Patty), Ruth Nerkin (Frenchy), and Karren Dille (Rizzo).

24

"Leader of the Pack"

The Geary Theater, San Francisco, June 1975

The first bus and truck tour played extended runs in San Francisco and Los Angeles before resuming its relentless schedule across the country. Richard Cox replaced John Lansing, who came to Broadway.

—TOM MOORE

RICHARD COX (*Zuko*): There are those roles you feel you just have to play, and playing Danny the first time *Grease* was in San Francisco was exhilarating. The reviews were terrific, and we were the toast of the town. What a part in what a show in what a city! The Geary Theater, home of the American Conservatory Theater, is a classic, gorgeous, traditional venue. Our company was given guest-artist status at the conservatory, and I took full advantage of the perk of being able to audit acting and other related classes. I just had to make sure I conserved my energy to kick ass as Danny every night.

Art can be a catalyst for bringing people you'd never expect together. Actors can be shamans, and *Grease* is so archetypal it transcends differences and speaks to all. The audiences in San Francisco were hugely enthusiastic and richly diverse, and many invitations to various gatherings came via the stage door. There were two particularly memorable ones. A gorgeous witch (this was San Francisco) introduced herself to me at the stage door one night and invited me to her coven. On my night off I had a lovely evening with a charming group of witches and warlocks.

On another night I was greeted enthusiastically at the stage door by a group of four Hells Angels. They passionately praised our company and me

170

Richard Cox (Zuko) and the first bus and truck company.

as Danny, saying that they were sure my fellow cast members and I must have had upbringings much like theirs as the scenes were so true to life. I diplomatically said my upbringing was probably quite different from theirs, but that's what theater was all about, because we could all find common ground and connect across the footlights. They very much wished they could come back to see it again and again, lamenting that the San Francisco run was almost over. I smiled and, as I waved goodbye, said, "Well, we'll be opening in L.A. next week! If you happen to be in the area, come see it there!"

Shortly after our opening in L.A., I emerged from the stage door to find the same group with a whole bunch more club members, who then gave me a Harley motorcycle escort back to the hotel, where we all chatted for quite a while before I went in.

The Hells Angel I'd connected with most was named Cisco. He was very bright and articulate, and had a warm affability about him. Some days later he and they surprised me by showing up and wanting to take me to lunch. I thanked them but explained that I had tickets to see the Alvin Ailey American Dance Theater that afternoon. Tom Moore was going, and we had planned to meet at Royce Hall (UCLA). I said, "Sorry, guys, but hey, if you want to see Alvin Ailey, some great modern dance . . ."

When I said that, Cisco stared at me for a really long beat and then somewhat emotionally pointed at me and said something unexpected: "You see, this is why you're a special and decent person. You didn't assume we know nothing about modern dance or wouldn't be interested. Your impulse was to include us . . . What the hell, we'll go."

Tom had no idea who was about to join us for Alvin Ailey. He's rarely lost for words, but he was definitely struck dumb that afternoon when the Angels and I came through the lobby door. The Angels sat behind us, and after each act I turned to discuss each piece. One dance was kind of mystical and esoteric, and Cisco said, "Sorry, but I don't know what the fuck that was about!" "Don't worry," I laughed, "I don't either. And neither do most people here. They just pretend!"

But the last piece was an Apache, in the tough Parisian bar-fight style, with a woman hanging in the balance. Cisco and his friends came alive like they had when talking about Greased Lightning and the Burger Palace Boys' rumble that night at the San Francisco stage door. Knowing far more about this milieu than Tom or me, they happily tutored us as we walked out of Royce Hall. What an extraordinary afternoon of unlikely togetherness *Grease* wrought. Who knew?

LEFT: Richard Cox (Zuko) and Marcia McLain (Sandy). RIGHT: Chick Vennera (Sonny), Richard Cox, Cosie Costa (Doody), and Vince Otero (Roger).

Richard Cox (Zuko) and Jerry Barkoff (Johnny Casino).

Ruth Nerkin as Frenchy, "Beauty School Dropout."

(Front) Chick Vennera, Cosie Costa, Vincent Otero, Larry Horowitz, (back) Denise Nettleton, Ruth Nerkin, Richard Cox, Kathy Levin, and Karren Dille.

The First Bus and Truck Company Hits the Road Again

When the B&T left Los Angeles to go back out on the road,
Lloyd Alan took over from Richard Cox.

—TOM MOORE

LEFT: Shannon Fanning as Sandy. RIGHT: Kim Herbert and Andrea Walters as Vince Fontaine and Marty.

Vince Otero (Roger), Clifford Lipson (Sonny), Danny Jacobson (Kenickie), Donald Russell (Doody), and Lloyd Alan (Zuko), "Greased Lightnin'."

First bus and truck, "We Go Together."

Stage Crew Warriors

MICHAEL MARTORELLA (*Production Stage Manager*): After San Francisco and Los Angeles, we headed out on tour again, and our terrific road crew worked their magic daily to set the stage in a variety of settings across the country.

Every audience in every city we played expected and deserved to see *Grease* in its original and perfect form. We did that with few exceptions, but when those exceptions occurred, well, we did our best to deliver! From city to city we performed in venues ranging from magnificent first-class theaters to high school auditoriums. No matter what the conditions, however, we learned to adapt quickly and efficiently.

OGDENSBURG, NEW YORK: A high school auditorium. I think we even performed as part of a high school assembly. Minimal props and scenery—and no Greased Lightning car! But where there's a bench, there's a way!

UNIVERSITY OF RHODE ISLAND: A lecture hall. Props and costumes were on racks neatly arranged on the lawn outside the back door of the lecture hall. Actors would run out, pull their next costume, hightail it to the restroom to change, then run back across the lawn, grab a prop, and smoothly make their entrance.

BURLINGTON, VERMONT: The Flynn, a grand old vaudeville theater. But not for a very, very long time. When the crew and I arrived early that extremely cold morning, we faced the sad sight of a stage and auditorium that had long lost its luster. We knew we could make the stage space work, but the freezing, dank dressing rooms were unusable. Up to the challenge, the crew soon rented Winnebagos to use as makeshift dressing rooms, hired some local carpenters, and in a matter of hours made a totally enclosed, weather-protected passageway leading from the Winnebagos to the stage door.

Just as we finished, our weary actors arrived and, amid a flurry of expletives, crammed themselves into the Winnebagos, which by then had frozen water pipes. But when the audience filled that broken-down theater and the houselights dimmed, we all rose to the occasion and brought the stage to life, and *Grease* soared. Drinks that night were on me!

However, at the other end of the spectrum, and without question, the highlight of our tour was this:

THE US MILITARY ACADEMY (WEST POINT): Eisenhower Hall. Our one performance there was toward the end of the tour. A harsh winter was closing in; we had been on the road for months, playing one-night stands all over the country; and we were all tired, as were the scenery, props, and costumes.

Our crew bus and trucks arrived at West Point at about 2:00 AM on a very cold December 7, 1974. We were directed to a parking area near the theater. The cast bus would arrive later that day.

The crew bus was our "home on wheels" for the nine-person road crew, and we were fast asleep at 6:00 AM sharp when there was a firm knock at the bus door. When our bus driver opened the door, he was smartly greeted by a cadet who asked to speak with the person in charge. Jay Geller, our road carpenter, and I stumbled to the door, where the cadet told us he was reporting for duty. He and his team were there to help us get ready for our evening show. Jay and I greeted the cadet. I looked at the rest of our crew, they looked at me, we all looked at the cadet, and in unison we bellowed out, "Yes sir, that works for us!"

Within minutes the loading-dock doors opened, and we were ready to start loading in the show with a platoon of cadets standing by waiting for their orders. Without hesitation the cadets quickly unloaded the trucks and asked if we would like them to clean and make any necessary repairs to the scenery and props. We felt like we had won the lottery! Our road crew gave the eager cadets guidance, and when it became clear our outstanding academy crew would do a great job, the cadet in charge offered us dressing rooms, showers, and a place to rest while his crew went to work. We gratefully accepted his offer and happily went off for showers and to catch up on some much-needed sleep.

When we regrouped onstage four hours later, we stared in awe at the amazing refurbishment the cadets had accomplished. Every prop, every piece of scenery had been repaired and repainted, and every costume looked like it had just come off the designer's rack! The trucks had even been washed, and our crew bus looked like it had just come off the showroom floor—go, Army!

When the cast arrived, they were thrilled to see their refurbished sets and costumes, not to mention the cadets.

It was like opening night that evening, with a packed theater. I can unequivocally say that there was nothing quite like experiencing a standing ovation from four thousand uniformed West Point cadets and their guests at our curtain calls!

It was a fantastic way to top off our tour. Those long six months on the road now seemed a very distant memory.

25 | *Broadway* 1974–1975

The best way to follow the Grease *chronology is through the progression of Danny Zukos that led each company. The multiple road companies became farm teams for the major league, which was of course Broadway. Some arrived directly, like Greg Evigan, and some through understudying on Broadway (Jeff Conaway, Richard Gere, Treat Williams); others came in from the road after a tour (John Lansing, Adrian Zmed, Lloyd Alan, Frank Piegaro, Peter Gallagher). It was an ongoing carousel of talent.*

—TOM MOORE

JOHN LANSING (*Zuko*): Barry Bostwick had moved on from *Grease* a year earlier, and Jeff Conaway was about to make the Greaser's migration to Hollywood fame. I was back in New York when I received the fateful call. They wanted me to play Danny Zuko in the Broadway company.

I was elated. But there was a caveat: I had to audition; I had one night to prove I could handle the New York company. I was pumped but a bundle of nerves. A dream come true—or crash and burn. I had one shot.

The show started without incident, although the cast didn't greet me with open arms. After the musical number "Summer Nights," Zuko stops Sonny, played by Jim Borrelli, in his tracks. Now, Borrelli was a powerful actor. No nonsense. Didn't suffer fools. The orchestra started the transition music, and Borrelli turned to head offstage. I slapped the back of his leather jacket. The

179

sound echoed in the theater, only challenged by the pounding of my heart. *Did I hit him too hard? Did I piss him off?* Jim Borrelli did a slow turn . . . and then I saw that glint in his eye, and I knew I'd passed muster. With Borrelli's nod of approval, the rest of the cast warmed up to the new guy. That was the beginning of one of the best years of my life—playing Danny Zuko on the Broadway stage.

PHILIP CASNOFF (*Understudy*): In the fall of 1974, I had just returned from a yearlong national tour of *Godspell,* and I was riding high, a working actor with an Equity card but, alas, no agent—only my copy of *Backstage,* where I saw an open Equity call for *Grease* on Broadway. I stood in line with hundreds of other hopefuls, most of whom had been performing in school musicals since elementary school. I had a BA in French literature and a minor in physics, but senior year I did a play. The bug bit me. Hard. I wasn't yet ready to teach French in some prep school, so I stood in line.

Four long hours later I was in a rehearsal space facing Tom Moore, Pat Birch, and Vinnie Liff. I was fucking nervous, but I was also pumped. I sang my rock 'n' roll version of "Summertime." My version started Bobby Rydell–ish and went into Robert Plant–land by the end.

The Rydell High prom: the dance contest.

Vince Fontaine declares Danny Zuko the winner of the dance contest.

When I had tried out for chorus in high school, I was rejected because Mrs. Barteletti said they had no space for boy sopranos. Humiliated, I almost never sang again.

Tom Moore intently stared at me when I finished my song. I was still breathing hard, red in the face. He leaned forward with a barely suppressed smile and a twinkle in his eye and said words I will never forget: "Where the hell did you come from?"

JOHN EVERSON (*Assistant Stage Manager/Understudy*): Tom Moore and Pat Birch were putting together a new Broadway musical called *Over Here!*, starring the Andrews Sisters. Needing several talented young men, they raided their own *Grease* companies, bringing in John Travolta, Treat Williams, and John Driver as well as the current production stage manager, Tommy Smith.

I had the good fortune of being in the right place at the right time because they also needed to replace the assistant stage manager/understudy, John Fennessy. I got the job, and moments later—actually three weeks—I was making my acting debut on Broadway.

JIM WESTON (*Vince Fontaine*): When *Grease* moved to the Royale, the show inherited an ancient stage doorman, Bill Hill. God only knows how long he had been there. At this point Bill only worked matinees.

One Saturday matinee day, not having an entrance until the second act, I was watching the first act from out in the house. The cast was in the middle of the park scene, sometime after Rizzo's "Look at Me, I'm Sandra Dee," when all of a sudden from stage left came Bill Hill, walking across the stage and right through the scene, calling, "Ben Lanzarone, telephone. Ben Lanzarone, telephone." And he just slowly walked across, never looking, never stopping. He just did it. The people in the audience were stupefied. As was the cast.

It was just one of those Broadway things.

FRANK PIEGARO (*Understudy/Zuko/Teen Angel*): On a Sunday in October after a matinee, Shannon Fanning (Sandy) and I were having dinner at Teacher's Restaurant when a guy walked in and the entire staff started congratulating him, patting him on the back, giving him hugs and kisses. I asked our waitress what it was all about. She told us he had run the New York City Marathon that day. I turned to Shannon and said, "There is no way I could do that."

But then my ego kicked in—no goal too high not be achieved. Doing Johnny Casino / Teen Angel wasn't so physically demanding. *Why couldn't I, in a year or so, train for this?* So it began. Long runs on the day off, shorter runs while performing eight shows a week. I went through a rough-and-tough application process. If I got in, great. If not, I tried.

Lo and behold, I got in. And then as fate would have it, the role of Danny opened up and I'm cast! *Oh no! No! No! Danny's a huge role. How in the hell am I gonna pull this off? Eight shows a week as Danny* and *the New York City Marathon? Maybe I can back out.* No, not part of my nature. The entire cast and crew knew, and everyone was thrilled for me and totally supportive. I was screwed.

My alarm went off at 3:00 AM. Besides finishing the race, I had a show to do that afternoon. Half-hour call at 2:30 PM for a three o'clock show. It was going to be tight. The start of the race was at Fort Wadsworth / Verrazano Bridge. Along the route our drummer cheers me on in Brooklyn, our sax player in the Bronx, and our bass player in Manhattan. Then the runners enter Central Park at the twenty-mile mark. The thousands of onlookers of all ethnicities cheering us on is one of the most exhilarating feelings I've ever experienced. I feel great. I've got it made in the shade.

By mile twenty-one I'm sure I'll never finish the race, but with the help of those great people cheering me on, I gut it out. The finish line is in the park by Tavern on the Green. As I run across it, a great feeling of accomplishment courses through me. *I did it!*

As all the runners are hustled along, I see our production stage managers Lynne Guerra and Bill Vitale. *Oh right, I have a show to do!* They whisk me away in a cab to the Royale. With the runner's high—endorphins, etc.—I have never been so pumped up to do a show.

For the show's opening announcements, Mike Martorella, our stage manager, said, "In the role of Danny Zuko is Frank Piegaro, who just completed the New York City Marathon in three hours and twenty-six minutes." The crowd went crazy! And seated in the front row were two people still in their running gear from the race. I couldn't let the opportunity pass; I wore my New York City Marathon number in the track scene.

The high from reaching my marathon goal carried me through that performance and many to come. It was truly an awesome experience. The race, the show—a perfect way to spend a Sunday in New York.

Frank Piegaro as Zuko.

Broadway Understudy Lament

Understudies in any theatrical production are perhaps the most underappreciated members of the cast, especially in a long-running production. By the time it closed, Grease *had become a multi-limbed organization of constantly rotating casts and replacements on Broadway and in its eight companies on the road. It was our group of exceptionally talented understudies who kept our well-oiled machine running smoothly, often under the most difficult of circumstances. The show always went on!*
—TOM MOORE

PHILIP CASNOFF: Understudying is a special kind of hell, mixed with the electric excitement of being *on Broadway.* The thing is, when you are an understudy, you're a target. Everybody is throwing darts of "wisdom." Hit your marks, sing the notes—basically do what the regular guy did. *Exactly* what he did. Not quite my style—I wanted to fit the role to me. Make my own mark. But getting respect as an understudy is not an easy task.

Ray DeMattis (Roger), Philip Casnoff (Doody), John Lansing (Zuko), Jerry Zaks (Kenickie), and Jim Borrelli (Sonny, back row).

Jerry Zaks (Kenickie) always had a few . . . let's call them "suggestions" for me. One night I'm on for Doody, and we're in a freeze. Zaks leans in and quietly says, "Casnoff, say the line, the one before 'Magic Changes.'" "Which line?" I say. "The line, idiot—'Has it got a C in it?'" "Why should I say it to you?" "Casnoff, just say the line." I say it. He shakes his head sadly. "See, that's your problem." "Fuck you, Jerry." And then Jerry, who became Jerry Zaks, the famous fucking director, says, "Casnoff—you're not saying the line, you're asking for a laugh."

Point taken. But what I defiantly said to him at the time was "Yeah, and I'm getting it!"

TOM MOORE (*Director*): When Jerry recently heard these stories of his backstage direction, he was mortified and said if he had been the director, he would have fired himself immediately.

JOHN EVERSON: During that year on Broadway, I had the distinction of covering future A-list directors Jerry Zaks and Walter Bobbie. Jerry was already honing his directorial chops. The first time I went on, he caught me in the wings and couldn't hold back. "John—brighter colors, brighter colors!"

PHILIP CASNOFF: Jim Borrelli (Sonny) scared the shit out of me and everybody else with his tough-as-nails attitude. Every time I went on as Zuko,

Ray DeMattis, Jim Borrelli, Jerry Zaks, Philip Casnoff, and John Lansing, "Greased Lightnin'."

I dreaded the moment when Zuko crosses the stage and gives Sonny a shot in the nuts. It had to be just right—no touching but close enough so Borrelli could milk it and get his guaranteed huge laugh. The first two times I was about five feet away when I pretended to jab his balls. It was obvious nothing happened. Still Borrelli grabbed his crotch as if I'd nailed him. No laugh! Egg on Borrelli's face. He was volcanically pissed. "Casnoff—just do it, you fucking pussy, but if you touch my nuts, you're dead. Understood?"

I was determined. *Yeah—I got you, Borrelli.* That night I waited for him to get close. Real close. I made the move and got him square in the nuts. I mean *square*. He almost dropped to his knees, eyes crossed. He gave me the look of death. Then the laugh came—it rolled into a tsunami. That took the edge off his need for revenge. Later in that same show, I screwed up the choreography in "We Go Together." Borrelli shoots me a "great work, Casnoff," with his trademark sneer. I turned around, gave him the finger, and said, "Fuck you, Borrelli!" loud enough for the front row to hear—which elicited a worried "Oooh" from the Pink Ladies. And a wicked smirk from Borrelli. Two months later he lost his dressing room–mate and requested me to fill in. Lesson learned: just go right for the balls!

ALBERT INSINNIA (*Understudy*): Like all young actors at that time, I had auditioned for *Grease* many times. It took a while, but when the call finally came, I was offered not one but many roles. It was a fantastic experience for a young actor like me: Tuesday night, Kenickie in "Greased Lightnin'," a growl from deep in my throat, and then Doody's tenor and falsetto at the Wednesday matinee.

NICK WYMAN (*Understudy*): The tough part for me was the existential quandary of an understudy on the road—standing by. Being an understudy is a challenge to one's self-esteem and emotional security in the best of situations. An understudy is like a neighbor: useful in an emergency but not part of the family. The understudies are sort of an outer ring of the show; they're like out-of-town relatives when you're making up your Christmas list. "OK, we'll give gifts to the nephews and nieces but not the aunts and uncles."

MALCOLM GROOME (*Understudy*): My understudy nightmare of all time occurred when I arrived at the Royale one night to find out I would be going on as Doody. I was definitely underrehearsed for that part, and Doody's song "Those Magic Changes" peaks in the stratosphere with notes I could barely hit even on a relaxed day. I was terrified but had no time to dwell on my terror, only to be professional and just go for it. Later I got confused in the choreography for "We Go Together" since five of my characters were in that number, all with their own specific dance moves.

After the performance no one said anything, and I didn't ask, so I'll never know how it came off. That was pretty much what happened every time I went on. I was always left wondering how I was doing in the job.

Truth to tell, it sometimes felt like my fellow understudies and I were considered second-class citizens by the first string. In many ways it seemed like a high school mentality, where the characters in the show had seeped into the actors playing them. That was a bit discouraging and dispiriting. But I loved being on Broadway, and when the time came, given my friends, it was oddly hard to say goodbye.

PHILIP CASNOFF: After a year of understudying, I took over from Bob Garrett as Teen Angel and Johnny Casino.

I became obsessed with Johnny Casino, with volatile results, both for me and the elegant Dorothy Leon, who had played Miss Lynch since the show opened. It started with me improvising one night, shoving the neck of Johnny's guitar between my legs and then straight up toward Miss Lynch. Let's just say *big laugh*. Dorothy had never heard that laugh before, and she shot me a sharp look, by which time I was "innocently" tuning my guitar. *Bigger laugh.* Now I was intoxicated, but Dorothy was not pleased. I kept it up. My guitar and I were doing a full-fledged three-act dumb show at every performance, to the delight of my fellow actors watching from below. I played by the rule that she could never catch me, until the night she did—with the guitar still sticking up between my legs. *Biggest laugh ever!* I guess she complained, because I received a written note from Tom that I was to stay three feet away from Dorothy at all times, and not to use my guitar as a phallic device. Sadly, so sadly, goes the way of unappreciated genius.

FRANK PIEGARO (*Zuko*): When I inherited the role of Zuko from John Lansing, I was all of twenty-three years old and playing the lead in a hit show on Broadway. Pretty heady.

It takes a while for things to mesh, but this time there was no time. Before it started it was over! Stagehands went on strike, and the musicians followed. The strike only lasted a few weeks, but it felt like years. The cast ran through the show a few times, then we reopened. I never felt comfortable. The show and I never meshed.

Hell, this is Broadway. A lot is expected and should be.

I was fired!

Oddly, when I was told I was to be replaced, it was like a boulder was taken off my shoulders and I relaxed, and during the two weeks I had left in the show, I gave some of my best performances.

When I left I met with Ken Waissman, the producer, thanked him, and told him if anything were to open up in the show, I hoped he would consider me. Just a month later I was back, this time as Johnny Casino / Teen Angel, taking over from Phil Casnoff, who was leaving. No audition.

But hey, how do you return to the scene of the crime like nothing happened? I don't know to this day how I emotionally did it. It was definitely the support of my soon-to-be wife, Shannon, that made it possible. Her faith in me and our mutual attitude of *no matter what, we will get through this together* carried me through. It wasn't easy, and sometimes it drove me nuts, but eventually the payoff was worth it.

I was originally the understudy who got hired as the lead, then got fired from the lead, and then got hired for another part. And through all of the crap, was it still worth it? Definitely!

"Definitely!" Frank Piegaro.

"I'm Walkin'"

ILENE KRISTEN (*Patty*): When Kenickie lifted that prom dress over my head and more than a thousand people laughed, it was a dream fulfilled. As a ten-year-old, I was mesmerized by "Dance at the Gym" in *West Side Story*, and at twenty there I was living out my own version of that in "Shakin' at the High School Hop."

My two-and-a-half-year journey in *Grease* from the Eden to the Broadhurst to the Royale was a joyride. We were the toast of the town. I remember looking out into a packed house of smiling faces and seeing Diana Ross and Cher staring back at me. And one time Tennessee Williams was backstage, probably waiting to meet Barry Bostwick. It was phenomenal.

At a certain point, though, I knew it was time to go. No job on the horizon, just the instinct that there was something else waiting for me out there. I would miss the adventure of the numerous cast changes, hanging out with the musicians downstairs, dressing room gossip, the late nights closing down Charlie's, and receiving a steady paycheck—but I knew it was time to move on.

Tom Harris (Eugene) and Ilene Kristen (Patty).

26 | Coconut Grove
August 27, 1974–
November 17, 1974

In the eight years our Grease *ran on Broadway, there were three national tours, three bus and truck tours, two licensed summer stock shows on the East Coast, and one licensed residency in Coconut Grove, Florida. We also created two first-class productions on the West End in London during that time. Each was the same, each was different, and all were a major part of the legacy.*
— *TOM MOORE*

LISA RAGGIO (*Frenchy*): In the early '70s I was underage and singing show-cases in the clubs of NYC. Pal Joey's on the East Side was one of my favorites. It was there after a late-night performance that a man approached me. "I'd like you to come audition for our show *Grease*. Have you heard of it?" On my no, he looked shocked. "Well, here's my card. Call the office tomorrow and we'll set up an audition." I took his card and, as he walked out the door, I said, "Sir, can you get me a record deal?" He looked back at me, smiled. "Call tomorrow, OK?"

His name was Vinnie Liff, the casting director for *Grease*. He would become my champion.

My auditions went really well, and everyone seemed to like me. Then right at the end they asked me what I thought of the show, and I said, "The people in the show are way too old to be playing high school students . . . they're really old." Fortunately the auditioners had a great sense of humor, but unfortunately, and needless to say, I didn't get a part.

But God bless Vinnie Liff; he kept calling me every time there was a *Grease* role I was right for. Finally, in the early summer of 1974, I hit the jackpot! They offered me the role of Frenchy in the new Coconut Grove company in Florida.

I was thrilled about the show, but I was very concerned about leaving New York, where I was slowly becoming the Queen of the Gay Bars. Why would I want to give up singing at Ronnie's Roost, where there was only a pool table between me and the audience? But after a brief consideration, it was clear: *Grease*, Florida, *no* parents . . . *Grease!* It was the beginning of the best years of my life.

MIMI KENNEDY (*Jan*): Following a few fallow months after the end of the first national tour, some of our cast members had joyfully regrouped in Coconut Grove, where we happily stayed in condos with palm trees and a swimming pool—heaven for young New York actors squirreled in tenement flats facing dark-all-day air shafts. There were piña coladas and sailboat rides on our days off—and on the days we worked, we were being paid to sing and dance!

Robin Lamont (Sandy), Lisa Raggio (Frenchy), and Mimi Kennedy (Jan).

"We Go Together," Coconut Grove, Florida.

"You Got What It Takes": Rehearsals

LISA RAGGIO: In Coconut Grove most of the cast were staying in the Tigertail Apartments, and we all thought we were in paradise: gorgeous weather, a pool, and the Grove still funky and quite bohemian. So life in Coconut Grove was going well—kind of.

I was struggling with my new career: acting. To say I was green would be an understatement. The only acting experience I had was in two high school plays: *Little Mary Sunshine* and *The Pajama Game*. Both directed by nuns. I knew nothing, and I was petrified I would be found out!

We were into tech rehearsal, and everyone was on overdrive trying to get everything down. We were about to go into the scene change after "Freddy, My Love." The scene changes were very fast and done by the actors in dim light. Tom brought us together: "Now, ladies, you have to remember; after the blackout when the lights turn blue, Rizzo, grab your clothes and get out that window as fast as you can. Jan takes the blanket, Marty clears the mic stand, and Frenchy, strike the wine bottle on your way out."

Then Tom said, "OK, are we ready to reset for the number? Let's do it with full pace and lots of energy."

We do the number, it's great, it's over, blackout. Everyone does her task. I start to leave and remember I have to strike the wine bottle. I do and then dance off the stage as directed. It seems to go great. But then everyone in the

Lisa Raggio (Frenchy) and Livia Genise (Rizzo).

house breaks into laughter. Tom comes down to the edge of the stage and sternly says, "Frenchy, come back out here."

I was shaking like a leaf. I thought, *They're gonna can me . . . I know it.* Tom said, "There seems to be a wine bottle still left onstage. Didn't I tell you to strike the wine bottle?"—I said, "Oh, I did, Mr. Moore"—I kept calling him that for a long while; Catholic school roots are deep—"I hit it hard like you said." He said, "Lisa, do you have any idea what *strike* means?" I said, "Hit, right?" "No, Lisa, *strike* means remove it—take it with you when you leave the stage." And he burst into laughter. He was so good-natured about it that I didn't even feel like a complete nitwit.

But oh, this acting thing was keeping me awake nights in my little trundle on Tigertail Avenue in Coconut Grove.

On the occasions when I did sleep, I would have nightmares. I would dream I was in the show *Grease,* but I didn't know any of the people onstage or any of the dialogue or music. I didn't know at the time that these were called "actor's nightmares." The nightmares were frighteningly real. As we

Lisa Raggio (Frenchy), "Beauty School Dropout."

got closer to opening, I was becoming a little unhinged. The pressure from knowing my parents were driving down from New York to see the next show didn't help.

My mother had been forwarding my mail, and when I got the most recent batch, lo and behold, there was this card from Equity. I knew I had to do something, and fast, so I went to the Coconut Grove Hotel, where Mr. Moore was staying, and I asked if they could ring his room. They did, he answered, and without even saying hello, I told him that there had been some mistake: I now knew I couldn't do Frenchy. I couldn't even act. I was a singer—and I kept going—*blah, blah, blah.* Mr. Moore interrupted: "Stay where you are in the lobby. I'll be right down."

When he arrived I promptly handed him my Equity card and said, "I'm sorry, Mr. Moore, but you can have this back. I'll fly myself back to New York. I just can't do this." He calmly said, "Yes, you can, Lisa. All I need is for you to be you. We picked you, and we know that you can do this. Just go out there and trust yourself."

I was dumbfounded. He continued, "Trust me. I know it will be all right." I must have looked like a deer caught in the headlights, but I finally said, "What should I do with this card?" He said, "Keep it. It may come in handy someday."

I took myself back to my little place on Tigertail Avenue, took a deep breath, and thought, *Well, he must know, he's the director.* I kept repeating his words: "We picked you, and we know that you can do this." It became my mantra. And Mr. Moore—Tom—became my friend.

Playing *Grease* in Paradise

MIMI KENNEDY: Ken and Maxine came down with Tom and Pat to spruce up the show, but I think mostly to join in the fun. At our opening-night celebration, I remember dancing with Tom to a nonstop club tape of Hues Corporation's "Rock the Boat." We were in sunny Florida, we were young, and we were on top of the world! For a moment it felt to me, and I'm pretty sure to him, that we were madly, unexpectedly soulmates. It was heady and memorable.

DAVID FRANK (*Music Director*): Monday, our one day off, was a time to forget about *Grease* as best we could and catch up on everything else in our lives. But this Monday was uniquely different . . . and memorable.

On Monday, October 7, 1974, the cast and I performed at the Orange Bowl for the NFL game between the Miami Dolphins and the New York Jets. Over sixty thousand fans attended, with a national television audience of over forty million on ABC's *Monday Night Football*.

Scott Robertson (Roger) and Mimi Kennedy (Jan) trying to win the dance contest.

MIMI KENNEDY: We got to sing the national anthem at a Miami Dolphins football game when Jim Kiick and Larry Csonka were national sports stars. We even got to hang out and joke with them—because they thought we were stars too.

Mimi Kennedy, Char Fontaine, Robin Lamont, and Livia Genise, the Orange Bowl.

Mimi Kennedy, Lisa Raggio, and Livia Genise.

DAVID FRANK: For the halftime show, I was set up with a portable keyboard and monitor at the twenty-yard line, while the cast was way down at midfield. I started playing the intro to "Summer Nights" and heard the cast singing through my monitor in perfect sync with the music; but within seconds "Summer Nights" was not coming through my monitor but booming over the stadium PA system. It was so loud that I had no choice but to just play along with what I heard. I was no longer conducting but following, and I was playing two seconds behind the cast vocals the whole way through. Fortunately the excited crowd seemed not to notice and loved it!

It was a memorable night for us all, performing in a gigantic venue with a worldwide audience of millions. And we got to watch the game from great seats just above the field!

SCOTT ROBERTSON (*Roger*): Life was at its youthful best when I was playing Roger at the Coconut Grove. I was in my early twenties, riding high and believing things could only get better; I decided that it was a great time to try dropping acid to highlight the experience. Of course, I was a responsible performer, so the great experiment would have to be on my day off.

A friend found our drug, and off we went into the Land of Oz. After we dropped the acid, my friend quickly turned into about five different people from my past life. For an hour I just stared at my hands and kept counting, discovering many more than ten fingers. The effects kept going for quite some time—thirty-six hours to be precise—but I was still confident I would be fine by showtime Tuesday evening.

But Tuesday evening seemed to come pretty quickly. I walked to the theater (I had never seen Florida so green), managed a good warm-up, and was primed, pumped, and ready for our eight o'clock curtain. I was the Rocky Balboa of Rogers!

It seemed a very long way as I headed down to the stage, but I finally arrived.

Wow! I had never seen the cast look so spectacular in their fluorescent costumes.

When we began to sing the "Alma Mater Parody," I looked around the stage. *Oh wow, wow, those lights are so beautiful! And so bright.* My knees were shaking just as choreographed, but they seemed to have a life of their own. As the show continued I floated above it, somehow managing, to my surprise, to end up at the right place at the right time. My lines seemed exceptional, my timing brilliant.

Everything was more intense, more incredible during the first act, but by the second, colors seemed to fade, lights seemed to dim, and I no longer thought this was the greatest performance I or anyone else had ever given. By the last scene at the Burger Palace, I was a shadow of the Roger who had begun the show. When we sang the last chorus of "We Go Together," I had never been so anxious to get off the stage.

FYI, that would be the one and only time I dropped acid!

A stoned Scott Robertson (Roger), Norman Meister (Doody), and Matt Landers (Kenickie).

Coconut Grove Highlights

LEFT: Frank Piegaro, "Summer Nights." RIGHT: Mimi Kennedy, Lisa Raggio, Livia Genise, "Freddy, My Love."

Char Fontaine, Robin Lamont, Livia Genise, and Mimi Kennedy.

Matt Landers with Scott Robertson, Lenny Bari, Frank Piegaro, and Norman Meister, "Greased Lightnin'."

Scott Robertson, Livia Genise, and Norman Meister, "Look at Me, I'm Sandra Dee."

Livia Genise and Matt Landers, "Hand Jive."

Char Fontaine and Lisa Raggio.

Mimi Kennedy, Robin Lamont, Char Fontaine, Lisa Raggio,
and Livia Genise.

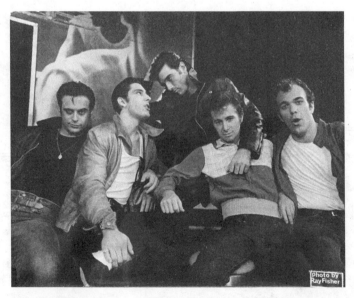

Matt Landers, Lenny Bari, Frank Piegaro, Norman Meister,
and Scott Robertson.

27

The Summer Stock Tent Tours

April 1975

The licensed summer stock tent shows were often cast with a mix of actors from one of our tours and new talent. Pat and I would do the auditions as usual, but our production stage managers (Tommy Smith, Steve Beckler, Michael Martorella) and dance captains (Kathi Moss, Carol Culver, Cynthia Darlow), using Pat's and my original choreography and direction, did the initial blocking and dance, putting the show on its feet. Pat and I would come in for the last rehearsal and usually see the show through its previews and opening.

—TOM MOORE

MARSHA WATERBURY (*Patty*): Valley Forge Music Fair, 1975. I am now in the cast, playing Patty. It's a summer stock contract, so no understudies.

We're going to have to cancel the matinee. Shannon Fanning has no singing voice. She can squeak out the scenes but can't sing. In the second act, when Sandy sings "It's Raining on Prom Night," the actress playing Cha-Cha (Joene Lewis) sings the counterpoint backstage.

"Hey, Peter, why don't I sing the songs from the back of house and Shannon can lip-sync and do the scenes?" Peter Mumford, the stage manager, starts laughing, and I start laughing "Let's do it!"

Valley Forge is in the round. We set up a mic stand at the back of the house, behind the seats at the end of one of the *verrry* long aisles. I sing. Shannon lip-syncs. It's working! Everything is going great until "Hand Jive/Raining on Prom Night." That's when I realize we haven't factored in how far away the mic is from me on the stage. I am going to have to really haul ass to get there for the beginning of Sandy's "Prom Night."

I break the freeze in "Hand Jive" and run, I mean *run*, up that very, very long aisle and across to the mic at the top of the next aisle over. Completely out of breath, I get to the mic just in time, and I start singing.

"It's raining on prom night"—I lean over and away from the mic, *pant, pant, pant*—"my hair is a mess"—more leaning, more panting. Joene, at the mic next to me, is laughing her head off. It's freaking hilarious. It goes that way for most of the song. Shannon is standing in her bedroom, which consists of a light halfway down one of the aisles, looking so beautiful, so heartbroken, so Sandy sad, mouthing the words. I see the audience sitting close to her looking at her quizzically. *Uh, there's no sound coming out of her.* They're just staring at her.

I can't help but think of Debbie Reynolds singing for famous silent-movie star Lina Lamont as she tries to lip-sync the lyrics in *Singin' in the Rain*—surreal but definitely the highlight of the tour.

Shannon Fanning gets her voice back.

Danny Jacobson, Kenny Morse, Cosie Costa, and Scott Robertson.

LISA RAGGIO (*Frenchy*): Wardrobe malfunctions, or the threat of them, are every actor's nightmare. Mine took place on the Guber and Gross summer tent tour.

My quick change happened at the end of the high school hop scene. It was lightning fast since I had to be back onstage for the very next scene in the front of the Burger Palace. That scene contained my big number, "Beauty School Dropout," so there was a lot riding on the costume change. A makeshift booth was constructed for me at the top of the designated aisle. I would run like crazy up the aisle and strip down completely, to my bra, panties, and tights. Off came my prom dress, Velcroed down the back, and then on went my Pink Lady garb. My dresser was a very young girl and a bit of an airhead, who constantly asked me for Frenchy's bubble gum. I always gave it to her. I figured it would be insurance for her not missing my quick change. Before every show I checked in with her and made sure everything was set in my change booth—and then said a prayer that the airhead would remember.

All went well until one fated matinee. I hauled ass up the aisle and—you guessed it—no dresser in the booth. You can't imagine my horror. So I did

Shannon Fanning and Lisa Raggio,
the ear piercing.

what any sane person would do. I looked around the audience to see if I could find some nice lady to help me.

It turns out that for that particular show, they had bused in a whole bunch of high school boys from somewhere, and only boys were seated in that section. Desperate, I went over to the nearest boy I could find, grabbed his hand, and said, "Come with me; you have to help." He was paralyzed with fear, especially when I took him in the booth and said, "OK, take off my clothes . . . hurry up. Just rip the dress up the back. Now help me with my sweater and skirt. You're doing great. Now my socks, my shoes . . . now get my lipstick. OK, we're good. Thanks so much." I tossed him the extra piece of bubble gum that I had in my Pink Ladies jacket for the airhead and ran like the devil, hitting the stage just as the lights came up.

I've often wondered how he tells that story. I'd like to believe I made his day. But mostly I'm just hoping he wasn't permanently scarred by the event.

The Motorcycle-Wagon Tour, September 23, 1975

TREAT WILLIAMS (*Zuko*): After a year as an understudy in *Grease,* I had been cast as Utah in the *Grease* team's splashy new Broadway production,

Over Here!, starring the Andrews Sisters. A few months after that show closed, in January of '75, I was knocking around New York when I got a call from Tommy Smith, production stage manager of the Broadway show. "Would you like to take over the last two weeks of a tent tour of *Grease*?"

There had already been national tours, a bus and truck tour, and a Guber and Gross tent tour. I called our tent show the Motorcycle-Wagon Tour.

I was absolutely determined to create the best Zuko I could because I felt like I had failed on my first attempt. It's difficult to create a character when you do the part only occasionally as an understudy, and you're trying to accommodate everybody else on the stage. Tommy Smith and I made a really exciting, fun little production of *Grease*, and with each performance I got braver with my Zuko. Ken and Maxine came down to see it, and two weeks later the whole creative team had approved me. I found myself back on Broadway—this time as Danny Zuko!

But when I got back to Broadway, it would be with a new and very different attitude. I wasn't going to let anybody in the cast tell me how to do it or what to change on their behalf. I was going to own this, just like I had on our Motorcycle-Wagon Tour!

Treat Williams (Danny) and Candice Earley (Sandy).

28 | *The Flight to Norf*ck*

SCOTT ROBERTSON (*Roger*): We Greasers are on a Guber and Gross tour, and the chemistry of this cast is amazing. The best and most fun group yet.

CYNTHIA DARLOW (*Jan*): It was a Fourth of July weekend, and somehow someone hadn't booked us on a commercial flight. That morning we had to fly from our last stop, Albany, New York, to open that night in Norfolk, Virginia. The company had no choice but to book us on a privately chartered plane, at great expense, to get us there in time.

FRANK PIEGARO (*Zuko*): The commuter aircraft was a nineteen-seater. You had to lower your head to get in your seat. Lisa Raggio refused to get on the plane. She had to be convinced this aircraft was safe. An omen?

SCOTT ROBERTSON: When we arrive at the airport, Lisa sees the plane and begins screaming and sobbing: "*No, no, no, no, I can't! This is* **insane!**"

CYNTHIA DARLOW: When we walked out onto the airfield, our hearts sank. There sat this tiny, tiny little plane. Marsha Waterbury and I had our dogs with us, and we panicked. The pilot assured us that they would be fine in the baggage compartment, despite the fact that the baggage compartment was merely a tarpaulin laced to the walls of the plane between the seats and the tail. He valiantly tried to assure us that their crates would be safely strapped down. We had grave misgivings but no options for alternative travel.

SCOTT ROBERTSON: The plane is small. *Really* small. It barely fits the cast and a few musicians. Luggage, musical instruments, drums—*way* too heavy! I turn to Lisa and gleefully say, "I think it has really good rubber bands!"

That does it. She lets out a bloodcurdling scream: "*I am not getting on that plane!*" Our very droll, very collected, and dear stage manager, Peter Mumford, manages to calm her down and walks her up the tiny steps.

CYNTHIA DARLOW: Shannon Fanning, who was playing Sandy, was afraid of flying as it was, and this toy airplane did nothing to ease her fears. On boarding, the fuselage was so small you couldn't stand up straight. The seats were tightly packed, but we meekly sat down, buckled ourselves in, and took off. Maybe it wouldn't be so bad after all.

SCOTT ROBERTSON: The door closes and we are on our way! Lisa begins to sob quietly: "Oh my God, oh my God." We take off for our one-hour flight into some very dark and ominous clouds. Somebody jokingly yells out, "This plane is *going down.*" We laugh our asses off as Lisa goes catatonic.

FRANK PIEGARO: Halfway there we had a violent storm.

SCOTT ROBERTSON: We are in the middle of a major thunderstorm.

CYNTHIA DARLOW: We ran into insane turbulence.

SCOTT ROBERTSON: Joking becomes more strained, and everyone starts to get a little nervous. Lisa's sobbing becomes just a bit louder: "Oh my *God,* oh my *God!*"

DANNY JACOBSON (*Kenickie*): We were literally bouncing over Chesapeake Bay in a twin-engine propjet. Stage manager Peter Mumford was in front of me, an arm's length from the cockpit, and Ruth Russell (Miss Lynch) was seated to my left. They were the only two calm ones aboard. The rest of us were ready to crash into the bay and die, surrounded by great Maryland crabmeat. If Ruth hadn't been holding a book, I'd have thought she was embalmed. I tap my buddy Mumford and point to the cockpit. "Ask them if it's all right." Mumford turns slowly and says drolly, "What if it's not?"

FRANK PIEGARO: We were, as the astronaut said in *The Right Stuff,* "Spam in a can." It was a roller-coaster ride. Everyone thought death was imminent. Lisa kept screaming, "I got to get out! I got to get out!" Peter Mumford, seated in front of her, responded, "Lisa, you can't get out!" and then proceeded to throw up in a bag.

SCOTT ROBERTSON: Lisa is still screaming, "I'm getting *off!* Let me *off!* Let me off *now!*" Danny Jacobson gets up, saunters up to her seat, and says in a deadly monotone, "Lisa, you can't get off." He then saunters back to his seat with a big grin. We are all screaming with laughter.

MARSHA WATERBURY (*Patty*): The massive storm has gotten bigger, and we're right in the middle of it.

SCOTT ROBERTSON: We are all still chatting and joking around like usual until the plane suddenly drops a thousand feet in three seconds!

CYNTHIA DARLOW: Suddenly, the plane took a nosedive!

SCOTT ROBERTSON: Almost everyone flies out of their unbuckled seats, along with their drinks and snacks. I see Ruth Russell, our Miss Lynch, flying through the air like a rag doll! Lisa screams. *We all scream!*

MARSHA WATERBURY: Cynthia Darlow and I stare at each other, terrified. We grab each other across the aisle and hug as the plane continues to fall out of the sky. Shannon Fanning's shoes go flying by. Everybody is screaming, everything is flying all over the tiny nineteen-seater we are taking from North Tonawanda, New York, to Norfolk, Virginia.

My dog Beard and Cynthia's dog Rhubarb are each in their cages in the back of the plane. I see everything in slow motion, like a series of still photos. I say out loud, "Oh wow, man," and then everything in my vision goes completely white.

CYNTHIA DARLOW: As we plummeted toward earth, our seat belts broke open, water began to spray inside the fuselage, and Marsha and I in the last row were sucked into the tail of the plane, holding on to each other for dear life and screaming the Lord's Prayer. In front of us we could see bodies being tossed all over the plane, our friends grabbing desperately to hold on to anything they could. Shannon was screaming, "Let me out of here!" as she tried to claw her way to the exit door!

MARSHA WATERBURY: Cynthia and I are still hugging. The plane drops again. More screaming. This all happens in maybe twenty seconds, tops. It feels like forever. It feels like the end.

CYNTHIA DARLOW: Then suddenly the plane somehow pulled out of its downward spiral, made a few vicious bumps and heaves, and steadied once again. Everyone was crying . . . bruised and bloodied. Vomit was everywhere. But incredibly, we were all right.

MARSHA WATERBURY: Somehow or other our hero pilot controls our tiny plane and saves our lives. But we are in complete disarray.

"You all right? How are you?"

"Shannon, here are your shoes."

"You OK, Lisa? Joene? What the fuck. Man, that was a freak-out."

SCOTT ROBERTSON: Then we check out dear Ruth. She is a bit disheveled but intact.

MARSHA WATERBURY: "Ruth! You OK, Ruth? How's everybody?" We're all checking in with one another. People start laughing now and cracking jokes. Some are still crying, and some are just frozen. Jimmie Skaggs (Eugene), who is at the front of the plane, turns. We catch each other's eye and try to smile at one another. He is green. I probably am too. Our dogs, Beard and Rhubarb, seem to be OK in their crates. Cynthia and I look at one another and know for sure that we are bonded for the rest of our lives.

SCOTT ROBERTSON: I notice Danny Jacobson writing on some blank sheets of paper. Danny is one of the funniest men I have ever met, and he is always writing. I ask him, "What are you writing?" He pauses, looks up at me, and smiles: "My will."

Lisa is still in a meltdown. We are howling. Complete mayhem. I have never laughed so much—before or since. The flight continues without incident, and we arrive safely.

CYNTHIA DARLOW: We miraculously landed in Norfolk. Our dogs, Beardsley and Rhubarb, although banged up and barking hysterically, were alive!

SCOTT ROBERTSON: Lisa is the *first* one off the plane.

A few hours later . . .

DANNY JACOBSON: That night we were opening at an impressive venue, Chrysler Hall in Norfolk, which our stage manager, Mumford, sarcastically called the "Lincoln Center of Virginia." After we all check in to our hotel, vomit, and call our loved ones, we have an unusually trying tech rehearsal, after which Mumford assembles the cast and introduces us to the theater manager. "This is Ms. Kate," he says, with as much contempt as he can inflect. She's blond, smart, and full of southern attitude, which may just be attitude with a southern accent. Mumford informs us that Ms. Kate was less than happy with what she saw in the tech and expects us to do the clean version of the show. Cynthia Darlow, who was playing Jan, immediately agrees. The rest of us look at each other. Some of us don't know the *clean* version. Mumford breaks the tension: "I told Ms. Kate how much actors love notes from theater management just before opening night."

The show went well—three-thousand-seat house and they loved every second.

I'm in my dressing room after the show. We each had our own! The shower was better than the one in the hotel. I'm dressed and about to leave when there's a knock on my door. It's Ms. Kate and she is pissed off. "*Eat me?*" is what she opens with, but even I know this is not a joke opportunity. Ms. Kate shreds my performance and says she knew I was trouble when she watched the tech.

A few minutes before, I had an appetite and was ready to go to the small opening-night bash at our hotel. Now my stomach is a knot. Nauseated for the second time in a day. Ms. Kate says she is calling Equity and will tell the producers in New York to have me replaced. In the meantime she wants the understudy to play Kenickie.

I started working when I was fourteen, and I had never been fired from any job. This was unlike any defeat I'd ever been dealt. I walked across the stage to leave the theater, thinking for sure this was the end of the ride. If I'd stayed on Broadway and didn't do this tour, I'd still have a job and wouldn't have had to endure that horrific twenty-five minutes yo-yoing over Chesapeake Bay. But I knew like the rest of us that no ride lasts forever.

I couldn't reach Mumford in his room, so I began to pack up my stuff. The ninth time I tried his room, the front-desk lady said the people "with the show" were in the restaurant.

First night in Norfolk, and every gay guy in Virginia is at Mumford's table. So I go to the bar and sit there staring, trying to get Mumford's attention. I ordered a Coke, and the bartender comes back with a big smile and a beer. "This is on the young lady." I look down the bar. It's Ms. Kate.

An hour later her powder-blue fuck-me panties and garters were on the floor of my hotel room, and for the second time that night I was getting fucked by Ms. Kate. Clearly she had no interest in the "clean version" of anything.

Joene Lewis (Cha-Cha) and Danny Jacobson (Kenickie) arrive at the Rydell prom.

29 | *Broadway*
1975–1976

NANCY ROBBINS (*Assistant to the Director*): *Grease* had become a jugger-naut of multiple companies, and auditions were always ongoing because of the continual need for actors in new companies and new replacements for Broadway. Of course there were the usual methods of agents submitting actors, open Equity calls, and recommendations, but these methods didn't always fit the bill. Vinnie Liff, however, was intrepid; he was known to walk up to any Danny Zuko type he saw in the Broadway area and ask, "Would you like to audition for *Grease*?" Fortunately no one reported him to the police.

Even with all these submissions, the *Grease* machine always needed more and more actors. Some of that no doubt was due to the fact that the creative team of *Grease* was not given to compromise. They knew exactly what they wanted and would settle for no less. Casting director: "But you've seen every-one." Director or producer: "No, there has to be someone out there who is perfect—just keep looking."

So . . . the *Grease* phone.

There were weekly ads in *Show Business* and *Backstage* that listed a dedi-cated phone number anyone could call to get an audition. You had to call on Friday afternoon between three and five o'clock, and you would get Vinnie, who would be crammed into a little cubicle at Otto & Windsor, cradling the *Grease* phone. He would give the actor an audition time and tell them what they had to bring—headshot and résumé and sheet music to sing a ballad and a rock number. When Vinnie was promoted, I inherited the *Grease* phone. I learned to approach Friday afternoons with great trepidation.

Now the wonderful thing about *Grease*, and perhaps the reason that the bonds are so strong, is that for many it was their first professional job. In fact it was how many got their Equity card. On the *Grease* phone, however, many were high school actor wannabes who didn't have a clue. Often when told that they needed to bring a photo and résumé, they'd ask if a Polaroid was OK. "Well, not really," I would say. Instead of singing, many wanted to bring a cassette tape: "Is that OK?" "Well, not really." They didn't understand that they actually had to sing at the audition. Getting past that fact, they were asked to bring music. Often they didn't.

And so it went—for years!

I'd like to think that many of those actors who called ended up in the show, and that those hours that Vinnie and I spent in that cubicle on the *Grease* phone helped launch some great careers.

BARRY TARALLO (*Doody*): It was sometime in late summer 1974. I was locking my apartment door and about to head down to the Jersey Shore. As I was leaving, the phone started ringing. I knew that if I answered it, I might have to adjust my plans for the shore, so I started to lock the door, but a voice in my head said, "Stop, Barry . . . answer the phone!"

It was my good friend and fellow Catholic University alum Ray DeMattis, who was now Roger in the Broadway show *Grease*. "Barry, what are you doin'?" he asked.

"I'm headin' down to the Jersey Shore."

"No, you're not," he said. "I got you an audition for the role of Doody in the Broadway company of *Grease*." At first I thought he was kidding, but he assured me that he was quite serious. "Do you know Doody's song, 'Those Magic Changes'?" It turns out I did. "OK, this is how it's gonna go. You're gonna come over to my place as soon as you can, and we'll rehearse the scene and I'll teach you the hand jive."

My first performance was December 9, 1974. I will always be grateful that I had the good sense to answer that phone, and I am eternally indebted to Ray DeMattis, who "greased" the way. Those were four of the most exciting years of my life.

"I Only Have Eyes for You"

ILENE GRAFF (*Sandy*): In the course of my two and a half years playing Sandy on Broadway, I did the show with no less than eleven Danny Zukos.

LEFT: Barry Bostwick. RIGHT: Jeff Conaway.

They were an extremely talented bunch. I was lucky enough to start my run with the original, definitive, charismatic Danny—the wonderful BARRY BOST-WICK. Barry had that rare talent of making you believe you were the most important person in the scene as he bestowed all his attention on you. He was pure magic.

My next and longest-running Danny was JEFF CONAWAY. Jeff was a wild child. Blond, blue-eyed, tall, and lean, he skated the closest to the edge. Unpredictable, exciting, and very, very talented, Jeff always had a twinkle in his eye and enough energy for everyone onstage.

RICHARD GERE and I had a few performances together as he got ready for his London *Grease* debut. He was just what you'd think he'd be: a little serious, a little intense, a little internal. He was a different Zuko from the others but very, very appealing, indeed.

TREAT WILLIAMS was totally adorable. He felt a little more mature than the other Zukos—a little more solid, so that when he played the goofy moments, they were totally unexpected and fun. He also had a megawatt smile that lit up the stage.

GREG EVIGAN was the Zuko that the little girls loved. He was so cute, and the only one I remember who had gaggles of teens hanging at the stage door,

LEFT: Richard Gere. RIGHT: Treat Williams.

hoping for a close-up look or an autograph. It didn't surprise me one bit that he became a big TV star.

PHILIP CASNOFF was smooth. He sang smooth, he danced smooth, he looked smooth. At the time, he was dating a young Yale drama student named Meryl, and I remember her waiting patiently for Phil at the stage door so they could go home. Yes, that girl waiting for Philip was *Meryl Streep*!

JOHN LANSING: dark, handsome, focused, and a little sly. He brought a bit of the bad boy to Danny.

JOHN DRIVER brought a James Dean thing to his Zuko. He was fair haired and attractive, and I always wondered what was going on behind those big eyes!

TONY SHULTZ had the most beautiful coloring, and he wore his costumes like he was a model. He also had that slight slouch that cool models have, but it just made me feel like his Zuko wanted to get closer.

And of course JOHN FENNESSY. John was an understudy and assistant stage manager, or ASM, and steady as a rock for as long as I can remember. More than once I handed him my valuables for safekeeping backstage as our ASM, and then when onstage, I'd turn all goofy teenager when he made his entrance as Zuko.

LEFT: Greg Evigan. RIGHT: John Lansing.

I was incredibly lucky to work with these young men. They each brought something unique and wonderful to the role, and I had the great pleasure of falling in and out and back in love with each of them.

"Jailhouse Rock"

TREAT WILLIAMS (*Zuko*): For some reason I decided it would be a great idea to perform *Grease* for the inmates at Rikers Island. Some of the actors were very against the idea.

Our Sandy was particularly terrified and wouldn't go, but Marilu Henner was always up for a new adventure, so she played Sandy and her understudy played Marty.

We got permission from the producers and headed out to Rikers Island with an electric keyboard and a guitar. We did the show with only a couple of chairs and tables. What I most remember is that when the girls sat at the cafeteria table, they all had their legs apart, and the Rikers guys were going absolutely bananas. Batshit! It was kind of scary. The girls were totally oblivious as to why.

Urgently I whispered, "Close your legs. Just cross your legs, OK? Please!" Once they did, it was one of the greatest audiences we ever had.

Rebecca Gilchrist, Ellen March, Marilu Henner, and Randee Heller.

"That'll Be the Day"

ALAINA WARREN (*Understudy*): I was standing by in New York when I got a call from our general manager telling me he needed me to fly to—honestly, this happened often enough that I don't even know, but I think it was Chicago—to go on that night as Rizzo.

I raced to the airport, by this time an old pro at catching last-minute flights, and ran down the gangway with my Rizzo costume slung over my shoulder. I made it just in time and settled down in my seat to study Rizzo's lines and my notes on her choreography.

I ended up with a lot of time to do both. The plane was late taking off, which meant we were late landing, and I was late getting to the theater.

I missed the curtain. The second understudy had gone on as Rizzo, but I was still there in time to play Cha-Cha. I made my entrance at the top of the stairs, missed the first step, and slid all the way down those stairs on my derriere. I may have forgotten the city, but I'll never forget that entrance.

JOY RINALDI (*Understudy*): One night after Johnny had become famous on the extremely successful *Welcome Back, Kotter*, he came back to visit his old pals at the Royale, hoping to show off his newfound fame and its perks in the form of a limousine provided by *Kotter* for his stay in New York. He gleefully walked into the theater looking for someone to share his good fortune with, but because he had arrived mid-performance, only the understudies (Alaina Warren and me) were available to go out for a spin.

The three of us raced out to the limo with great excitement. Johnny was younger than all of us, and we still thought of him as the kid. Well, the kid had arrived! And we were going to celebrate!

I had never seen such a decked-out limo. Incredibly soft leather seats, crystal glasses, every kind of booze imaginable—and all free for the taking! Much to Johnny's disappointment, we couldn't go far from the theater because understudies have to stay close in case of emergency. So we just kept going around and around Times Square, Broadway and Forty-Fifth Street, all the while feeling quite superior to the people staring in from the outside.

Understudies are often overlooked, but not that night. We were the two queens of Broadway, and Johnny was our king.

REBECCA GILCHRIST (*Jan*): Having originally opened on Valentine's Day, *Grease* was tailor-made for romantic promotions. In 1975 a contest was launched to find a bride and groom who wanted to be married on the stage of the Royale Theatre following the *Grease* performance on Valentine's Day, with the cast serving as attendants.

Rebecca Gilchrist, Joy Rinaldi, Ilene Graff, Carol Culver, Ellen March, and Randee Heller, "Summer Nights."

A couple weeks before the event, a drawing was held on the *Grease* stage, employing one of those cage cylinders used for bingo or a gerbil. The chosen couple then returned on Valentine's Day, and following the curtain call, the audience was asked to stay while the cast jumped back into our prom costumes.

While we were changing, the stage was bedecked with flowers. Well, not exactly bedecked, but a few flowers were placed on the double staircase. This was *Grease* after all!

Ilene Graff, Alaina Warren, and I sang "Goin' to the Chapel" as the bride made her way down the theater aisle to join her intended onstage. The cast formed a semicircle around the happy couple while our trio stood down left in front of the microphone and sang in perfect three-part harmony.

I don't know about the bride, but I truly thought I had died and gone to heaven. Singing three-part harmony with those two women that night was one of the happiest moments of my years in *Grease*. I felt like I was singing with the angels. I really did.

"Breaking Up Is Hard to Do"

ALAINA WARREN: I'd been with the show three plus years, and what times they'd been.

I was on as Cha-Cha the night of my last performance. At the curtain call, Zuko stopped the music and told the audience that I was leaving the show after a long run. He asked them to help say goodbye. The band started playing "Auld Lang Syne," everyone was singing, and I was weepy. All of a sudden whipped cream on a foil plate smacked me in the face! I got pied! What a send-off! I remember thinking that wardrobe was gonna be really pissed.

JOY RINALDI: It was bittersweet. *Grease* was a permanent connection for me, and finally getting my favorite role of Marty had been everything I hoped it would be. However, leaving was almost anticlimactic. All the original cast, crew, and musicians were long gone, and although many talented cast members had joined the show, I missed the originals dearly.

Performing Marty eight times a week had been a dream come true, and I reveled in it. When I was finally cast, I thought I'd never leave. But life had other plans for me. I was in a horrible personal relationship, and I thought the only way to escape was to quit *Grease* and move to Los Angeles. So off I went . . . to be a Hollywood star!

Turned out Hollywood was *not* waiting for me, but many of my *Grease* pals were, and it turned out to be the right place to go and the right time to say goodbye.

30

The Grease Tours Circling America

1976–1980

Second National, *October 10, 1976*
Second Bus and Truck, *September 14, 1977*
Third Bus and Truck, *February 7, 1978*
Third National, *April 13, 1979*

The Auditions

ADRIAN ZMED (*Zuko*): Several months after I graduated from the Good-man School of Drama, and after countless auditions all over Chicago, things were looking bleak. In defeat, I decided to go to architecture school. At least I would have something to fall back on in case this acting thing didn't work out, which it clearly wasn't at the time.

And then I got a call from Lisa Mionie, a casting associate, who was reaching out to young Chicago actors for *Grease*. She thought I would be perfect for the role of Danny. Based on my lack of audition luck in Chicago, I had no expecta-tions, but I thought, *What the heck, it's my last shot before architecture school; I have nothing to lose.* And for the first time, I walked into an audition very relaxed. I read, sang, and danced the Lindy with abandon. I left thinking, *Great, that's done. I can now move on.* When I got home my mom told me someone from the country of Greece had called and wanted me to call them back immediately.

The producers had liked my audition and wanted me to fly to New England to audition for the director. *Wait . . . what?* I had a couple of problems: I was about to start architecture school, and I had just gotten married and was about to go on a honeymoon. *And* I had never been on a plane before!

I left the next day. Terrified, I was sure the plane would crash at least twelve times before it landed somewhere in Massachusetts. I had been told by the general manager, Eddie Davis, to take an $80 cab ride (he promised they'd pay) to somewhere God lost his shoes (Williamstown, Massachusetts) to meet the director. I was rattled, nervous, and a little grumpy.

When I arrived, I was sure I was in the wrong place because the guy waiting for me was this preppy college student who looked younger than me. Turns out it was Tom Moore, the director, who was directing *Our Town* with Geraldine Fitzgerald at the Williamstown Theatre Festival.

He saw I was pretty flustered (who wouldn't have seen it?), but it turns out Tom has a great talent for calming people and focusing them. I sang and read with his stage manager on a grass hill outside the theater where Tom had just finished working with Ms. Fitzgerald. He made me feel so comfortable and important that the audition went from highly stressful to something just plain fun. When I left I realized that I had just given the best audition of my life; on my tortuous way home, I thought, *Why weren't all my auditions in Chicago this easy and fun?*

I left on my honeymoon the next day and was offered Danny in the second national tour at a phone booth somewhere in the Canadian Rockies.

Adrian Zmed as Zuko and the cast of the second national company.

PEGGY LEE BRENNAN (*Frenchy*): On a hot August Sunday in 1976, I left my mom's backyard barbecue on Staten Island and began my two-hour trek to the city via bus, train, ferry, and subway to my first Broadway callback.

I had dreamed so many times about reliving Peggy Sawyer's *42nd Street* journey from small-town girl to Broadway *to be a star!* Maybe this was my chance.

At the callback there were twelve of us vying for the part of Frenchy. After the readings there were six! They brought us back onstage, and Pat Birch and her assistant, Carol Culver, demonstrated the hand jive. It seemed like everyone knew it but me. I sheepishly asked Pat to demonstrate one more time, "if that's OK?"

After dancing, two of us were asked to stay. We took turns reading and dancing some more. It felt like an eternity. Then they brought us center stage, side by side. The other girl and I exchanged glances and smiled. She seemed even more scared than me. Then from the middle of the orchestra, Tom calls the girl's name and asks her to wait outside. As soon as she leaves the stage, I start jumping up and down, gushing, "Thank you, thank you, thank you" over and over until I realize that Tom is yelling back from his seat in the theater: "No, no, no, Peg! Hold on! The audition's not over."

Then I reversed course, gushing over and over, "I'm so sorry, I'm so sorry, I'm so . . ."

They sent me out and brought the other girl back to read again. I was a wreck. She then returned, silently picked up her bags, and left.

At center stage once more, I stood, heart pounding. Someone walked down the aisle and said, "Are you ready to start rehearsing tomorrow at 9:00 AM?"

I jumped up and down one last time. "*Yes, yes, yes* . . ."

It was 9:00 PM. I finally found a working pay phone to call my mom and gave her the great news. I then hopped on the downtown number 1 train to begin my two-hour trip home. I pulled out my script to study my lines and gushed to an older man sitting next to me, "I just landed my first hit Broadway show and my life will never be the same." He smiled.

DAVID PAYMER (*Sonny*): It's early 1976, and I'm a twenty-one-year-old University of Michigan graduate with a double major in theater and psychology. Psychology was the fallback position favored by my parents, but I was giving myself two years to see if this acting thing that I loved was for real.

In June of '76 there was an open call listed for a national tour of *Grease*. I thought, *This is my chance—a real shot!* Maybe I wouldn't have to study gestalt

Vince Otero (Roger), Bill Vitelli (Doody),
David Paymer (Sonny), Adrian Zmed (Zuko,
on steps), and Paul Regina (Kenickie).

therapy after all. For my audition song I chose "Who Put the Bomp (in the Bomp Bomp Bomp)," and I rehearsed the hell out of it, singing along with an old 45 rpm record. Not having the sheet music, my dad, a talented pianist and classical musician, forgetting his showbiz reservations, jumped in to help. He transcribed it, writing out the chords and arrangement—and all in my key!

On the big day, when my name was finally called, I walked onto the Royale stage, handed Dad's arrangement to the accompanist, and dove right in. When I got to the first "bomp bomp bomp," I did a little hip move and heard a titter of laughter. *OK.* I felt hopeful. When I got to "rama lama ding dong," I got a couple of really good laughs. *Encouraging!* And then I read Sonny's first lines: "I got old lady Lynch for English again!" Big laughs. *They're with me!*

Then came my Achilles' heel: the *dance callbacks.* I couldn't even "move well," as it had stated in the trades. Choreographer Pat Birch set up an improvisational dance, with boys on one side of the stage and girls on the other. We were each told to ask a girl to dance and do a little dance routine. I summoned the courage to ask an unlucky dark-haired Rizzo type to dance and stumbled through a self-conscious, very unimpressive Lindy hop, tripping over my feet at every turn. I sulked back to the corner, totally defeated. I had blown it. Big time!

Traveling back on the Long Island Rail Road to my dad's house, I sank into a deep depression. *Grease* was known as the "dancingest show in town," so clearly I didn't have a chance. Days passed. I barricaded myself in my room and pondered my future as a marriage psychologist. About a week later the phone rang. "David, we'd like to offer you the role of Sonny in the national tour of *Grease.*" Before he had a chance to reconsider, I quickly accepted, mumbled my thanks, and hung up in shock. *Of course! Sonny doesn't have to be a great dancer! During "Shakin' at the High School Hop" and "Hand Jive," he's too busy getting drunk and falling down the stairs—and I will be great at that!*

Psychology would have to wait. My life had just changed forever.

PETER GALLAGHER (*Zuko*): When I was a junior in high school, I saw *Grease* in its first week of previews, and all I remember was thinking that Barry Bostwick as Danny Zuko looked really cool in that red jacket during the Rydell prom. I never in a million years imagined a day that I might be wearing that red jacket too.

Five years later, after college and a season with the Boston Shakespeare Company, I arrived in NYC with my economics degree in hand, hoping to become an actor. I was going to audition for *everything.* When I got an audition for *Grease,* I prepared by seeing the show again at the Royale.

Patrick Swayze as Zuko was so amazing, I didn't see the point in even trying to audition. When I told my college pal Henry that there was no way I could do what I saw those guys do, he said, "I thought you were going to audition for *everything.* You're quitting now?"

Couldn't argue with that, so I showed up for the *Grease* open call. By 7:00 AM, three hours before the auditions even started, there would already be more than two thousand names ahead of you on the clipboard posted on the door. So after adding my name at the bottom of the list, I joined the blocks-long line wrapping around the corner and down Eighth Avenue.

After about six hours the guy that had been in front of me all this time was suddenly in the room, wailing, "Jeremiah was a bullfrog . . ." I started to lose all confidence in myself and my song. Why hadn't I picked a cool song like his? I was a heartbeat away from chickening out, running back down the stairs and out of showbiz forever, when all of a sudden I found myself

Peter Gallagher and Gail Edwards in the second bus and truck tour.

handing over my sweaty sheet music to Phyllis Grandy, the accompanist, and my soggy headshot and résumé ("Special skills: Driving") to Vinnie Liff, the casting director.

Phyllis Grandy started to play, and I started to sing "Put Your Head on My Shoulder." I had been up half the night coming up with some really inventive ways of performing the song, which I thought were pretty clever and kind of funny but didn't have much to do with the meaning of the song. Fortunately I didn't do any of it; I just sang like my life depended on it.

Vinnie looked up and said, "That was beautiful!" My knees buckled and my eyes filled with tears because he had just given me a reason to keep going, to keep believing. It was huge.

Over that summer I was cast in the first revival of *Hair*. During a lunch break while we were rehearsing *Hair*, I walked from the Biltmore to the Royale for yet another callback for *Grease*. Vinnie was there, this time along with the director, Tom Moore, and all the big shots. It seemed to go well, but . . . you never know.

After the audition I started heading back up Eighth Avenue when I heard Vinnie shouting behind me, "Peter! Wait! Stop! They want you! You've got the part!"

It was probably a good thing that I happened to be doing a show about peace and love, because when I got back to the Biltmore I found our director, Tom O'Horgan, and our producers, and asked them if I could leave the Broadway *Hair* for a bus and truck tour of *Grease*. They were speechless and looked at me like I was crazy. *Are you serious?*

I told them I was. It was an opportunity to play a lead role and get a ride on an airplane—*Grease* was flying me all the way to Utica for press! They were still looking at me like I was out of my mind, but after a long pause someone said, "Let me talk to the boys," meaning the authors, Gerry Ragni and Jim Rado.

A couple days later Tom O'Horgan made it easy: "Sure, man, go and have fun." And I did.

CHERI EICHEN (*Frenchy*): It's 1977. I've just graduated college, and I'm working as a page at NBC. I see an ad in the *Hollywood Reporter*: NON-EQUITY OPEN CALL FOR *GREASE*. I tell my best friend / audition buddy we should go. He tells me no. *The ad says you have to sing a song from the '50s. We don't have any of those in our songbooks. We're not going.*

On my way to the audition (alone), I stop at Hollywood Sheet Music to pick up a '50s song. The man behind the counter suggests "Johnny Angel." I pay my $2.50 and go merrily on my way to audition with a song I've never sung before. I am unprepared, winging it and clueless. Happily they're looking for a Frenchy, so it might just all work out.

I get a callback, then another. I tell NBC I'm sick so I can skip work for the final callback. I don't remember reading or singing. I just remember jumping around a lot.

Then—I am plucked from obscurity to replace the current Frenchy on the second national tour. Casting director Vinnie Liff asks if I can fly to San Francisco Monday and offers me Equity scale plus per diem. I don't know what these words mean. He translates: a weekly minimum salary that is twice what I'm earning at the Peacock. Plus living expenses. I find a pay phone, borrow a quarter, and quit my day job. NBC does not pay per diem.

JAMES REMAR (*Kenickie*): Not long after the big blackout of 1977, around dinnertime, I was warming up a can of soup in my cold-water, walk-up apartment when the phone rang. Pretty unusual in those early actor starvation days.

In those days all I did besides trying to learn more about acting was drive a truck for P. J. Clarke's, purchasing fresh fruits and vegetables at night from the Bronx Terminal Market. It was a lonely, hungry time, but I was young and I was nothing if not resilient. And I wanted to be an actor more than anything—more than I wanted to eat.

I answered the phone, and a voice asked if I was James Remar. *Uh . . . yes, I am . . . who's this?* "I'm calling from Johnson-Liff casting, and we would like you to come in and audition for *Grease*." I thought it was one of my jerk friends messing with me. I said, "Who is this really?" "It's really Johnson-Liff, and we would like you to audition." I responded, "I sent you guys my picture six months ago for another show." "Oh yes, we keep them, and we would like you to try out for Kenickie in the musical *Grease*."

I floated around for the next few days really excited and bewildered—and terrified. I was no song-and-dance guy. I was a dramatic actor—fresh out of *not* being asked back for year two at the Neighborhood Playhouse . . . devastating.

Finally the day of my big tryout came. I figured I would have an intimate, nurturing audition and show them how serious and sensitive James Remar really was. Stepping into the backstage area of the Royale, I was overwhelmed by what seemed like a thousand other actors, all great looking and way better trained as singers and dancers than me. I almost split right then, but something told me to stay . . . and fight!

The many rounds of singing and dancing were overwhelming. *Hand jive . . . what the heck is that?* I don't remember how many rounds over how many days I auditioned, but it seemed endless. And I knew, at best, I was mediocre. At worst, I was horrible.

But on the last day, after waiting for what seemed like forever, and wound up tighter than a drum, I finally got back onstage to read a Kenickie scene. At least I knew how to do that. After all, I was a serious actor!

After the scene a very young, midwestern-handsome, white-bread kind of guy walked down to the front row to give me some acting suggestions. I did them all, and it seemed to be going well. And then . . . the guy in the front row stood up. "Thank you very much."

"Thank you very much?" I said. I was pissed! How the hell do you torture someone all day like that and then just say, "Thank you very much"? I said, "That's it?"

Guy said, "Yes, that's it. We'd like you to see the show."

I said, "Go see the show?"

Guy said, "Yes, please go see the show."

I was profoundly rattled at how these guys just didn't get it! I walked to the edge of the stage and said, "*Go see the show?*" They didn't even offer me a ticket! I would have to pay for it! How was I gonna do that?

I got down on one knee. "If I could afford to go see your show, I wouldn't be walking around wearing shoes with holes in them." I pointed to the holes in my boots. "And I wouldn't be driving a truck at night buying vegetables!"

In retrospect I'm sure he, or someone, made clear that I wouldn't have to buy a ticket; the stage manager would walk me in. But by that time I was hearing none of it; I was *on a roll!* I stood up and somewhat—maybe all what—belligerently said, "Who are you?"

He said, "I'm Tom Moore, the director."

I said, "Oh shit!" thinking, *I'm fucked! I'm really fucked!* And then I quickly walked/ran straight off the stage and out the stage door.

I was already halfway up the block when a voice called, "*Remar! Remar!*" I ran back in world-record time as the casting director, Vinnie Liff, put a calming hand on my chest and said, "You got the part."

I couldn't stop saying "Thank you, thank you," and my joy was like floating—truly cloud nine! I was officially gonna be a professional actor—a member of Actors' Equity. Some rent money! Food! I was on my way!

I have been a professional actor for over forty years, but my audition for *Grease* was the toughest one I ever experienced, and as such it is the most memorable and doubtless the most formative one of my career.

Appreciation to Tom for seeing the actor hidden beneath the bad (terrible) singing and dancing.

MEGHAN DUFFY (*Frenchy*): I'm sitting in a frozen tundra, a.k.a. Chicago television studio. I was there to promote *Dames at Sea*, which I was doing at the Candlelight Dinner Playhouse. Warren Casey and Vince Otero were there to promote *Grease*, the other, bigger musical happening in Chicago in the spring of 1977. The host was far more interested in Warren and Vince. Every once in a while, he would glance in my direction, realizing he should probably ask me a question. The problem was that he just asked the same question over and over.

I had not yet refined my poker face and diplomatic skills, so I'm rolling my eyes a lot and letting him know that he had already asked me that very same question. I'm not rude—just young.

When the interview is over, Vince tells me that auditions for *Grease* are happening in a few days and that I'm perfect for the show. Of course I agree—even though I'd never even seen the show.

A few days later I'm backstage at the Civic Opera House. When my time comes, I walk out onto the stage and am immediately thrilled to look out at the massive house of this theater. It's huge. The stage is huge. It's all huge—including this moment.

A voice comes from one of the people sitting several rows back: "What's your name?"

"duffi."

"Duffi?"

"Just duffi." I went by one name in those days. With a small *d*. Don't be judgmental!

I hand the music to the piano player in the orchestra pit. I had never seen a pit before, except in the movies. It's huge too. The music I brought was "Da Doo Ron Ron." I had no idea what key it was in. I had no idea about the arrangement. But I knew this song in the core of my being. I'd sung it over and over again, daily—with Bette Midler and Barry Manilow on the Bette Midler album.

A voice floats out of the pit: "I'll give you four bars."

I am off like a bat out of hell. I'm flying, in my zone, body and soul. It wasn't choreographed. It wasn't premeditated. It wasn't contrived. It was just me doing what I love to do. When I finished, you could feel the energy in the room. They loved "Da Doo Ron Ron"!

I was in heaven. I was doing what I was supposed to be doing.

There were some encouraging words about how talented we all were, and then, "OK. Thank you all very much." And then we were dismissed.

"Thank you all very much!" Am I understanding this correctly? I was great. How could I not be hired? I wasn't.

Fast forward: It is the day Elvis Presley dies. I'm doing an improv show at a comedy club. The director of our group informs us that Jim Jacobs, who wrote *Grease*, is coming to our performance. When Jim comes in, we eagerly gather around his table. He tells us how heartbroken he is over the death of Elvis Presley. We commiserate. But I don't think any of us are quite feeling Jim's heartbreak. He then turns to me and says, "You did a great audition."

"I know. I can't believe you didn't hire me." Everyone at the table gasps. I'm not rude—just young.

Jim says, "You'd be a good Frenchy."

"I think so."

Two days later I'm in bed. The phone rings. It's Vinnie Liff. "We've been looking all over for you. We want you to do the tour of *Grease*."

And that's how it came down. All because I happened to be doing a television interview in a frozen tundra along with Warren Casey, Vince Otero, and a talk-show host who paid me little attention.

BUDDY POWELL (*Eugene*): Just out of college, I was teaching high school theater in a small town in southern Illinois. I saw a newspaper ad promoting the *Grease* tour coming to St. Louis. Though I had not actually seen the show, it had to be a great field trip for my young teenage drama students.

The day of the matinee, our school bus driver let us out under the huge yellow and red *Grease* marquee. Excitement filled the air. A real Broadway show in St. Louis!

I sat with a couple of parent chaperones directly behind my eager students. The lights dimmed. Fifties rock 'n' roll filled the air! Just five minutes into the show came the raunchy "Alma Mater Parody." My jaw dropped. Sweat poured. I cringed in my seat. I stared at my knees. I was absolutely not prepared for what these innocent midwestern kids were about to see. I knew I would be fired. Hell, these kids would be in therapy for years!

Despite my fears, those kids laughed and giggled for the next two hours. What they didn't understand was left that way. Seems I was the only prude in the group.

As luck would have it, several years after I saw *Grease* with my high school students, another tour of the show was playing in Chicago. They were auditioning for future replacements. By this time I was no longer teaching. I was an actor, and I auditioned for the role of Eugene—the same pathetic character who was subjected to horrors by the Burger Palace Boys and Pink Ladies in that *same* scene that had filled me with terror with my young students!

Who would have known three years before—when I sat frightened in St. Louis, worried that I'd scarred my young students for life—that I would eventually be cast as Eugene Florczyk in the 1978 bus and truck tour? And have the time of my life!

GREASE TOP TEN: ROCK 'N ROLL PARTY QUEEN • SHAKIN' AT THE HIGH SCHOOL HOP • BEAUTY SCHOOL DROPOUT • BORN TO HAND JIVE • FREDDY, MY LOVE • ALL CHOKED UP • THOSE MAGIC CHANGES • SUMMER NIGHTS • ALONE AT A DRIVE-IN MOVIE • IT'S RAINING ON PROM NIGHT

grease

A NEW 50's ROCK 'N ROLL MUSICAL

KENNETH WAISSMAN & MAXINE FOX
in association with ANTHONY D'AMATO
present

grease

Book, Music, & Lyrics by
JIM JACOBS & WARREN CASEY

Musical Supervision
& Orchestrations by
MICHAEL LEONARD

Vocal & Dance Arrangements by
LOUIS ST. LOUIS

Scenery by
DOUGLAS W. SCHMIDT

Costumes by
CARRIE F. ROBBINS

Lighting by
KARL EIGSTI

Sound by
BILL MERRILL

Production Stage Manager
JOE CALVAN

General Management
THEATRE NOW, INC.

Hair Styles Created by
JIM SULLIVAN

Musical Numbers & Dances Staged by **PATRICIA BIRCH**

Directed by **TOM MOORE**

EDEN THEATRE 189 Second Ave. 260-5200 (2nd Ave. & 12th St.)

LEFT: Carrie Robbins's costume design for Sonny LaTierri. RIGHT: Carrie's design for Rizzo's dance dress. BELOW: Carrie's costume design for Patty Simcox.

Doug Schmidt's early conceptual design for the *Grease* set.

The Eden marquee.

Marya Small in Frenchy's memorable red wig, created by costume designer Carrie Robbins.

The *Grease* cast album.

The Eden Theatre original cast on Greased Lightning. Top, L to R: Timothy Meyers and Barry Bostwick. Middle, L to R: Jim Borrelli, Walter Bobbie, Garn Stephens, and Adrienne Barbeau (reclining). Front, L to R: Katie Hanley, James Canning, and Marya Small.

"BROADWAY'S MUSICAL KNOCKOUT!"
—Leonard Probst, NBC

Grease

THE NEW 50's MUSICAL COMEDY HIT!

ORIGINAL CAST ALBUM ON MGM RECORDS
Tickets also available at Ticketron outlets, call 644-4400.

ROYALE THEATRE 45th STREET, WEST of B'WAY

The first national tour company made a promotional appearance in Farragut Square when the show played Washington, DC. ABOVE: L to R: Rebecca Gilchrist, Ellen March, and Marilu Henner. BELOW: Judy Kaye and John Travolta in Farragut Square.

In the first national tour company, Walter Charles (Vince Fontaine) declares Judith Sullivan (Cha-Cha DiGregorio) and Barry Bostwick (Danny Zuko) the winners of the hand-jive contest.

John Travolta and Barry Bostwick with the first national tour company at the Shubert Theatre, Los Angeles.

Jerry Zaks, Ray DeMattis, Barry Bostwick, Judy Kaye, and John Travolta in the first national tour company.

The first bus and truck company on the road. Top: Jerry Barkoff. Back row, L to R: Vince Otero, Shelley Barre, and Clifford Lipson. Middle row, L to R: Joene Lewis, Kristin Jolliff, Donald Russell, Andrea Walters, and Lloyd Alan. Front row, L to R: Shannon Fanning, Jimmie F. Skaggs, Marsha Waterbury, Cynthia Darlow, and Danny Jacobson. Front right, standing: Ruth Russell and Kim Herbert.

Marya (Mews) Small as Frenchy and James Canning as Doody performed together on Broadway and in the first national tour in Chicago.

Sandra Zeeman, Lorelle Brina, Adrian Zmed, Peggy Lee Brennan, and Pippa Pearthree on Broadway in 1978.

ABOVE: Melody Meitrott and Greg Zadikov represent *Grease* with other stars of Broadway in this poster campaign for the New York subway system.

LEFT: This huge billboard was hung in Times Square every year right across from the New York Times Building, where the New Year's ball drops, offering holiday greetings from *Grease*.

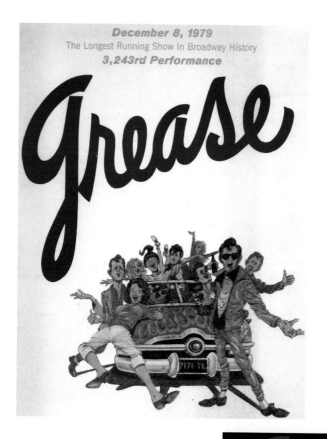

December 8, 1979
The Longest Running Show In Broadway History
3,243rd Performance

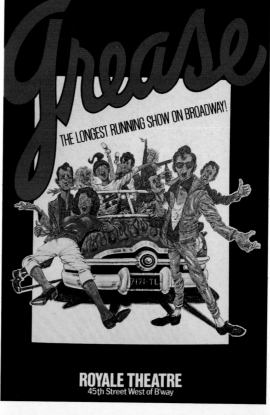

THE LONGEST RUNNING SHOW ON BROADWAY!

ROYALE THEATRE
45th Street West of B'way

Congressional Record

United States
of America

PROCEEDINGS AND DEBATES OF THE 96th CONGRESS, FIRST SESSION

Vol. 125   WASHINGTON, TUESDAY, NOVEMBER 20, 1979   *No. 164*

Senate

GREASE

Mr. MOYNIHAN. Mr. President, the American musical "Grease" became the longest running show in the history of Broadway on the evening of December 8, 1979, with its 3,243d performance, surpassing "Fiddler on the Roof" which played 3,242 performances from September 22, 1964, through July 2, 1972.

"Grease," set in the 1950's, portrays adolescence and the universal growing pains that every generation experiences. Since it opened in New York at the Eden Theatre on February 14, 1972, "Grease" has introduced to the public a whole new generation of young stage, film and television stars including such celebrated names as Adrienne Barbeau, Barry Bostwick, Jeff Conaway, Candice Early, Greg Evigan, Richard Gere, Randy Heller, Marilu Henner, Judy Kaye, Ilene Kristen, Rex Smith, John Travolta, Chick Vennera, Ted Wass and Treat Williams. The play is a triumph also for its director, Tom Moore; choreographer, Patricia Birch; cocomposers and authors, Jim Jacobs and Warren Casey and for its producers, Kenneth Waissman and Maxine Fox.

In March of 1972, "Grease" received seven nominations for the American Theatre Wing's Antoinette Perry Awards (Broadway's equivalent of Hollywood's "Academy Awards").

On June 7, 1972, the production moved to the Broadhurst Theatre on 44th Street and November 21, 1972 moved once again to the Royale Theatre on 45th Street, which has been its home ever since. On December 23, 1972, Waissman & Fox sent out the first National Touring Company of "Grease." Since then nine touring companies have crisscrossed the United States and Canada, playing engagements in Washington, D.C., seven times; Philadelphia, eight

times; Baltimore, seven times; Detroit, six times; Miami, four times; Los Angeles, three times; Boston, three times; as well as repeat engagements in many other cities. The large number of return engagements caused Washington, D.C., Drama Critic Richard Coe to comment, "We look forward to this show each season. A year without 'Grease' is like a year without the Circus."

Total gross in the United States on Waissman & Fox productions of "Grease" New York and National companies is approximately $70,000,000. Capitalized at $110,000, the musical thus far returned a 4,000-percent profit to its investors.

The film version released by Paramount Pictures on June 13, 1978, starred Olivia Newton-John and former Broadway cast member John Travolta. The film has grossed approximately $200,-000,000 to date in the United States and around the world, making it the highest grossing film ever made. It is also the highest grossing film in the history of Paramount Pictures.

In Mexico City, entitled "Vaselina," and performed entirely in Spanish, a live production of "Grease" played for 2½ years. Other foreign productions include: London, Melbourne, Sidney, Tokyo, Johannesburg and a Paris production to be called Brilliantine is in preparation.

Awards that "Grease" has received include citations from the Actors Fund of America, the American Theatre Wing, Cue magazine, the Shubert Organization, the city of New York, the city of Los Angeles, the city of Baltimore, the Variety Club of New York, the Television "Clio" Awards, and the League of New Work Theatres & Producers.

"Grease" began as a local workshop project in 1971 in Chicago. At this embryonic stage, it was more of a play with

music than a full-scale musical. Dr. Philip Markin, a Chicago dentist and a former college friend of Kenneth Waissman, suggested he see the workshop production. Mr. Waissman and Miss Fox flew to Chicago to see the play and fell in love with the basic idea of the piece. They brought the authors, Jim Jacobs and Warren Casey to New York to rewrite the play for Broadway and compose a full score. The producers then chose Tom Moore to direct and Patricia Birch to choreograph. Mr. Moore spent each day for 2 months assembling the original cast and each evening working with Jacobs and Casey on the play's structure. Rehearsals began on January 2, 1972, and following 3 weeks of previews, "Grease" premiered on Valentine's Day. The initial notices were mixed but the theatre-going public immediately embraced the show with an enthusiasm that has persisted right into its current eighth season on Broadway.

Kenneth Waissman and Maxine Fox, husband and wife in private life, are 36 and 33 years of age, respectively, and are Broadway's youngest producing team. Other Waissman and Fox productions include the musical "Over Here!" which starred the Andrews Sisters, "And Miss Reardon Drinks a Little" which starred Julie Harris and Estelle Parsons, and "Fortune and Men's Eyes" directed by the late Sal Mineo. The Waissmans produced the entertainment for New York's salute to Congress October 10, 1979, at the Washington Hilton. They also produced the all-star "V.I.P. Night on Broadway" at the Shubert Theatre, April 22, 1979, which netted $150,000 for the purchase of bulletproof vests for New York's policemen.

The phenomenal success of "Grease" is a living tribute to Irving Berlin's immortal phrase "There's No Business Like Show Business!"

Grease was read into the *Congressional Record* for November 20, 1979.

Broadway's *Grease* alumni and the cast of the movie celebrate the beginning of filming at a party given by Tom Moore. L to R: Louis St. Louis, Pat Birch, Alan Paul, Jeff Conaway, Marya (Mews) Small, and Barry Bostwick.

The *Grease* gals from multiple companies celebrate an anniversary. Back row: Char Fontaine, Forbesy Russell, and Robin Vogel. Front row: Lori Ada Jaroslow, Peggy Lee Brennan, Gege Martorella, Jill Rose, and Randy Graff.

The original cast gets together to celebrate *Grease*'s thirtieth anniversary. Back row: Barry Bostwick, Tom Harris, Ken Waissman, and Don Billett. Front row: Joy Rinaldi, Carole Demas, Tom Moore, Adrienne Barbeau, and Jim Jacobs.

Celebrating *Grease*'s twentieth anniversary at the Sheraton Universal in Los Angeles.

The original cast gathered for the 23rd Annual Gypsy of the Year Awards. L to R: Don Billett, Dan Deitch, Ilene Kristen, Alan Paul, Joy Rinaldi, Tom Moore, Pat Birch, Barry Bostwick, Carole Demas, Walter Bobbie, Adrienne Barbeau, Katie Hanley Storer, James Canning, Mews (Marya) Small, Tom Harris, and Ken Waissman.

The original cast performing at the 23rd Annual Gypsy of the Year Awards, December 6, 2011.

LAURIE GRAFF (*Frenchy*): Walking onstage felt like entering a scene from *Funny Girl*, the theater dark and empty but for the creative team seated in the first few rows. Adjusting my navy-blue sweater over my white-collared shirt, I checked to make sure my brown bangs were in place.

I took a breath and sang. "We've never heard that song before!" said someone important. Hell, they were all important. Naive me didn't know one person I was auditioning for from the next.

I got a callback. And then another the following day, to dance. We were given some steps to do for the dance at the prom. I am not a dancer.

Pat Birch came up on the stage, pulled me aside, and gave me a tip. "Laurie, you don't have to be a great dancer," she told me. "It's a bunch of kids at a school dance. Use your personality in the movement."

From then on I hand-jived and bopped about that stage until I heard "Thank you." We were dismissed.

I was just about to leave the theater when I heard someone say, "Laurie—they want to see you. Will you go back onstage?"

I raced back. A voice from the house said, "We'd like to offer you the role of Frenchy in the national tour of *Grease*."

"*Yes! Yes!*" I shouted. Two men, whom I came to learn were producer Ken Waissman and director Tom Moore, had already put on their coats and were walking up the aisle.

"Hey, you guys. You guys. Wait!" I called out, sounding a whole lot like Frenchy. "You mean I'm going to get my Equity card? And when I rewrite my bio, it will say, 'Laurie Graff, who just returned from playing Frenchy in the national tour of *Grease*'?"

They nodded.

"Thank you. Oh, my goodness, thank you so much."

They smiled. They could go now. They got their show cast. They would get lunch. But I . . . I just floated up to cloud nine.

LORI ADA JAROSLOW (*Understudy*): While most kids I grew up with went to college after high school, I went for a year, had a nervous breakdown, and then matriculated to Rydell High.

At the time of my last of several auditions, I was working as a waitress in a janky ladies' bar on West Third Street that was upstairs from a fortune teller's parlor. This was a win-win: an endless supply of alcohol, and I slept with the head gypsy.

A few nights after the callback, some friends picked me up after my waitress shift for a road trip to the Jersey Shore. We arrived in Lavallette so late that it was impossible to find lodging, so we did what any idiotic teenagers would do: drank blackberry brandy and passed out on the beach. Bleary-eyed, we stumbled into the morning sun, and I ducked into a phone booth to call my answering service. There was a message that I was cast in the third national tour of *Grease*. I was shocked, ecstatic, and screaming with joy.

I careened into my new life with a steamer trunk and talent; absolutely no training, life skills, or support system; and perhaps too much of a fondness for drinking and smoking pot.

Katherine Meloche, Lori Ada Jaroslow, Melody Meitrott, and Lorelle Brina.

Rehearsals

ADRIAN ZMED: When I walked into the Minskoff Theatre rehearsal studios, I was nervous, but I soon discovered that everyone was in the same boat since it was pretty much the first Equity production for all of us. Plus I found out that we were the first cast to be close in age to actual teenagers. I think that was the magic of our particular company. We were kids, excited to be in our first show. We weren't seasoned and experienced enough to have egos. It was like the first day of summer camp; we bonded immediately. I distinctly remember meeting Paul Regina (Kenickie) and Billy Vitelli (Doody). In time they became my best friends.

Rehearsals picked up right where I left off with Tom when I auditioned the week before. He encouraged us to try things. I was a kid in a candy store, exploding with ideas and trying new things all the time. But our young director definitely knew when to pull in the reins and wasn't afraid to make the call. As many times as I heard "I like that, keep it in," I also heard "Uh, no, Adrian. I don't think so."

It was one of the few times in my career a director was not dictating but collaborating with the actors. And it was the same with Pat Birch, the choreographer. She coaxed movement out of each of us and somehow magically made it into dance. This collaboration made each company special and unique—and a big reason why audiences always kept coming back for more.

MEGHAN DUFFY: I had never enjoyed the reputation of being a person who was on time for pretty much anything. But today would be different. Today I would make sure that I was on time for my first day of rehearsal because I was now a New York actor. Today being early would be my first major accomplishment.

Crossing the threshold into the rehearsal studio was like entering Oz, the mythical land where I would find the wizard who could make my wish come true. The room was electric. Everyone was kind, excited, nervous, and thrilled to be there.

The director blocked the opening of the show, and we were quickly into the cafeteria scene preceding "Summer Nights." When Patty Simcox enters, she plops herself right in the middle of the Pink Ladies, hip-slamming Frenchy (me) as she pushes her way onto the bench. I'm blocked to fall off the bench. I take it one step further and fly off the bench! This would be my second major accomplishment of the day—thanks to Lucille Ball and Carol Burnett.

There is another pivotal moment in the cafeteria scene. I was going to give it a little humor from the Three Stooges—with a little Jackie Gleason flair. I decided to switch the scripted line from "Hardee har har" to "Yuckity yuck yuck," and as I exited on the line, it got a big laugh from the room.

I'm standing there smiling with my cafeteria tray, just outside the white line on the floor that indicates where onstage ends. Tom stops the rehearsal, drawing everyone's attention to me—*Oh Lord!*—and the fact that I had changed the line. *Oh Lord!* My smile fades. I say nothing.

Tom then tells us that we should all continue to approach rehearsal in this playful way, feeling free to experiment. Although we should be respectful of the original Broadway production, we need not imitate it. We should make the show our own, and that's what would make our company unique and special.

I breathed a sigh of relief and smiled again. I had done something right. This was my third major accomplishment of the day.

"We Go Together," second national company.

Peter Gallagher as Zuko and Mary Garripoli as Cha-Cha win the dance contest.

PETER GALLAGHER: The *Grease* rehearsal I remember most vividly was with Pat Birch teaching us the hand jive. I was not a dancer—I had only taken one dance class in my life.

Pat showed me where and when I was supposed to spin like a top, and I really didn't know how to do it, but I gave it my all, spinning with surprising speed, and fell literally flat on my face. The noise was deafening, and I was pretty sure my face was cracked like glass. The embarrassment, however, was way greater than the pain, and it propelled me right up off the floor just milliseconds after my face had made full contact with it. To my surprise, no one seemed to be looking at me with horror. I glanced at the rehearsal mirror and I wasn't even bleeding, so I casually turned to Pat and said, "Got it!"

JOHN KELLY (*Kenickie*): After our short two-week rehearsal period, as our official opening at Paper Mill Playhouse drew near, you could have filled Madison Square Garden with the excitement that I and everyone in that room was feeling, but my nerves were on edge, and I was trying my best not to show panic. So at the end of our last rehearsal, I walked out into the nighttime air, where the sudden coolness brought comfort and exhilaration. As I walked I thought about my fellow castmates and how we had already formed a bond of trust and cohesiveness, and were ready to grab that brass ring. When I got to my destination, I looked up at the Royale Theatre marquee with the big, bright letters spelling out *Grease*. I was about to be part of a theatrical phenomenon. Into the night air I whispered, "Bring it on."

"We Go Together," second bus and truck company.

31 | *Danny Takes Sandy to the Drive-In*

It's a fact: every teen boy wants to be a rock 'n' roll star, and every clean-cut teen girl wants to be a slut . . . if only for a couple of hours onstage. Therein lies the appeal of Grease *to every professional, amateur, and school production since the early '70s!*

—BARRY BOSTWICK

TOM MOORE (*Director*): The drive-in movie scene and Danny Zuko's attempted seduction of Sandy was a pantomime masterpiece, sometimes taking a full five minutes or more, and it was richer each time I saw it. It is always such a joy to watch an actor totally in control of his craft and skills, with charisma to burn, blazingly take down an audience. And take them down he did. Every single night.

Every Danny Zuko in our productions and all to follow added some bit of business to that scene. And the additions were often brilliant. Each of our Dannys was special in his own inimitable way, but they all owed the template from which they worked to the original Danny Zuko.

BARRY BOSTWICK (*Zuko*): The second-act drive-in scene was like Zuko's eleven o'clock spot—his big second-act showstopper—and "Alone at a Drive-In Movie" the eleven o'clock musical number. You could try anything to get a laugh, and believe me, I did—from using the grease in my hair to get the ring off to getting my hand slammed in the door when Sandy storms out.

The scene begins with Zuko's expansive yawn, allowing him to finally get his arm around Sandy. I had done that many a time at my local drive-in

Carole Demas and Barry Bostwick.

when I was in high school. It always worked until you accidentally brushed up against a breast.

My real inspiration for Danny was what I wore around my neck: one of those stamped aluminum coins that you got from those machines at a carnival. You printed your name on the coin and who your steady was at the time. Mine was Tracy Moyer, and she was with me for every *Grease* performance, to remind me of how innocent and full of promise our lives had been back then. She was the head cheerleader and the school senior beauty queen. Tracy was my Sandy, and I was apparently the creep of her dreams.

TREAT WILLIAMS (*Zuko*): While I was in acting class trying to learn how to really be an actor, one of the things we worked on was a sense of place. If you're going to do a scene and it's in a drive-in, really imagine what it's like when you were a kid at the drive-in. So as we rehearsed the drive-in scene, I thought to myself, *OK, this isn't an empty stage with Danny and Sandy in a single car. This is a car surrounded by hundreds of cars, and I've got people all around me.* When Sandy says she'll go steady with him, Danny gets very excited, fist pumps in triumph, and beeps the car's horn. Because of that sense memory of being surrounded by other people, all of a sudden I heard an imaginary voice say, "Shut up!" so I turned to the asshole and said, "Hey, fuck you, man," and gave him the finger. The audience immediately recognized the moment, and the laughter exploded. That was my addition to the *Grease* drive-in scene.

Mike Nichols used to say, "The reason people laugh is that they have an unconscious acknowledgment that this has happened to them." That kind of moment, recognizable to all of us, is so painful, so funny, and so stupid that everybody enjoyed it. Every day I would be thinking about things I might try in the drive-in scene that night. It never stopped.

Barry Bostwick, who originated Danny, was the premier Zuko of all time. The whole structure of the drive-in business—the unspoken physical activity—was created by Barry, and every Zuko since has just sort of added their own layer to it.

In addition to Barry using the grease in his hair to get the ring off for Sandy, another great piece of business was the moment when Sandy is running away and Danny is crawling across the seat to stop her. She slams the door directly into Danny's crotch. There's like three minutes of agony, and the audience can't stop laughing. I first saw this moment when Jeff Conaway was playing Danny and I was understudying. Probably some of this was invented by Barry, but in Jeff's Zuko, the moment definitely grew. And then with me it grew some more.

Tom came backstage one time after a show and said, "Treat, that was very funny. It's a great piece of business. Take about two and a half minutes out of it."

BARRY TARALLO (*Understudy*): Now that I was an understudy, I had a lot of time to watch Peter Gallagher and the drive-in scene. While I watched I kept thinking that something was missing. Then it hit me. In Act 1 the character of Doody returns a set of foam dice to Kenickie, who makes a point of putting them back in Greased Lightning. But for some reason those dice had never appeared in the car in the drive-in scene in Act 2. That's what was missing. So during my week as Zuko, when Peter was out of the show, despite the prop master's objections, I put the dice back in the car before the scene. Then, instead of fondling my own breast (à la Treat Williams's hysterical bit), I would slowly bring my hand up into the audience's view, fondling the foam dice. It worked. The crowd went wild.

JOHN LANSING (*Zuko*): "Alone at a Drive-In Movie" was in my estimation one of the best comedy scenes in American theater, and a joy to perform. I honed my skills for "Drive-In Movie" on the road, playing opposite the wonderful Marcia McClain. She was the perfect Sandy, an ingenue with a killer

Marcia McClain and John Lansing.

singing voice. She was so effervescent I could lie back and not go overboard with broad physical comedy.

The scene was a winner in any venue—a first-class stage or a gymnasium somewhere in the Midwest, with folding chairs standing in for Greased Lightning.

I made it my mission every night onstage to see how many laughs I could get. Being able to perform the drive-in scene, where a raised eyebrow or a slight hand gesture could bring down the house, was a once-in-a-lifetime experience, and it never grew old.

DEREK KUCSAK (*Understudy*): In the second act comes the drive-in scene, the big test for any Zuko understudy. I had nightmares about the car brakes not working, or that I would somehow put the car in motion when I put the moves on Sandy and we'd wind up in the orchestra pit. As Sandy and I began the scene, all the actors from our show came out to the audience, one by one, and lined up against the wall on house right (stage left), all waiting and watching to see what I could do.

I got to the part where Danny yawns and puts his arm around Sandy. But before I did, I leaned back, opened my eyes as wide as I could, and without turning my head, looked to the right at Sandy and checked her out from top to bottom, then looked straight back. It got a big laugh, and I saw all the guys fall all over themselves laughing. That got me through the rest of the night!

ADRIAN ZMED (*Zuko*): Each Danny Zuko did his own unique version of the drive-in, and of course each of us thought we made it better.

Andrea Walters and Adrian Zmed.

We all left our signature. Mine was the disappearing Danny. After Sandy slammed the car door into Danny's crotch and I gave my high-pitched "It's nothing" response, I completely melted down into the car seat and disappeared under the dashboard—for quite some time. I was the only one who could physically do it because I have this ability to contort myself like a pretzel. When the laughter started to die down, my hand, as if reaching for life, would shoot up from underneath the dashboard onto the steering wheel and then I would slowly pull myself up.

Other Dannys tried the move after me, but they could never figure out how to completely disappear. This bit did have its dangers, however. In fact it almost got me and most of the orchestra killed.

Greased Lightning was built around a golf-cart chassis. To prevent the car from moving forward by accident, it was imperative to turn off the ignition when Sandy and I parked. Well, in Boston at the old Shubert, which had a twenty-five-foot drop from the stage into the orchestra pit, I forgot to turn off the ignition. When I contorted down under the dash, my knee pressed the gas pedal. I looked up to see Sandy (Andrea Walters), who was standing outside the car, start to move toward the back of the car. *Why is she moving?* Then I heard the screams. She wasn't moving, Greased Lightning was, and it was moving right toward the pit—with me in the car and the band at the bottom. Just in time, I slammed on the brake.

When I finally had the courage to look up, I saw that I was just inches from the edge of the stage.

I never ever forgot to turn off the ignition again.

More Nights at the Drive-In

Ilene Graff and John Lansing.

Marcia McClain and Richard Cox.

Shannon Fanning and Lloyd Alan.

Gail Edwards and Peter Gallagher.

32 | *The Last Tours on the Road*

ADRIAN ZMED (*Zuko*): For a kid who had never been out of Chicago, there were countless exciting times for me as we played thirty-six American and Canadian cities.

One of my greatest moments of the tour was when we played my hometown, Chicago. My father had not been very happy with me pursuing an acting career. He was a Romanian Orthodox priest (they can get married!) who understandably wanted his son to be a doctor, lawyer, architect, or even a priest—*not* an actor.

The only theater available when we were booked for Chicago was the immense thirty-five-hundred-seat Civic Opera House. As popular as *Grease* was, there was no way we were going to fill that theater. Mike Martorella gave me two of the greatest pieces of news I ever got on that tour. One was much later, when he told me I was going to Broadway, and the other was that they were going to offer comp tickets on opening night in Chicago and my father's *entire* congregation was invited. That night, every time I came out onstage, several hundred Romanians cheered. It was one of the greatest moments of my life because that night I finally gained my father's approval. He never did quite understand the acting profession, however. When he saw my first television show he said, "You're on TV for one hour. What do you do the rest of the week?"

CHICK VENNERA (*Sonny*): When the second national tour of *Grease* performed in Philadelphia, we were asked to appear on *The Mike Douglas Show*, which was doing a series of shows focusing on music and events from different decades. Our show was, not surprisingly, a salute to the '50s, and the cohost was Liberace.

COSIE COSTA (*Doody*): Fifties week with Mike Douglas and Liberace!

CHICK VENNERA: The guests included '50s icon Annette Funicello, *Your Hit Parade* stars Snooky Lanson and Gisèle MacKenzie, and chief counsel of the McCarthy hearings, attorney Roy M. Cohn.

COSIE COSTA: Annette Funicello! Growing up, I had never missed an episode of *The Mickey Mouse Club*, mainly because I had fallen in love with Annette. And there I was, a little Italian guy from a tiny mining town in Northern California (Grass Valley), being asked to sing on the same show with Annette, my long-loved beautiful Italian star!

She was very sweet to me, and I enjoyed every minute I spent with her . . . *and* her husband. Oh well—no fantasy goes on forever!

CHICK VENNERA: I was standing off to the side, watching the taping, when Liberace looked directly at Roy Cohn and accused him of being responsible for the destruction of the careers and lives of a lot of his good friends. And he didn't stop there. Liberace wouldn't let up with his accusations, and Roy Cohn turned red and stormed off the set.

The director cut to a commercial. Someone yelled, "Get the *Grease* kids ready. Now!"

COSIE COSTA: It was a big deal for me to sing Doody's number, "Those Magic Changes," on national television.

Andrea Walters and Adrian Zmed as Sandy and Danny.

CHICK VENNERA: Our musical number went really well, and Liberace later apologized. He told us he hated Roy Cohn for his part in the McCarthy witch hunt, which had resulted in many of his friends being blacklisted, ending their careers. I've never forgotten that heated exchange between Liberace and Cohn. It gave me tremendous respect for Liberace.

COSIE COSTA: We invited both Annette and Liberace to come see our show. Sadly for me, Annette wasn't able to make it, but Liberace came on a Saturday matinee, a day I will never forget.

CHICK VENNERA: Liberace liked us.

COSIE COSTA: Five minutes before the curtain went up, our entire cast was standing onstage behind the now-opaque scrim. About two minutes before the curtain, we heard a buzzing in the crowd: *There's Liberace! Oh my God, is that Liberace?* and the like. Liberace slowly made his way to his seat and then slowly turned and waved to the audience! They went crazy and gave him a standing ovation. Now *that's* a superstar!

CHICK VENNERA: Liberace loved the show and came backstage to speak with us.

COSIE COSTA: And how cool is this? When he talked to us backstage, he asked *us* to autograph *his* program!

Denise Nettleton, Chick Vennera, Cosie Costa, John Lansing, and Karren Dille on *The Mike Douglas Show.*

Paul Regina, Joene Lewis, Adrian Zmed, Char Fontaine,
David Paymer, Cynthia Darlow, and Vince Otero.

Joene Lewis and Adrian Zmed winning the dance contest!

MICHAEL BRINDISI (*Understudy*): Due to an emergency, I was notified on Friday at midnight that I would be going on at the matinee as Vince Fontaine, the role I had not yet played and was the least suited for—"Vince in a pinch" casting.

The next morning Mike Martorella was pinning my costume and running lines when he casually said, "Oh yeah, and Tom Moore"—as in *director* Tom Moore—"will be in the audience this afternoon taking notes."

You have to be f**king kidding me—not in this role!

I made my entrance, ran up the stairs to the upper deck, and announced the rules for the dance contest and eliminations in my best radio-DJ voice, which really sucked, I'm sure, but I missed not one line.

Proud of myself, I made my way back down to the stage deck for the dance eliminations when I suddenly realized I had forgotten to review the sequence of eliminations. I am so f**ked

As I turned to the first couple and gave them the Vince heave-ho gesture, they just looked at me with blank expressions and shook their heads. *Nope.*

I moved to another couple and precisely on cue gave them a stronger ejection gesture. Again the negative nods. *Nope.*

Never missing a beat, I tried yet a third couple, and once again they sniggeringly shook their heads. *Nope.* It was a total clusterf**k.

Flustered and at a total loss, I just jumped to the end of the scene and declared Danny and Cha-Cha the winners.

At our notes session in the theater lobby, Tom complimented my performance. He said my upper-deck performance was fantastic. The cast applauded me. He then said my lower-deck performance was . . . somewhat confused. We all laughed together.

CHICK VENNERA: After performing the show all over the United States, we had a good feel for which lines and what bits the audience would react to or laugh at.

But when we got to Canada, it was quite a different story. One night in Ottawa, at a performance with Pierre Trudeau in attendance, there was little or no laughter throughout the entire first act. The cast, in despair, gathered backstage at intermission and admitted that the show was bombing, and we needed to get through the second act as fast as we could and just get out of there.

We finished the second act, warily went out for the curtain call, and then, to our great surprise, were given a five-minute standing ovation!

What? How? Wow!

We were later told the Canadian audience loved the show but were much too polite to applaud or laugh over someone's lines. I guess they didn't want to miss anything.

Cynthia Darlow, Vince Otero, and the second national company at the Rydell High prom.

The second national tour Burger Palace Boys and Pink Ladies

STEVE YUDSON (*Teen Angel / Johnny Casino*): Life on the road can be very stressful, and playing one- or two-night stands across the country was not easy for me.

John Everson, who had joined our cast on the road as understudy and assistant stage manager, couldn't help but notice my anxiety. He wanted to help. John taught me a meditation technique, and I've been meditating using various techniques ever since. I am very grateful to John for showing me the way.

On our tour there were a number of stressful situations; not least were the long bus rides between cities. In those days the smokers were able to smoke in the back of the bus. And they would sing. One of the standards they sang most often was "L-O-V-E," made famous by Nat King Cole. None of them could remember the lyrics, so they sang, "*L* is for the way you look at me, *O* is for the way you look at me, *V* is for the way you look at me, *E* is for the way you look at me" over and over and over again.

Meditation was of no use.

To this day the sound of all my *Grease* friends on the bus singing with their inane, simplified lyrics still spins in my brain. Stressful then, but now when I remember, it makes me smile . . . and I remember often.

Meghan Duffy (Frenchy) and Steve Yudson (Teen Angel).

PEGGY LEE BRENNAN (*Frenchy*): I was so excited! I don't even remember what city we were in, but we would soon be at the Pantages Theatre in Los Angeles. In anticipation of Tom's cleanup rehearsal, Michael Martorella gave me extra rehearsal time to nail down every single beat in the pajama scene. After the show we gathered for our notes session.

Tom opened with, "So Peggy Lee Brennan thinks she's Ethel Merman! This is not *The Peggy Lee Brennan Show!*" He then proceeded to edit out all the bits that I had added to the scene. For the remainder of the long notes session, I sobbed quietly with my head down, body shaking convulsively, all the while hoping no one noticed. But they did. Bill Vitelli, my Doody, leaned over to whisper, "*Everyone* is looking at you, Peggy."

At the end of the long notes session, I jumped to my feet and started running out of the room. Tom stopped me in my tracks: "Peggy, will you please stay for a few minutes?"

As the others exited in silence, I stopped, turned, and wiped away my tears. When it was just the two of us, Tom looked directly at me and said, "Peggy, I only come down hard on those I believe in, and I believe in you." (Tom had directed me the year before in *Once in a Lifetime* at the Arena Stage in Washington, DC.) As I turned to leave, he gave me a big hug and said, "And you are also my friend." I cried again, but this time they were happy tears!

JIM SHANKMAN (*Sonny*): When the second national company landed in L.A., our opening night coincided with the wrap of the movie version of *Grease*. Someone had the great idea to combine their wrap party with our opening. So our big night (which we had waited a whole tour for) was eclipsed by a glitzy wrap party at the Pantages for the movie's cast and crew. They were all there: Travolta, Olivia Newton-John, Jeff Conaway; our cast was pretty much the least of it that night. Wandering around star-sighting, and just about ready to leave, I sighted a longtime crush, Valerie Bertinelli of *One Day at a Time*, sitting all alone on the staircase that led to the balcony. She was wearing a stunningly beautiful sequin gown. And she was not on TV. She was there in real life. Right in front of *me*. She had a glass of champagne in her hand, which she was staring at forlornly. I said, "Why aren't you drinking your champagne?" "I'm underage," she said. "I'm only seventeen." I was so taken aback. She was a child! And I was a grown man, all of twenty-three. I mumbled something unintelligible and then it was over. I never saw her again.

I often wonder if that moment is seared into her brain the way it is seared into mine. No, I don't. And honestly I'm not even sure it really happened. But she was definitely there.

The second national opens at the Pantages Theatre, with the cast of the film as their special guests.

Tom Moore, Pat Birch, Maxine Fox, and Ken Waissman celebrate opening night at the Pantages.

CHERI EICHEN (*Frenchy*): The *Grease* company flies me (*They. Fly. Me.*) to San Francisco to replace Peggy Lee Brennan, who was going to Broadway.

I am living the dream. I meet the cast. They are living in reality. They've been on the road for months. That's years in tour time. They are hyper-bonded and hyper-bored, and haven't got the bandwidth for a hyper-enthusiastic newbie who just got her Equity card and thinks scale is the best!

I rehearse and get put into the show. I discover the dancing is more than just jumping around. I cannot French inhale. I have trouble holding the harmony in "Freddy, My Love," and the harder I try, the flatter I go. I develop digestive issues.

I share a dressing room with the Jan. She doesn't talk to me, only to her cocker spaniel. The Doody misses his real-life girlfriend, the former Frenchy, who has left him to do the role on Broadway. He'd rather be there. It feels like they all would rather be there. It feels like I'm the only one who wants to be here.

LEFT: Bill Beyers, Char Fontaine, and Douglas Barden in the second national tour. RIGHT: Katherine Meloche and Bill Beyers in the second national tour.

Joene Lewis and Paul Regina in the second national tour.

The second bus and truck tour. LEFT: Dan Woodard, Nita Novy, and Michael Riney. RIGHT: Linda Lyons and Stephen Groff.

33 | *Broadway*
1976–1977

LLOYD ALAN (*Zuko*): For over a year I stood by on the road for John Lansing, Richard Cox, then John Lansing *again*, and then Treat Williams on Broadway. But when Treat left to do a film, the director and producers finally asked me to play Danny on Broadway.

It was worth the wait! Playing Danny was a dream come true, and there was never a moment I wasn't amazed at my good fortune at being there.

Well, maybe one moment . . .

It was a Wednesday matinee, and the Royale Theatre was filled with hundreds of high school girls. They were singing along and clapping in time with the music, and after I sang "Alone at a Drive-In Movie," there were a few girls who rushed the stage and had to be dragged off by the ushers. When I came offstage, the other actors had heard the ruckus and were waiting in the wings to find out what was going on. I said I didn't know, but I guess they liked it!

After any show there were usually a few girls waiting for an autograph, but today it seemed like every girl who saw the show was waiting at the stage door. As I exited the theater, I saw a sea of young girls—it looked like hundreds—and all of them were screaming my name. The girls nearest to me were pulling at me from all directions, and I was being pushed into the street. It was for all intents and purposes a crowd very much out of control.

I was starting to fear for my safety. I could be hurt. So what do you do when you are scared you could be hurt? I ran away. I mean, I literally just ran away.

MIMI KENNEDY (*Jan*): From time to time Tom came back to tune up the show and often to remove the "improvements" we actors had managed to

257

sneak in. He was determined to keep the show in opening-night condition, its tone and pace sparkling through all the cast changes and the often-grinding routine of eight shows a week. After Tom watched the show, he gathered the company in the orchestra seats for notes.

In the park scene at the end of Act 1, Roger asks Jan to the prom. Acting like she has a busy social schedule, Jan pulls out her datebook and says, "Lemme check." Roger, hurt, slings a retort, so Jan flips him the finger and says, "Right here, lard-ass!" I loved that moment when I saw the show at the Eden, and I really dug into it. Tom's note was to soft-pedal because I was hitting too hard.

"But I want to get the laugh!" I protested. "Don't you want me to get the laugh?"

Tom, slack-jawed, responded, "Mimi Kennedy! Of all people, I never thought I'd hear you say you want to play something just for the *laugh*!"

Looking back, I realize it wasn't the first time I'd been thought of as a method actor. *How did this happen?* I have often wondered. And why did it matter in *Grease*? I traced it back to Curt Dempster, a wonderful but strict teacher of the Sanford Meisner method. He produced my "devotion to the real." And directors like Tom reminded me that the more real a situation is played, the funnier it will be. Genuine delight can't be bullied or provoked by tricks.

Tom was right; I stopped pushing for the laugh . . . and got an even bigger one.

Mimi Kennedy as Jan.

"Every night at the Royale Theatre, the '50s come to life!"
Grease's first TV commercial.

Lloyd Alan takes over as Zuko at the Rydell High reunion.

CYNTHIA DARLOW (*Jan*): When Mimi Kennedy left the show, it was my turn; my Broadway debut was to be on Christmas Eve. The cast had had several turnovers recently, and they were exhausted from all the extra rehearsals. And it was Christmas Eve. Only Ray DeMattis (Roger) agreed to at least run through our duet, "Mooning," and practice the handstand at the end of "Hand Jive." And that was it!

The show went well enough, and although everyone was congratulatory, they had other places to be. After the final bow everyone took off for a big dinner party at Tavern on the Green in Central Park.

I had just opened on Broadway! I was exhilarated and bereft all at once. As I came downstairs from the dressing room, our conductor, Jeremy Stone, was just leaving; he was Jewish, and I guess no one thought to include him either. He congratulated me on my performance and asked what I was doing to celebrate. When I admitted I didn't have any plans, he invited me back to his apartment, where we shared a bottle of wine, listened to wonderful music, and watched the fresh snow gently falling over the city. It was a lovely Christmas Eve. I'll always be grateful to Jeremy for putting the *sweet* in my bittersweet Broadway debut.

GREG ZADIKOV (*Understudy*): It's October—autumn in New York—and I'm at Joe Allen's after the *Grease* matinee; a bunch of the cast and crew are crowded around the bar. Baseball. Yankees. Always the Yankees.

Rizzuto with the call: *Two and two . . . Torrez stretches, pitches . . . a high fly to left! Holy cow!*

The Yankees win the championship! Everyone is cheering. Drinks clinking. No better way to begin the evening.

I'm about to head over to the Royale when I see Lynne Guerra, our stage manager, push through the front door of Joe Allen's. She immediately heads in my direction.

"Greg," she says, "let's go!"

It seems I am going to Philadelphia. Although it's always exciting to play Zuko, the excitement is definitely heightened when you're going to play him a hundred miles away with less than two hours before curtain. I don't even have my ticket. But Lynne is there and she figures it out. Lynne figures everything out.

When the taxi stops, I look up to see where I'm putting my life for the next thirty minutes—a tiny seaplane. *Sky King* stuff. I give her a look and try to yell, "*Are you kidding me?*"

She just gestures at her watch. "Best we could do."

White-knuckling it through the windy skies, we finally touch down on the water. No time to worry. In what seems like five, ten minutes at most, I'm at the Merriam Theater in hair and makeup (pompadour perfect!).

When I make my entrance as Danny Zuko, I realize the cast is my old national tour castmates—and suddenly it feels like I'm home. I'm welcomed with open arms and great appreciation for "saving the day."

Yankees win the championship. *Grease* wins Philadelphia!

MELODY MEITROTT (*Understudy*): I especially loved the outreach opportunities we had because we were part of the *Grease* cast: performing for schools, hospitals, and fundraisers like United Way. My favorite was the iconic poster shoot that we did for the MTA (New York's Metropolitan Transportation Authority). They ran a poster campaign in the subway cars with the headline The Only Way to Make It to Broadway and photos of actors from all the Broadway shows that were running at the time. Greg Zadikov and I represented *Grease* and were honored to be photographed standing beside Carol Channing (*Hello, Dolly!*), Stephanie Mills (*The Wiz*), Eartha Kitt and Melba Moore (*Timbuktu!*), and Reid Shelton (*Annie*). I proudly have that poster up in my theater school, the Performing Arts Conservatory of New Canaan.

FORBESY RUSSELL (*Understudy*): Before every performance, we'd hear the cast warming up, especially before the 7:30 PM call, when the stairwell was generally quiet. Danny Jacobson (Kenickie) could be heard singing one of his two favorite warm-up songs—"The Hills Are Alive with the Sound of Mucus" and "Nothing Could Be Fina than to Be in Your Vagina in the Morning"—followed by yells up and down the stairway: *"Danny!" "Jake!"*

STEVE BECKLER (*Production Stage Manager*): Antiapartheid bomb threats also took their toll on *Grease*. The bomb threats had started at the Majestic and wound their way east on Forty-Fourth Street, through Shubert Alley, and down Forty-Fifth Street past us at the Royale to the Golden Theatre. If memory serves me right, *A Chorus Line* got hit a couple of times.

Our bomb threat was at a matinee during the high school hop. I was backstage calling the technical cues and Lynne Guerra (stage manager) was standing behind me when a substitute house manager came rushing through the pass door and announced, "It is the policy of the Shubert Organization to evacuate the theater when a bomb threat is called in. What is your policy?"

Without missing a beat, Lynne (with Jackie Gleason "away we go" arms) said, "To evacuate the theater."

Lynne went up the stage-right escape stairs and got Jim Weston's attention. Within seconds, Jim went to the mic and, as Vince Fontaine, silenced the band and the dialogue onstage. It sounded something like *Hey, boys and girls and you guys and gals out in the audience, we've got to take a break and leave the hop . . . and the theater as quickly as possible.* Clearly in reaction to the confused faces of the cast staring up at him, he assured them that this wasn't a joke.

We got the houselights on, and the house manager instructed the audience to exit through the doors out to Forty-Fifth Street. The cast and crew also exited to Forty-Fifth and were instructed to gather across the street in the box-office lobby of the Music Box Theatre. As the fire engines and police cars pulled up to the marquee, they found young men and women dressed for a 1950s dance hop scurrying to get out of the way.

Since this was just the next in a sequence of bomb threats, no one seemed particularly worried except one of our cast members, who was visibly nervous. He came over to me and asked if I thought that the cops would go through the dressing rooms. I guessed that they probably would, and he volunteered that they "might" find a couple of joints on his dressing room table.

We eventually got the all clear, and after getting the cast and audience back into the theater, we resumed. That was our one and only bomb threat. We never heard another word about those joints.

RAY DEMATTIS (*Roger*): After the show one night (long into my run), I was leaving by the stage door, and standing right outside was the quintessential '70s dude: tall, long hair, muscle T-shirt, muscles everywhere, bell-bottom jeans, and cowboy boots.

He said, "You're Ray DeMattis!" (and I thought, *Thank you, God*). "My name is Patrick Swayze, but my friends call me Buddy. I'm going to audition to play Danny Zuko, and a mutual friend said you might be able to help me." (Again, *Thank you, God.*) I said, "Yes!"

We worked hard, but when he auditioned, he was turned down. I think it was the deep Texas accent. Anyway, we became friends, and not long after, he was cast as Riff in a production of *West Side Story* somewhere in New Jersey. So of course I went to see it. He was extraordinary! I was sitting next to the very definition of a New Jersey Italian housewife, who was instantly in love with him. In the second act, when Riff gets knifed, she spontaneously yelled out, "No! Not him!"

I went back to work lobbying our stage management, casting agents, and director, and begged that he be seen again. And guess what? They did see him again, and Buddy got cast! His first performance was a Saturday matinee. I was out of the show with a hematoma on my right knee from jumping over Greased Lightning a thousand times. But I was definitely at the theater to cheer him on.

As the power of the theatrical universe would have it, the entire theater seemed to be filled with what had to be housewives from New Jersey. They were his from his opening entrance. And when he appeared bulging out of his track suit in the second act, they went hormonal! I was standing in the back of the house with Ken Waissman and Tom Moore. Tom, more than pleased with his performance, asked, "Where did you find him?" I said, "I didn't. He found me!" Then Ken said the prophetic magic words, "He's going to be a star!"

God bless you, Buddy!

TESSA RICHARDE (*Frenchy*): When the second national had played in San Francisco, Marilu Henner (Marty) was visiting her then boyfriend, Lloyd Alan, who was soon to take over the role of Danny. After seeing one of our rehearsals, Marilu came up to me and told me I was her favorite Marty. Surprised, I asked why. She smiled, "Because your Marty is more like Frenchy." We both laughed.

After the tour ended I got a call from the *Grease* casting director, Vinnie Liff, asking me if I wanted to play the role of Frenchy in the Broadway company. I was confused. When I asked why Frenchy and not Marty, who I had just played on tour, Vinnie replied, "Because you are so much like Frenchy in real life, we just thought you would be perfect for the part!"

So Marty on tour, Frenchy on Broadway. Not many—actually no one—can claim that particular distinction. And as a special bonus of my Broadway run, Patrick Swayze was playing Zuko!

FORBESY RUSSELL: We knew him as Buddy, but *Playbill* listed him as Patrick. Buddy Swayze was a young, innocent Zuko whose sweetness went all the way to his soul. He was a fabulous dancer, spectacularly dazzling everyone at the Rydell dance at the gym, but one night at the end of "Hand Jive," doing his fancy spin-around move, which brought the audience to a frenzy as we all watched and clapped, his happy grin suddenly became a white mask of pain.

Buddy was down. We knew something terrible had happened. It was as clear as having red lights flashing and an alarm blaring. Instinctively we all moved in to help him up, but somehow . . . he slowly rose, in character, and raised his arm high in victory for winning the contest. We all cheered.

Then the Burger Palace Boys gently carried Buddy offstage. He was replaced by his understudy for the rest of the show. It took a few weeks for him to heal and play Danny again. But Buddy had managed to leave the stage in triumph that night.

"Memories Are Made of This"

RAY DEMATTIS: In honor of making their Broadway debut, actors were given house accounts at Sardi's, Joe Allen's, and Charlie's (our favorite), which was right across the street from the Royale.

CYNTHIA DARLOW: Broadway Night at Studio 54 was one of our favorite events.

RAY DEMATTIS: One night it was hosted by the original cast of *Saturday Night Live*.

CYNTHIA DARLOW: And we could walk right in because our press agents, Betty Lee Hunt and Maria Pucci, were their press agents too, and would put us on the VIP list.

RAY DEMATTIS: The Tony Awards featuring Ethel Merman coming down Forty-Fifth Street singing "There's No Business Like Show Business," with Broadway casts coming out of their theaters and following her.

CYNTHIA DARLOW: The Merry *Grease*mas tree dedication in Times Square.

RAY DEMATTIS: The Phoney Awards, our yearly Tony parody awards presentation. The awardee received a clunky '70s pay-phone handset painted gold.

CYNTHIA DARLOW: Held on our anniversary, every Valentine's Day, at Sardi's.

RAY DEMATTIS: Encountering Brooke Shields at a gala years after *Grease*, and her calling to me by name to tell me that she had won the Hula-Hoop contest at one of our anniversary performances when she was twelve, and that I had given her the prize.

CYNTHIA DARLOW: *Grease* Day at Yankee Stadium! Hanging in the locker room and then driving onto the field in Greased Lightning at halftime. Thrilling to see ourselves perform on the jumbotron.

RAY DEMATTIS: I had a fan club! Actually only two girls from Brooklyn: Toni Marie Ornorato and her friend Ginger. They came to Saturday matinees, sat down in front, saw the show over sixty times, and always paid for their tickets! When *Grease* became the longest-running musical on Broadway, the producers gave them tickets to the celebration. They were ecstatic!

CYNTHIA DARLOW: Flying with my fellow Greasers on National Airlines' inaugural flight to Amsterdam for the I♡NY campaign. A party in the sky!

RAY DEMATTIS: And just to cap off with a personal best: I performed *Grease* close to a thousand times.

"Earth Angel"

KATHI MOSS (*Cha-Cha*): I finally left *Grease* in 1977, after five years. Everyone I'd begun the show with was long gone, and many of those I was currently working with likely couldn't understand the gut-wrenching thing it was to see my final day arrive. One person, though, did—Treat Williams. He decided I needed a very special commemoration, and he certainly provided one. Treat had a pilot's license, so to celebrate my long run and departure, he took me flying up and down the New England coast. It was one of those perfect, beautiful days in New York and along the whole East Coast, and the views were dazzling. As was the company. I'll always be grateful to Treat for making that last day so special.

CARRIE ROBBINS (*Costumes*): Kathi Moss played the original Cha-Cha on Broadway, the comic centerpiece of the big dance number, "Hand Jive." She was heavy at that time but unafraid, and she brought great warmth and sympathy to the character, and the audience responses were roars of laughter and love. They felt for her, this vulnerable chubby girl in the bright yellow dress, dancing alone and picking her nose. Kathi was the first Cha-Cha on Broadway, and she made a strong mark and set the standard.

One day, after the show had been running for several years and Kathi had long since moved on to more challenging roles, I got a call from the *Grease* office telling me they had talked to Kathi Moss about coming back to reprise her iconic role. Although she had agreed, it turned out that Kathi had lost a huge amount of weight and obviously would not be putting it back on for *Grease*. "Could you design a fat bodysuit for her?" management asked. I suggested that it would be nice to make a new yellow dress with padding instead. Management agreed to the plan, as did Kathi.

When the work was done, the shop delivered the dress and the padding to the theater, and Kathi put everything on and did the show. I left the theater pleased, feeling like we had achieved what was asked of each of us.

Later I heard the news—Kathi would *not* be playing the part. She just couldn't do it. She could no longer be a fat girl for laughs, even sympathetic laughs. She had obviously worked too long and too hard to lose the weight. Kathi was not going back to that person she played in 1972. Not now, not ever.

CODA: Some years later Kathi became quite ill with a genetic illness. It was relentless. Friends from *Grease* and *Nine* raised money toward her doctor and hospital bills by performing a concert tribute. When I finally went to buy my ticket to the event, it had totally sold out. Of all the great shows I have missed, this is the one I kick myself most for. Every actor, every singer who knew her or had just heard of her was there. In the inside world of Broadway, talent knows talent.

Kathi died in 2013.

Kathi Moss.

34 | Hanging Out with Liz and Dick
March 1976

MATT LANDERS (*Sonny*): Word was out that Richard Burton was coming to see our show *Grease* at the Royale Theatre. It was possible. He was rehearsing next door at the Plymouth to replace Tony Perkins (who replaced Anthony Hopkins) in *Equus*. But why would the great British actor-turned-film-star come to see—of all shows in town—*Grease*?

RAY DEMATTIS (*Roger*): The rumor was that Richard Burton asked his personal assistant, Brook Williams (the son of Welsh playwright and actor Emlyn Williams), what this *Grease* was. Brook raved and said he should absolutely see it.

JOHN FENNESSY (*Assistant Stage Manager*): Over the previous few weeks, I had struck up an acquaintance with Richard Burton's driver, who told me he was going to tell Richard he should see *Grease* before he opened in *Equus*.

MATT LANDERS: Whatever. It seemed unlikely. This was Richard Burton, of the longest-running *Hamlet* in Broadway history. The man who rocketed to international superstardom in the film *Cleopatra* with Liz Taylor. I mean, we were a commercial monster, sure—a big, fat, moneymaking hit—but a universally undisputed artistic lightweight. I was astonished that the living legend Richard Burton would consent to see our show.

MIMI KENNEDY (*Jan*): Luckily, about the same time I made my Broadway debut, Richard Burton came to see *Grease*—to "get to know the neighbors," he graciously explained.

MATT LANDERS: It was early 1976, and Burton's star was decidedly on the descent, his greatest roles behind him, his personal demons legendary.

But in my opinion he was still the embodiment of class and, with the possible exception of Olivier, the greatest living actor.

ELLEN MARCH (*Frenchy*): It wasn't easy, but our stage managers and the *Equus* company worked out Mr. Burton's schedule to make it possible.

RAY DEMATTIS: So one night he came! We were beyond excited.

MIMI KENNEDY: We were beside ourselves.

MATT LANDERS: Ensconced in a big Broadway hit, I was a smug and cocky twenty-three-year-old working actor, and I was thrilled he was coming. I invented for myself a kinship between us. Hey, we were both actors on Broadway. He was a replacement—I was a replacement. I was consumed and convinced by the idea that I, too, was destined for a stellar career in the theater world. I wanted what he had. What actor didn't?

I also wanted him to recognize the potential in me. I needed his approval, his acknowledgment that I, too, would one day "make it."

Just then a sneaky, conniving, insidious little idea formed in my one-track, wanton, grasping actor brain. It was surefire, a slam dunk. I knew from having skimmed his biography that he was a working-class boyo from Wales. Surely he could relate to the street-kid character I was portraying. I also remembered that Burton was not his real name. It was Jenkins. Richard Jenkins. I decided to embellish my role with three additional words.

In the dance hop at the top of Act 2, my character identifies a rival gang member's girlfriend by saying, "She goes steady with the leader of the Flaming Dukes." So that night, who was the leader of the Flaming Dukes? Why, none other than Dick Jenkins, of course! What the hell, I'll alter the line to "She goes steady with the leader of the Flaming Dukes—dirty Dick Jenkins!" Brilliant!

I could be fired. I didn't care. I was resolved. *The play's the thing wherein I'll catch the notice of the king!* Or something like that.

The fateful night arrives. Our spies (the understudies) reconnoiter and confirm Burton is indeed in the house. We even knew the seat number.

RAY DEMATTIS: He was hosted in the stage manager's office, then shown to his seat just as the houselights dimmed so that he wouldn't be recognized and besieged by the audience. And then at intermission, he was whisked backstage. He was carefully protected throughout the evening.

MATT LANDERS: *To do it or not to do it—that is the question.* I can barely contain my excitement. I notice the show is moving very fast tonight. Everyone is picking up their cues and really overacting.

We are finally in the dance scene. I don't dare look out at the seventh row, aisle seat. My cue approaches. My pulse is doing its own *rama lama lama*. Cue! *Can I do it?* Conscience does make cowards of us all—but not me! Yes, I say the words: "dirty Dick Jenkins." The die is cast. Sure, I get some weird looks from the other guys in the scene. But we keep going.

RAY DEMATTIS: After the show he came onstage to greet us all. I—well everybody, actually—was in absolute awe. *Are you friggin' kidding me? C'mon!* To this formerly fat Italian kid, I was meeting British royalty!

MATT LANDERS: After the show none of us changes out of wardrobe. We race to the backstage area. There he is. Himself. Shorter than I imagined but still, larger than life. He is cool. Tan, trim. Rugged, craggy features. Bright, darting eyes. He wears an all-black Nehru suit, the kind the Beatles made famous.

MIMI KENNEDY: We gathered onstage to hear him praise us effusively and tell us that in England, there were few actors who could do it all as he'd just seen us do: sing, dance, and act brilliantly, all at the same time! We glowed.

MATT LANDERS: As uncool as he is cool and in the spirit of our show, I shout, "Hey!" Startled, he jumps around. I grab his hand. Someone snaps a

Richard Burton backstage with the *Grease* cast.

picture. I ask, "Did you hear me say your name?" With an abjectly disapproving, withering look he mumbles, "Yeh."

Oops. I realize too late, of course, that he is a purist with the highest respect for stagecraft and stage etiquette. I may have achieved the opposite of my desire to impress him.

JOHN FENNESSY: Richard Burton's verdict on *Grease*: "I was helpless with mirth."

MATT LANDERS: Someone asks if he really liked the show. He says yes, he did indeed. So much so that he is going to be sure to have Elizabeth attend soon. He didn't need to say the rest of her name. First the king and now the queen!

Then Richard Burton singles me out (*gulp*), and no, he does not chide me with Hamlet's advice to players, "Let those that play your clowns speak no more than is set down for them. . . . That's villainous, and shows a most pitiful ambition in the fool that uses it." No. Thankfully, and in the presence of our stage manager, he tells me to be sure to also put Elizabeth's name in the show tomorrow! In response to the stage manager's puzzled look, I shrug. What could I do? It was a royal command.

Matt Landers eyes his king, Richard Burton.

Richard Burton and Matt Landers.

MIMI KENNEDY: The next day there was a handwritten letter on the backstage bulletin board saying how much he'd loved the show. He could not have been more generous in his praise. He said he hoped Elizabeth could see it because she would need entertainment in the evenings while he was performing *Equus*.

RAY DEMATTIS: After his visit Lynne Guerra suggested we all chip in and send him an opening-night gift. The gift? A tortoise-shell comb from Tiffany's with a sterling silver handle engraved with BEST WISHES FROM THE GREASE CAST.

Soon after we sent the gift, we arrived at the theater to find another note from Mr. Burton tacked to the callboard with an invitation to join him and Elizabeth (yes, *that* Elizabeth) for dinner at Sardi's between Wednesday's matinee and evening shows!

MICHAEL MARTORELLA (*Production Stage Manager*): The note went on to say that Elizabeth would like to see the evening performance and then come backstage to greet the cast.

RAY DEMATTIS: We were thrilled!

Richard Burton

Sat., 14th., Feb.., 1976.

Dear Cast of "Grease" and Everybody,

Sorry I couldn't accept your marvellous invitation which I meant to, but I played the matinee this afternoon and the crowd was so great outside the stage door that I couldn't make it to Sardi's. Had to get police help! (Said he showing off!)

However — how about Sardi's next Wednesday? Elizabeth will be here — she arrives tomorrow — and we'll all get drunk!

Affectionately,

Richard B.

The invitation!

Dinner at Sardi's with Liz and Dick

MATT LANDERS: The day of the Richard Burton / Elizabeth Taylor dinner at Sardi's has arrived. Richard is here on time, the perfect host. He has a woman with him—a tall, beautiful blonde. He introduces her as Susan Hunt. Does this mean Elizabeth won't be coming? I had read in the rags that Liz and Dick were first separated, then divorced, and possibly getting married again. Where they were in all that on this given day is hard to say. Susan is lovely, and the Sardi's staff is all over them, and us. We arrive at the tables and who else is there? Barry Bostwick, the Tony-nominated original lead in our show. He has been out of the show for two years, but news travels fast and (who can blame him?) he also wants to be here with the legends.

MICHAEL MARTORELLA: Richard Burton, his friend Susan, stage managers Lynne Guerra and John Fennessy, director Tom Moore, about eight cast members, and I were sitting at two round tables in the middle of the first-floor dining room at Sardi's. Directly across the table from me were Richard and Susan. There was one empty chair. And it was next to me.

MATT LANDERS: In my own selfish way, I hustle a seat right next to Burton and Susan. He is the king of cool once again, dressed a little more mainstream today in a blue blazer and open shirt.

MIMI KENNEDY: I unfortunately arrived too late to be at Richard Burton's table and was seated at a smaller table, with my chair's back right up against whoever was sitting opposite Burton, so I wasn't even facing him. This was a major disappointment, but I consoled myself with the fact that the person to my back was his new girlfriend, Susan, and if I was quiet I could eavesdrop on the celebrity chat.

MATT LANDERS: For small talk I fall back on my familiarity with his biography (which I never actually read but heard about from a guy who did). "Richard," I say, "is it true that you once bet someone that you could drink a bottle of booze during a performance of *Camelot* and that no one would notice?" Mr. Tact.

Silence at the table. Burton, who by now surely cannot believe there actually exists a creature such as yours truly, allows himself a little smile. He takes a moment and I think, *Maybe I will be beheaded or at least banished.* He replies, "Actually the wager was with five gents. Two hundred dollars a man, that I could drink an entire fifth of vodka during the show and that Julie Andrews would not know I was drunk." Add to the silence the looks of astonishment and dropped jaws of everyone at the table.

I say, "Yeah? And . . ."

"I drank a fifth during the first act and another fifth during the second. In order to win, I was required to go into Julie's dressing room and ask her what she thought of our performance." We all groaned, imagining the regal Burton in his Arthurian drag tottering into Guinevere's digs hammered. At our table he continued, "'How do you think the performance was this afternoon?

Did you think I was a little slow on the uptake?' She replied, 'No, actually I thought it was quite better than usual.'"

RAY DEMATTIS: Needless to say, we all laughed hysterically.

MATT LANDERS: *Wow, Richard Burton rocks.* And here I thought I was being such a bad actor by adding three little words. This guy did a show adding thirty-three little shots of vodka. My feeling of kinship with him grew. We were both a couple of devil-may-care, rowdy guys who tried to insert a little life into our long-run-itis. He in *Camelot,* me in *Grease.*

RAY DEMATTIS: As we all animatedly chatted away, Mr. Burton's assistant ran up to Richard and said quietly, "She's on her way."

MATT LANDERS: Burton displays a mild look of concern. He gives Susan a little nod and says, "Elizabeth is coming." I'm thinking, *Uh-oh. Let's see him get out of this. Here is Dicky with another woman, and Elizabeth will be here any second. He is so screwed.*

Wrong again. There is no look of panic on his face. (Not like the one I had when my brother and my best friend threw me a surprise party and invited all the girls from my little black book.) Nope. He is a man with a plan. He gives the high sign to his aide, who brings an additional chair and places it next to Barry Bostwick. Susan gives Richard a peck on the cheek, vacates her seat adjacent him, and moves to the other side of the table. Smooth.

RAY DEMATTIS: The blonde gracefully took her place just as the Sardi's doors were pushed open by paparazzi backing into the restaurant while photographing *her.* Vincent Sardi threw the paparazzi out and, accompanied by her bodyguard, Elizabeth Taylor swept into the room.

MICHAEL MARTORELLA: The red-jacketed Sardi's waiters formed a double line facing each other, extending all the way from the front door to our table. When the front door opened, Elizabeth Taylor made her entrance. Jaws dropped throughout the restaurant as Elizabeth made her way to our table.

MIMI KENNEDY: Suddenly all the energy in the room seemed to tilt toward the door, and throughout the restaurant there was a flurry of activity. Elizabeth had arrived!

MATT LANDERS: Coming through the restaurant were two big guys in suits, escorting a mink-coat-bedecked, gloriously smashed Elizabeth Taylor.

MIMI KENNEDY: As Vincent Sardi led her through the room of awed diners, Susan quietly appeared at our table.

MICHAEL MARTORELLA: Oh yeah, that empty seat next to me was instantly filled by Richard Burton's friend Susan.

MATT LANDERS: Richard Burton stands, as we all do, and he gallantly offers his chair to Liz (the one next to mine!). He takes Susan's former chair, and we all sit.

MIMI KENNEDY: Liz took the vacated seat directly behind me. I heard every word, beginning with her call for a bottle of Johnnie Walker Red. It was clearly not her first cocktail of the evening.

RAY DEMATTIS: When she joined us, Elizabeth was in high dudgeon about one of the photographers, Ron Galella (who *Newsweek* dubbed "Paparazzo Extraordinaire").

MATT LANDERS: Can you believe this? Now Liz Taylor turns to me, caresses my cheek, gives it a playful little slap, and says, "Blue Eyes." A waiter is there instantly with not one but two Jack Daniel's on the rocks for the lovely Elizabeth. I take a good, full look at her, and it is true—her eyes are violet. Talk about court intrigue.

ELLEN MARCH: An amazing, surreal, fun time, and my lucky night. I got to sit right across from Elizabeth Taylor! I remember staring at her luscious cleavage and into her truly violet, gorgeous eyes while my dinner was no doubt dribbling down my chin most of the night.

KATHI MOSS (*Cha-Cha*): High point of the evening? Elizabeth needed to use the bathroom, and I was elected to accompany/protect her. I had no idea how necessary that would be. Women in the ladies' room behaved like jackals—some even shoving *Playbills* under the stall for her to autograph. I'd always wanted to be famous—what actor doesn't?—but I think I knew at that moment that I never wanted to be *that* famous.

RAY DEMATTIS: There was a silent agreement among the cast that at some point in the meal, we would all change places so that each of us could experience her. When it was my turn, she was complaining that while Richard was working, she was left all alone and stuck in her hotel, that she didn't have many friends in New York, and that being with young New York Broadway actors was great fun.

I don't know where the hell I got the chops to say it, but I did. "Well, our show is dark on Monday, so while he's working, we'll get some cast members together. I'll make pizza, and we can all hang out at my place!" To my shock she immediately said, "Yes! That would be wonderful! But you can't tell any press!" *Are you friggin' kidding me?* I was ecstatic. Mimi Kennedy grabbed my leg under the table and mouthed, "Me!"

JOHN FENNESSY: Amazingly fun night—all kinds of things to watch!

BARRY BOSTWICK (*Zuko*): I spent a good bit of the evening flirting across the table with a pretty young woman named Susan. I didn't find out till a few days later that Susan was Burton's new companion. I had wondered why she hadn't seemed that interested in me! This Rialto lothario was clueless and totally out of his depth.

MATT LANDERS: Burton now turns his attention to three eager beauties from the show and chats charmingly. Bostwick is charmingly and eagerly engrossed in conversation with Susan. And I am trying to determine if Elizabeth Taylor is just having a fun little flirt or is seriously coming on to me. *Really?* Of the three groupings, I am the one most decidedly in over his head.

Unable to hold my gaze into the depth of those violet eyes, I notice Burton looking back at us. He catches my eye and winks. I detect a little sadness in his smile. The romantic in me is convinced Elizabeth Taylor is the true love of his life. I have my out. My path is clear. I can't betray my new pal—my king.

BARRY BOSTWICK: I could see my portrait on the wall above where we were sitting, but as much as I wanted to, I didn't point it out. When Richard turned to me and said, "I hear you're like a younger version of me," I still didn't point to the drawing, but I did "Wonder What the King Is Doing Tonight." He was sitting to my right, and all evening he made me feel like a prince.

Liz and Dick and the *Grease* cast at Sardi's.

MIMI KENNEDY: Elizabeth was raucous and funny, and we leaned close to hear her stories and comments. But she seemed equally interested in hearing about us—our lives, our backgrounds, how it felt to be young and in love and acting on Broadway. It amazed and elevated us to find that Liz, perhaps the most enviably famous actress in the world, was doing a role reversal. She—or so it seemed—envied *us.*

MATT LANDERS: I politely excuse myself from the table and reluctantly take my leave from Lady Elizabeth. I make my way to a bank of telephones and place a call. While I wait for the connection, I look back across Sardi's to our table and savor the scene.

"Hello, Mom? Guess with whom your son the actor is lunching at Sardi's? Liz and Dick! Liz and Dick who? Liz and Dick . . . Jenkins!"

MICHAEL MARTORELLA: Now for the fun part: How do you sneak Elizabeth Taylor into the Royale Theatre? Fennessy and I had devised a plan—walkie-talkies. Fennessy would go back to the theater and alert us when the show was about to begin. It was arranged that the band would play the opening alma mater several times through, without the actors, as the houselights dimmed, and then Elizabeth, her bodyguard, Barry, and I would walk down the aisle to the producers' house seats. Sounds simple, right?

ELLEN MARCH: We never thought it would really happen! But it did. Needless to say, we were very, very excited. Lynne had been told to have a bottle ready so that Ms. Taylor could have a cocktail at intermission and when she came backstage after the curtain call. Jack Daniel's was the lady's choice.

KATHI MOSS: When you're talking stars, no one—maybe ever—was bigger than Elizabeth Taylor. When she, then at her publicity height, came to the show, everyone went berserk.

BARRY BOSTWICK: It was my pleasure to accompany Elizabeth to the performance of *Grease.* I felt like her bodyguard the whole time.

RAY DEMATTIS: Unlike with Burton, there was no waiting for the houselights to dim for Liz Taylor. In full light, she took her orchestra seat, and not unexpectedly the house went crazy!

MICHAEL MARTORELLA: Well, it just wasn't possible for Elizabeth Taylor to simply walk down the aisle of a Broadway theater, or anywhere else, unnoticed. Audience members instantly recognized her, and the murmurs quickly spread throughout the theater. *Time to crank up the band!* The show started, the actors began to sing the alma mater, and like every performance of *Grease,* the enthusiasm of the cast and audience was a match for this most extraordinary distraction.

MATT LANDERS: As I had promised the king, I have the perfect spot to work in Elizabeth's name: the picnic scene at the end of Act 1. It is a greaser picnic in the park. My character, Sonny, so excited while looking at a borrowed fan magazine, crumples the pages. His girlfriend, Frenchy, says, "Quit wrinkling my magazine, Sonny." And I say (with singular intensity), "I was just looking at Shelly Fabares's jugs!" I kid you not—that is the actual line. An easy substitution: "I was just looking at Elizabeth Taylor's jugs!" *Oh, she's gonna love this.*

MICHAEL MARTORELLA: As we were closing in on the end of the first act, Elizabeth, her bodyguard, Barry, and I made it to the pass-through door to the backstage and spent the intermission in the stage manager's office, where we talked about the show as the cast and crew kept popping in and out to say hello to an unfailingly gracious Elizabeth Taylor.

BARRY BOSTWICK: At the intermission the stage managers, as instructed, had a bottle of Jack Daniel's waiting for our arrival.

MICHAEL MARTORELLA: We made it back to the seats for the second act and then backstage again during the curtain calls. Elizabeth met with the cast, sharing her appreciation for their performances and her thanks for a wonderful evening in the theater.

RAY DEMATTIS: As the house doors opened, the paparazzi came running in and tried to follow her onstage. The house staff and ushers shooed them away. As we gathered onstage to greet her, she beamed at me and said, "Honey, you stay with me!" *Are you friggin' kidding me?*

MATT LANDERS: When Liz sees me, she grabs my arm and says, "Blue Eyes!" Then with a pained expression, "Why did you say that about me in the show?" "Oh, you caught that?" "Caught it? The whole audience caught it!" "It did get a pretty big reaction," I reply with a helpless shrug. "Richard made me do it." She gives me a mock slap and says, "He would!"

ELLEN MARCH: We were basking in the glamour of it all. It must have been at least forty-five minutes before the staff thought it was safe for her to leave the theater. In order to avoid the massive crowds, she was to exit through the Forty-Fifth Street door across the stage.

RAY DEMATTIS: I stayed right next to her, and as she and I were crossing the stage to the exit, she stopped midstage and said to me, "I've never been on a Broadway stage." (*The Little Foxes* came much later.) Then she crossed down center stage and said to the empty house, "To be, or not to be . . ." and then turned back to me and said, "How does it go?" I said, ". . . that is the question." She repeated the full line and then howled!

ELLEN MARCH: The only light onstage was the traditional ghost light. As Liz and her entourage walked across the stage, she took hold of the ghost light, looked out at the orchestra, and said, *Oh, the theater . . . to be or not to be . . . there's nothing like the theater.*

Or something like that. Who can remember? It was Elizabeth Taylor! The moment was very dramatic, maybe even a little over the top, but it was thrilling!

When her security men opened the Forty-Fifth Street door to escort her to the limo, we were shocked to see there were still hundreds of fans waiting, screaming and begging for her autograph.

MICHAEL MARTORELLA: *Now what?* There was no way we were going out the door leading straight on to Forty-Fifth Street. There was only one clear path. The Royale stage door in the alley was close to the Majestic stage door. Our getaway team made its way through the alley into the Majestic and exited through the Majestic lobby on Forty-Fourth Street, safely leading Elizabeth to a prearranged spot where her car was now waiting.

RAY DEMATTIS: As we walked to the exit, she said, "Honey, I'll see you Monday! Give Brook your address." When we opened the door, another group of fans rushed toward her, but Liz's bodyguard deftly got her through the crowd and into the limo. As it pulled away she waved at me. *Are you friggin' kidding me?*

MICHAEL MARTORELLA: When the car drove off, we made our way back through both theaters to Forty-Fifth Street, where I let the waiting, soon-to-be-disappointed *Grease* audience know that Ms. Taylor had already left the theater. I walked across the street to our after-show hangout, Charlie's, to join the cast and crew and gleefully share stories of our day with Elizabeth.

ELLEN MARCH: The next day on the bulletin board, there was another handwritten letter to the cast and stage manager. This one said, "Elizabeth LOVED the show!" We were as giddy as teenagers. Over the moon!

MATT LANDERS: So forget about it. Liz and Dick and me! We're all goofing around together offstage and on—on Broadway! I've made it, haven't I?

RAY DEMATTIS: And Monday night? We found out that she and Richard had a big fight over that blond woman, and she bolted out of New York and back to L.A. Monday afternoon. *Are you friggin' kidding me?*

35 | *"Words of Love"*

FRANK PIEGARO (*Zuko*): On the first day of rehearsal for the Guber and Gross tour, I was introduced to Shannon Fanning. That was April 1, 1975. Who knew she would become my Sandy for life?

For starters, professionally she was open and easy to work with. Truly her innocence and honesty rivaled any Sandy I had worked with. But these were qualities Shannon displayed offstage too. For me there wasn't too much not to like/love about her. Oh yeah, I did leave one thing out. She was married.

Initially I tried to approach our relationship totally on a professional level. But some things are meant to be. Shannon and I were a perfect match, always on the same page. How could a guy from a tough city like Newark, New Jersey, meet a girl from a city like Albany, New York, and have it seem so right?

Throughout the tour I blocked out any idea about the two of us. Hell, I knew it was wrong, so I went about my business, focusing on the show.

But as fate would have it, after that harrowing, storm-tossed plane ride to Norfolk, when Shannon and I were alone in our hotel, we finally kissed. Well, the stage thing ain't nothing like the real thing. *What the hell do we do now?*

We were met with extreme criticism from everyone. We didn't care. In the *Grease* family, for some it was gossip, for others it was an affront. An affront to whom? We had family we had to confront with our love for each other. And how about Shannon's husband? Hard emotionally? You bet.

But through the good and bad of life, we could always do what we had to, as long as we were together. Later, Shannon's belief in me carried us through

Frank Piegaro and Shannon Fanning.

Shannon and Frank have been married for forty-five years—*Grease's* longest run!

an awful professional time in our lives. She's my best friend and I'm hers. If you don't marry a girl like Shannon, don't get married.

LISA RAGGIO (*Frenchy*): *Grease* in the round: I kept thinking, *How in hell are we going to get the Burger Palace and Greased Lightning up and down those ramps?* So I was already nervous and got to rehearsal early; not many were there yet. Suddenly a guy rushes in. He's kind of stocky, maybe a jock, with blondish/brown hair, and he's carrying a gym bag. He heads over to me and says, "Is this where practice is happening?" I look at him and say, "You mean, rehearsal?" He says, "Yeah, yeah, that." I nod yes, and he goes away but comes right back. "Where's the locker room?" he asks. I say, "There is no locker room." He goes away, comes back, and says, "Who are you playing in the show?" I tell him Frenchy. He asks, "Have you done the show before? Where?" The questions were endless. I wasn't amused; I was annoyed. He then looked me straight in the eye and said, "You'll be living with me soon," and walked away. I called after, "Fat chance."

By the middle of the week, he was still very annoying but rudely amusing. By week two he became funnier and a bit less annoying. It seems something was going on between this pesky guy and me.

I had never known anyone like Danny Jacobson, and I was soon finding his brand of wackiness irresistible. By the time we hit the next stop on the tour, his first-day-of-rehearsal prophecy had come true. I was living with him! I really don't even know how it happened. Maybe it was that he had given me nicknames like "Pumpy"—short for "Pumpy Wumpy Pumpkin." Of the many things that always kept me up at night, the main one became Jacobson.

SUSAN McANENY (*Patty*): A year before I even knew of a show called *Grease*, I went to see a psychic who told me I would get a dog named Charlie, I would be single within the year, and there was a lot of grease around my aura. I thought she might be talking about my then boyfriend, who had Greek ancestry, but she said no, it was very specifically not Greece she was seeing in my aura. It was *grease*—as in oily, greasy grease.

A year later Charlie the dog was gone, along with the ex-boyfriend, and I was playing Patty Simcox in the first bus and truck company of *Grease*.

Two years later I was married to Larry Horowitz, who played Kenickie in the show, and nine years later I married Jerry Boyd, who had played guitar in the pit band. No Greeks, but plenty of *Grease* to last me for many years.

GEGE MARTORELLA (*Stage Manager*): When my husband, Michael, told me the producers wanted me to make my debut as the assistant stage manager on their next tour, it didn't take me long to say yes. Little did I know what unique problems lay ahead!

MICHAEL MARTORELLA (*Production Stage Manager*): Gege and I shared duties like most good stage-managing teams.

GEGE MARTORELLA: We didn't always see eye to eye as husband and wife, but when it came to the tour, our relationship was professional and successful.

MICHAEL MARTORELLA: We worked well as a team.

GEGE MARTORELLA: After a couple of months on tour, I am sure you can imagine the actors were getting very close. So close in fact that at one point, there was a case of an "unexplainable itching" making its way through the closely knit company. It is true that on rare occasions this itchiness can spread through clothes and linens, but, well, I think you get the picture.

MICHAEL MARTORELLA: Gege came to me with the news. "And I'm supposed to think that the 'unexplainable itching' is a result of the restrooms or the sheets? Who's kidding who?"

GEGE MARTORELLA: "What do you want me to do about it? You're in charge!" After a few minutes of unrepeatable outbursts, we calmed down and gathered our professional demeanor to present to the cast. I gave Michael the special opportunity of talking to the guys, and I, in turn, was given the delightful task of talking to the girls. Remember, it was 1977.

MICHAEL MARTORELLA: I remember bringing the guys together to get a better understanding of what they thought might be the cause. I patiently (not always easy for me, which Gege can affirm) listened to a variety of absurd reasons, like "Maybe it's the toilets" and "I just woke up one day itching." My response was the phrase "Uh-huh" over and over again.

GEGE MARTORELLA: I was twenty-seven years old. The girls and I were all about the same age, and I wasn't really sure where to begin, when one of the more experienced cast members came to the rescue by suggesting an over-the-counter remedy. I quickly ended the meeting and ran to the closest pharmacy, returning with the goods that did the job. The unexplainable itch soon became a thing of the past, and as always, at 8:07 PM the houselights dimmed. "As I Go Traveling Down Life's Highway" ("Alma Mater") began, and we were back on track.

————————————

LORELLE BRINA (*Rizzo*): When I played Rizzo on Broadway, Kenickie was played by Danny Jacobson. He played my boyfriend onstage and was my boyfriend offstage as well, making this even more emotionally complex. Danny is an extremely talented, funny human being, and nothing amused him more than to crack up his fellow cast members or the guys in the pit. I loved that he could make me laugh—offstage. Onstage? Not so much.

One afternoon during our fight scene in the park, Danny raised himself up when he should have been down, and my fast-moving elbow smashed into his head, sending the bottom half of his nose over to the left side of his face. The sound was loud and unmistakable. Danny stood in a daze and, with both hands covering his face, walked offstage.

I was very upset that I had hurt him. I was very upset that he had put his face in the way of my elbow. And I was also upset that I was upset with him, because, hey, he was the guy with the broken nose! Danny was taken straight to the ER while the rest of us, shocked and Kenickie-less, were left onstage to finish Act 1. Greg Zadikov went on in Act 2.

Danny returned to the theater during the evening performance, bruised and bandaged, to let us know that he was OK and to show off his new look. He missed a number of performances and then, just to remind us, continued to wear what turned into a frayed and tattered little scrap of a Band-Aid across the bridge of his nose for a long, long time. Annoying . . . but funny!

FRANK PIEGARO: A unique stop on the Guber and Gross tour was playing the Shady Grove Music Fair, a five-thousand-seat theater in the round. It was the first time *Grease* had ever been presented in that format.

Everything changes in the round—even the costume changes. We all would run up aisles, stripping off the clothes from one scene to finish changing behind a booth at the top of another aisle, and then run down to the stage for the next scene. In the round the audience has very close contact with the performer, and one night, on my way up the aisle after the curtain calls, I got attacked by a group of female fans who congratulated me by trying to rip my shirt off!

As if *Grease* isn't strenuous enough, running to make an entrance on the other side of an arena is challenging. PB&J in the morning, ice cream sundaes in the afternoon, and I was still losing weight. Somehow two female fans found out about my dilemma and at least three, maybe four times a week they came backstage with a large layer cake and my favorite—brownies. They were soon dubbed "the Cake Sisters."

In Pennsylvania we checked into our hotel and went to a sound check, and then Cosie and I went to the King of Prussia Mall for something to eat. Suddenly he grabbed my arm and yelled, "Run!"

I said, "What?"

"Run! It's the Cake Sisters!"

They had followed the show from Maryland to Pennsylvania, this time with their husbands. Earlier they'd gone to the hotel where we were staying, looking for me. And guess what they brought? A cake and brownies—pretty sweet!

Frank Piegaro and the Cake Sisters: Kathy Johnson (L) and Leslie Homann (R).

JOY RINALDI (*Marty*): Sex, drugs, and rock 'n' roll—there was a lot of it! After all, it was the '70s, and we were all mostly in our twenties. Many years later we girls got together and took a little survey on who we had slept with during our time in the show, to figure out which guy had slept with the most women. It was an anonymous survey. We just put the names of all the men of *Grease* we had slept with in a big jar and started counting.

Who was the winner?

Imagine our surprise to find out it was one of the Doodys. The *Doodys*! I'll never tell.

MARA JOYCE (*Frenchy*): The on-the-road romances and crushes were endless. We were innocent and young and just having a good time. I loved, loved, loved being on the road. I loved going to the theater every night. Loved putting on my costume and makeup. Loved playing the show. Loved special appearances, like being on *The Mike Douglas Show* in Philly, where we performed "Freddy, My Love" and "Beauty School Dropout." In fact, I loved everything about all of it. I felt like a star! I loved that too.

36 | *Playing the Odds in Las Vegas*

Summer 1977

MICHAEL MARTORELLA (*Production Stage Manager*): The second national tour had originally been scheduled to finish up in San Francisco, but we got word that the Bagdad Theatre at the Aladdin Hotel in Las Vegas had been booked, and the show would extend. We were asked to extend with it.

Las Vegas only wanted "tab" productions, running no more than ninety minutes, so that they could have two performances a night with no intermission. The two-hour show would have to be shortened, the scenery would have to be modified to fit into the smaller space, and there would be a whole new Aladdin hotel crew.

GEGE MARTORELLA (*Stage Manager*): Michael returned to New York for two weeks to supervise and rehearse a new *Grease* tour, while Tom Moore and I went on to Las Vegas. Tom hated Vegas, but except for the fact that it was Vegas, things went very well.

JIM SHANKMAN (*Sonny*): The Bagdad Theatre at the Aladdin Hotel was in fact just a glorified cocktail lounge. The show jarringly went straight from the park ("We Go Together") to the prom ("Born to Hand Jive"). They couldn't have an intermission because the audience would be away too long from the blackjack tables and slots. You could often hear the activity on the casino floor as we were performing. When Rizzo cranked it up to sing "There Are Worse Things I Could Do," the cash register started ringing up the patrons' tabs—*ding, ding, ding, ding, ding*—as the saxophone wailed and Rizzo poured out her heart . . . *ding, ding, ding, ding.*

LLOYD ALAN (*Zuko*): It's opening day in Las Vegas and, like any responsible actor, I was checking my props before the show. While looking over the

287

Mike Martorella (production stage manager) gives notes to Jim Shankman (Sonny).

new Greased Lightning, I noticed there was no on-off switch like we had in New York. I promptly went to one of the crew guys and said, "There's no on-off switch on the car." His response was "Yeah, and?" At which point I said, "Well, it would be a lot safer and make me a lot more comfortable if we could put one in." He said in that way stagehands do, "Don't worry about it. It'll be fine. When you drive it out, just put it in neutral. It ain't going anywhere."

I said, "Well, OK." But I thought, *Well, not OK. Not OK at all!*

So the opening night is going well, and it's time for the drive-in scene. As usual I drive the car out, put it in neutral, and start the scene. I get big laughs, and I forget about the car. I'm wrestling with Sandy for a kiss and unbeknownst to me, my knee kicks the gearshift out of neutral. Nothing happens, so I notice nothing.

Now Sandy gets out and slams the door, hitting me in man's most uncomfortable spot, and as usual I do the slide under the dash, and my knee hits the accelerator. *Oh shit,* my worst fears. I feel the car lurch off the stage onto the cocktail tables right up against the stage. It was Vegas—nightclub seating. I can't see anything—I'm still under the dash—but I can hear people screaming, glasses breaking, and chaos everywhere. I lift myself up from under the dash just in time to see Sandy running off the stage screaming. Kind of appropriate for the scene . . . except the screaming part.

I get out of the car as I'm blocked to do, and I see everyone in the wings motioning to me to get off the stage. I don't. The show-must-go-on thing kicks in. I motion to the orchestra to start playing as I reach under the car for the mic to sing "Alone at a Drive-In Movie." The mic is smashed flat, but miraculously it still works.

As I'm singing "I'm . . . all alone," all I can think is *How am I going to get the car back onstage?* I finish the song, get back in the car, nervously shift it into reverse and, miracle of miracles, the car backs up onstage and I drive it into the wings as if it were all part of the show.

A new on-off switch was installed the next day.

CHERI EICHEN (*Frenchy*): When we got to Las Vegas, we had to rehearse a whole new version of the show. So I get a second chance, a do-over, a fresh start! The new version is what they call a tab version, which roughly translates to cutting the dialogue in half and double-timing the dances to squeeze in two shows a night. My hand jive fails at high speeds. "Freddy, My Love" still eludes me. Doody still wishes I were Broadway Frenchy. Jan still shuns me, and my stomach is now beyond help.

In Las Vegas, night is day. I live alone in a cinder-block room with fluorescent lights at the D-I 500 (*D-I* for "Desert Inn"). I am lonely. I bring my cats to live with me at the D-I. It doesn't help. I am lonelier. I invite my best friend to come see me. He dates Teen Angel and in time moves in with Cha-Cha. I'm the loneliest. And my cinder block smells like a litter box.

I become so accustomed to seeing my reflection in a red Frenchy flip that when I take off the wig, my own hair looks approximately the color and shape of what we now recognize as a poo emoji. I dye my 'fro Frenchy red. Now I look like Bozo the Clown.

LORI ADA JAROSLOW (*Understudy/Jan*): After a somewhat magical tour across the country, *Grease* sat in Las Vegas for a chunk of time. There I upped both my blackjack game and my Black Russian consumption. Most nights I would sit at a blackjack table drinking and playing till the sun came up.

In Vegas I took flute lessons, had a scary car accident because I was driving hungover, and nearly starved to death because now that I was an actress, I felt it was incumbent upon me to be skinny. Jan's onstage Twinkies and potato chips were often my only repast for the day. An eating disorder goes nicely with a drinking disorder, and I was far more interested in Kahlúa, quaaludes, and junk food.

CHERI EICHEN: The Vegas run ends at Christmastime. The show is closing. Some of the cast members are going to Broadway. Others are going out with the bus and truck tour. I am going home.

Thanks to the miracle of per diem, I have saved enough to buy a new Honda Civic. I drive back to L.A. in my new car with my new red hair, my two old cats, and a bunch of new lessons I never expected to learn.

I learned I could live alone in a flophouse on Geary and in a cinder block off the Strip. I learned to French inhale, hand jive, and hold for a laugh. I learned that the preshow songs you hear over a dressing-room speaker at half hour stay with you for life. And I learned that if I ever go looking for my heart's desire at a non-Equity open call for a national tour, there's no place like home.

37 | The Great New York Blackout
July 13, 1977

STEVE BECKLER (*Production Stage Manager*): It had been a particularly good two-show Wednesday at the Royale, and our well-oiled production was running along smoothly. Lynne Guerra (stage manager) was on deck, and John Fennessy (assistant stage manager) was on book calling the show. I was on the second floor talking to Greg Zadikov, one of our understudies.

FORBESY RUSSELL (*Understudy/Sandy*): It was a hot summer night, Saturday, July 13, 1977. I was on as Sandy opposite Treat Williams as Danny Zuko. Good show, good audience.

STEVE BECKLER: As Greg and I talked, I heard the transition music into the drive-in movie scene.

JOHN FENNESSY (*Assistant Stage Manager*): I'm calling the show from stage left. Greased Lightning pulls into the drive-in movie scene, and as it begins I notice that the stage is not quite as bright as it should be. There's also something odd about the sound. I call Jimmy Limberg on the soundboard at the back of the theater: "What's going on?" Jimmy comes back with an answer you never want to hear: "Fenn, I have no idea in hell."

DANNY JACOBSON (*Kenickie*): As I grabbed the phone to call up for the result of the Roosevelt daily double horse race, I noticed the stage lights fading. I grabbed the doorman's flashlight. He was listening to the Mets game and naturally was asleep.

JEREMY STONE (*Music Director*): *Grease* was in the middle of the second act just as Sandy abandons Danny at the drive-in movie, when the movie soundtrack ("Look, Sheila! . . . ") started to slow down and then stopped altogether. Immediately the stage lights dimmed and went out, leaving the theater lit only by automatic, battery-powered emergency lights.

FORBESY RUSSELL: The audio *slooowed* way down, and then the whole theater went dark except for a few dim safety lights. What was happening? Treat and I waited for the lights to come back on—they always did—but not this time.

STEVE BECKLER: Through the window I saw the marquee of the Imperial Theatre directly across from the Royale glowing in all its glory, when suddenly it was gone! I rushed closer just in time to see Forty-Fifth Street go dark from west to east as the blackout sped toward Times Square.

JOHN FENNESSY: Then it occurs to me . . . there's something familiar here. I whirl around and race to the pass door and shove it open onto Forty-Fifth Street. I look down the block toward Times Square, and there it is, boys and girls, "the Great Black Way."

JEREMY STONE: At around 9:30 PM, a series of lightning strikes and cascading malfunctions culminated in a citywide power outage that lasted well into the next day.

DAVID PAYMER (*Sonny*): When the blackout plunged *Grease*'s 2,251st performance into darkness, there was a collective groan from the audience and total confusion onstage as the actors retreated to the wings, stumbling all over each other.

TREAT WILLIAMS (*Zuko*): A few emergency lights went on, but we were mostly in the dark. The audience was confused and a little scared.

STEVE BECKLER: Carefully but very quickly, I made my way down the dressing room stairs (dimly lit by emergency light) to the stage and the call desk. As I looked out onstage at the very dark scenery, I could see John Fennessy at the edge of the stage speaking to the audience. He was in profile, bathed in the pale glow from the emergency lights out in the theater. John was assuring the audience, telling them we'd just had a power failure and asking them please not to leave as we would be resuming the show momentarily.

JOHN FENNESSY: I ran onstage and said to the confused audience, "Guess what?" And then a few words more.

STEVE BECKLER: By the time I reached Lynne Guerra, she had already developed a plan. All available understudies, stagehands, dressers, and so on would have a flashlight; the solo piano, drums, and other nonelectrical instruments would accompany the cast, and in the best show business tradition, the show would go on!

DAVID PAYMER: Lynne Guerra and the crew, the ushers, and all us actors started rounding up all the flashlights and lanterns we could find to provide what lighting we could to complete the show. Treat Williams shouted out to the restless audience, asking if they wanted to watch the rest of the show even with limited lighting, a single piano, and drums.

TREAT WILLIAMS: Having been playing Zuko, I was fearless, so I said, "How do you all feel—do you want to continue? You wanna see the rest of the show?" The audience shouted back, "Yeah, yeah, yeah!" So I said, "Well, stay in your seats and give us five minutes to reset."

DAVID PAYMER: He was greeted with very enthusiastic, affirmative applause. This audience was already excited to be part of a one-of-a-kind experience.

STEVE BECKLER: I took over the technical revamp and anticipated a lighting plan, which meant deciding where the flashlights should go for each scene so that the show could proceed as seamlessly as possible. Grabbing my call script, I headed to the stage-right fly rail to cue the necessary scenic moves.

FORBESY RUSSELL: Somehow enough flashlights appeared to light us. *The show must go on!* And we did, with intense focus from everyone as we were startled into hyperawareness. Something big had happened, and we were a part of it.

DAVID PAYMER: Onstage the cast crowded closely around Greased Lightning, flashlights in hand, shining them at Treat and Forbesy as they performed the drive-in scene. The laughs were as big as ever, and there was a wonderful sense of shared intimacy and companionship among the cast as we attempted to light our fellow actors.

DANNY JACOBSON: The show became more intimate than ever before. This was liver than live theater.

TREAT WILLIAMS: The band was right there with us and said they'd play what they could with piano, drums, and acoustic guitar.

JEREMY STONE: One of my guitarists, Jack Cavari, had an acoustic guitar in his locker. He brought it out, and the band for the rest of the performance consisted of him on acoustic guitar and me on acoustic piano.

TREAT WILLIAMS: The ushers and crew became our spotlights and, because they knew the show, put lights on whoever was speaking.

JOHN FENNESSY: No sound, no lights other than the theater's own emergency lighting, and all the ushers and available crew at the foot of the stage, training flashlights on the cast. Since they were our own stagehands and ushers, they knew the show. They could anticipate entrances and exits, and move the flashlights with the blocking.

TREAT WILLIAMS: That night of the Great New York Blackout made for an extraordinary performance of *Grease* and got me one of the biggest laughs I ever got on a stage.

FORBESY RUSSELL: The drive-in scene resumed; I broke up with Danny.

TREAT WILLIAMS: We continued the drive-in scene just at the moment when Sandy slams the door on me—hitting me in the worst possible place—and runs away from the car. As usual I walked to the front of the car, and since I was the only one onstage at the time, all the flashlights were on me. It was very cool. I reached down to the coiled mic and picked it up, and as the piano played the arpeggio intro to "Alone at a Drive-In Movie" and I opened my mouth to sing, the audience and I had a shared revelation. I looked at the microphone. The audience looked at the microphone. And we all realized together that there was absolutely no power in the entire state of New York, much less in that mic. The laughter started to rise up, so I swung the mic up and did the first mic drop I ever did. The audience roared. And I sang "Alone at a Drive-In Movie" to the very last row of the balcony.

DAVID PAYMER: This improvised lighting continued for the rest of the show, from Jan's basement to "All Choked Up," with actors trading flashlights to provide lighting for each other's lines. The audience was totally with us, and it was an oddly moving communal experience.

FORBESY RUSSELL: By flashlight I eventually transformed into the cool, leather-clad, "What's it to ya, Zuko" Sandy.

STEVE BECKLER: *Grease* proceeded in limited but unique style all the way through the big finale and into the curtain call.

JOHN FENNESSY: Blackouts were blackouts. But *Grease* was *Grease*. We finished the show.

STEVE BECKLER: And it was a triumph. The crowd, all of whom had stayed with us, registered their appreciation with a standing ovation . . . and cheers!

FORBESY RUSSELL: We also applauded the audience, as we were just as grateful for them hanging in there with us.

STEVE BECKLER: As we were finishing the fifth bow, a security person from the Shubert Organization came running onstage instructing the audience to leave the theater immediately because the emergency lights had a limited life span, and he wanted the crowd out before the theater went totally dark.

TREAT WILLIAMS: "All right, everybody's got to get out." The audience responded, *No, no, no,* and the guy said, "Pretty soon you guys are gonna be in pitch-black dark. You gotta go. Now!" And they did, while we Greasers all scrambled to collect our belongings and leave the theater too.

DAVID PAYMER: It was one of those rare moments in the theater where interaction between performers and the audience is collective and spontaneous. We had all shared something remarkable together—and we knew it. No one asked for a refund!

STEVE BECKLER: In the days that followed, the stage managers of our neighboring shows reported that they had all sent their audiences home. We were one of the few that finished that night, and we were justly proud.

TREAT WILLIAMS: But we couldn't go home. People were all over the streets, and Charlie's was cooking up steaks for everybody 'cause they still had gas and they knew all the meat was gonna go bad by morning.

STEVE BECKLER: Many of us went across Forty-Fifth to celebrate at Charlie's with other Broadway shows and to eat the now-unrefrigerated food that they were giving away. After a suitable period of self-congratulation, the conversation turned to how to get home. Several of us headed east to Times Square for this once-in-a-lifetime opportunity.

FORBESY RUSSELL: Even Times Square was dark. It was baffling; it was freeing. It was an alternate world. But it felt safe because everyone in the city seemed to be coming together in a new, magical universe. The night was warm, and we were in wonder.

TREAT WILLIAMS: New York had turned into one big happy village. It was unforgettable—and just a little magical.

FORBESY RUSSELL: The big city had turned into a small town, full of New Yorkers who realized once again why they were glad to live in the greatest city in the world, where amazing things happen all the time.

STEVE BECKLER: And there we stood in the middle of the unprecedented and pitch-black square, quietly staring up at the now stunningly visible stars.

FORBESY RUSSELL: At 8:15 PM Treat and I had sung, "But *ooh*, those *su-hummer nah-yights*," and just a couple of hours later, when the lights went out, July 13, 1977, became a summer night we would all remember for the rest of our lives.

38 | *Broadway*
1978–1979

KEN WAISSMAN (*Producer*): Six months before the release of the *Grease* film, Paramount lawyers discovered a clause my attorneys had snuck into the final draft of the contract. The clause stated that Paramount could not engage in any paid-for publicity or paid advertising until after the opening of the film in New York. We realized they couldn't open the movie without doing any up-front advertising or publicity, but my concern was protecting the Broadway production for as long as possible.

I offered a proposal: Paramount would pay for producing and running a new TV ad campaign with the theme of seeing *Grease* live onstage. They would also put a tag at the end of the film in every movie theater within a hundred-mile radius of New York promoting the Broadway production. In addition the Broadway show would cohost the New York premiere of the film. They agreed to it all.

The New York premiere of the movie *Grease* took place on June 13, 1978. The Broadway cast hosted a pre-party celebration in Shubert Alley and cohosted the premiere screening, followed by a big party at Studio 54.

Up to this point, when a movie version of a Broadway musical opened, attendance for the show dropped drastically, and it would usually close. *Grease* was the first time a show went back to sold-out status following the release of the movie. The show's national visibility as host of the New York premiere, the thirty-second Broadway promo (featuring a then-unknown Sharon Stone) at the end of the film, and the major TV campaign Paramount financed had a big impact on maintaining the Broadway grosses.

ADRIAN ZMED (*Zuko*): When I got to Broadway, my dream come true wasn't quite the fairy tale I was expecting it to be. *Grease* on Broadway was a runaway train with lots of egos, and this kid from the touring company with no credits is taking over as Danny? I had left the safety and comfort of my road family to become the new kid on the Great White Way block. My Danny fit into my touring company but not into this long-running dynamo of a *Grease* train. It took a while to get used to their interpretations and avoid stepping on the toes of everyone else's performances. As I was trying to make my adjustments, I realized my Danny had to grow up and become a tougher leader in order to gain their trust and respect. Only then was I able to infuse my Danny into the show.

After a few months, playing Danny on Broadway was everything I ever dreamed of. To walk out onto the stage every night to a full house, feeling the electricity of a Broadway audience, many of whom by this time had seen the show multiple times but just kept coming back for more, was the ultimate high. The New York company and I had become one, and I was in heaven and never wanted to leave. It was one of the greatest times of my life.

KATHERINE MELOCHE (*Patty*): We were going into the Act 2 final scene at the Burger Palace. I was sitting in the banquette onstage right where the Burger Palace Boys were gathered around, poking and teasing me. All of a sudden there was a booming reverb feedback from the bass guitar in the orchestra pit. Without missing a beat, Danny Jacobson (Kenickie) reacted as if I had cut a loud, smelly fart. He and all the Burger Palace Boys held their noses and waved the air as Kenickie exclaimed, "Oh, *Patty!*" It stopped the show. Laughter from the audience, musicians, and cast members went on for what seemed forever. Patty turned a lovely shade of red, and for the rest of the scene I was alone onstage right because everyone had moved over to stage left. When the Pink Ladies made their entrance, they also stayed stage left and reacted as if Patty had ripped a big one.

Uncle Jake!

ROBIN VOGEL (*Cha-Cha*): Thought *Grease* was raunchy onstage? You should have been backstage! When an actor joined the Broadway show, it was like adding a new family member; and like any family, the older kids loved to torture the younger kids. In my case it was my friend Danny Jacobson who did the torturing, both as Kenickie onstage and as Jacobson offstage.

Cha-Cha's costume for the prom was a huge, school-bus-yellow dress with three crinolines, weighing as much as the country of Liechtenstein, making me stand out like a large ballerina cake topper. The dress was extremely hot and uncomfortable to wear, so when I came offstage, I would immediately take it all off down to my very modest slip.

One particularly hot night backstage, Danny, tiring of my nonstop complaints about nonstop hot flashes, asked if he could make me more comfortable. He then took hold of my slip and bra straps, my yellow dance pants, and my stockings, and all at once yanked everything down to my ankles.

I collapsed to the deck, flopping around like a trout out of water as I attempted to cover myself, trying desperately to muffle my screams and laughter. Definitely of another era, but an oddly odd bonding experience; Danny and I are still great friends.

PEGGY LEE BRENNAN (*Frenchy*): It was Broadway Show Night at Studio 54. My twelve-year-old sister, Eileen, and my eighteen-year-old brother, John, were excited to visit the famed 54 and see some of their favorite stars. Eileen had been given an extreme makeover by Barbara Zmed (Adrian's wife) and the girls, miraculously transforming her into a twelve-year-old grown-up. Adorned with a cool hat, hippie jewelry, and lots of makeup, Eileen confidently walked into Studio 54 arm in arm with her handsome escort, Treat Williams. My brother John, at his "cool" best, escorted me into the wildly packed mob scene.

Around midnight, while I was hunting for my sister, who I had last seen dancing with a tall, colorfully attired transvestite on pink roller skates, a ruckus erupted on the other side of the room. Someone from the Broadway company of *Hair* had "hit on" my brother, who instinctively pushed the guy away. It quickly devolved into a brawl between John's *Grease* protectors—the Burger Palace Boys—and the entire cast and crew of *Hair*. It was the '50s guys dueling the Age of Aquarius!

Thankfully, although a few egos were bruised, no one was hurt, and the night concluded with everyone laughing and arguing about who got to treat whom for the next round of free drinks at the Broadway cast members' open bar.

LORI ADA JAROSLOW (*Understudy/Jan*): Shortly after the tour was over, they brought me into the Broadway company to understudy the same six roles I covered on the road, and eventually I became the full-time Jan.

When you're ensconced in addiction, it's not uncommon to be unaware of your problem—well, unaware of most everything. There are huge swathes of time I have no recollection of, and alternatively I remember tremendous detail about certain moments. Whenever I went on for Rizzo, for example, Danny Jacobson would do his best to make me howl with laughter when the lights were down and we were lying on top of each other on the park bench. He would whisper lesbian jokes with a faux Yiddish accent as I tried desperately not to laugh.

One night I went to work stoned, or it's entirely possible that I got stoned in my dressing room on the sixth floor, or maybe both—you never know. In the middle of the show, my friend Cynthia Darlow broke a limb, and boom, I was on for Jan. Apparently, maybe even miraculously, I made it down the six flights of stairs. I have no idea how the show went, but here I am, so Jan and I lived to tell the tale.

There I was in a big Broadway show, a quintessential dream job, loving every minute of it, and unknowingly sabotaging my life at every turn. I was destroying my spirit and robbing myself of my own presence, quelling demons by self-medicating—sending my life and career up in smoke.

Lori Ada Jaroslow.

39 | *Broadway*
1979–1980

REX SMITH (*Zuko*): In 1977, at twenty years old, I already had a six-album deal with Columbia Records. My band REX had just completed its second nationwide tour, and I was signed to star in a movie called *Sooner or Later*. The single from that soundtrack, "You Take My Breath Away," would eventually go platinum and make me a "teen idol" when the movie was released. But all that was yet to come.

Since the movie was not going to be released for six months, I was a bit at loose ends, riding my motorcycle around New York City. One of my pastimes was "second-acting" Broadway shows. I would wait outside a theater, and when the crowd came outside for a smoke at intermission, I would saunter in like I owned the place and find an empty seat. I always knew how the story ended but not how it began. Oh well, you couldn't beat the price. Funny that the only show I was unceremoniously kicked out of was . . . *Grease*.

One evening over beers, a friend listening to me complain that I was going balmy with nothing to do said, "Well, why don't you go down and audition for Danny Zuko in *Grease* on Broadway?"

"You mean just walk in?"

"No, it's called an open call, and anyone can try out for it. The actors have a union, and they require one open call because it gives someone off the street and without representation the chance to get through the door on Broadway."

It was something to do, and since I had been kicked out the front door, the thought of reentering through the back (stage) door appealed to the rascal in me.

The next day there's a line around the block. I ended up behind a fellow who grew increasingly nervous the closer he came to the stage. While I watched

300

from the wings, he froze center stage and launched into the most agonizing, brutal attempt at singing a song I'd ever heard. I could have kissed him.

There were about eight of us at the callback. To be considered for the iconic Danny Zuko, it seems one was required to survive a combination of stagecraft tests with the stamina of an NFL player. We were sequestered down in the subbasement/greenroom of the Royale Theatre. A serious flight of steps in darkness led up to the stage. I was playing gin rummy with the other Zukos when my name was called over the loudspeaker.

Leaping from the table, I started up the treacherous staircase three steps at a time. I could see the stage worklights as I was bounding up the last flight when—*Bam! Bing! Bongo!*—I dented my skull on a low overhang with a sign stating WATCH YOUR HEAD. *Well, too late for that!* I stumbled onstage holding my dented head with both hands.

"You OK?" I heard Tom Moore's voice coming from the fifth row.

"I just banged the shit outa my head!" I cried.

The next moment, I received the first direction I ever received from a Broadway director: "*Use it!*" The ensuing laughter gave me a chance to take a standing eight count before I tore into my audition.

It was great. I was in! And I have *used it* ever since.

Tommy Smith (production stage manager), Michael Corbett (Kenickie), Rex Smith (Zuko), and Paul Greeno (understudy).

JEREMY STONE (*Music Director*): It's well known that *Grease* through the years discovered and employed a vast number of exceptional young performers, many of whom went on to stellar careers. Some became big stars! Less thought is given to the talent we missed—all the gifted folks we did *not* hire.

One day when we were auditioning for the role of Danny Zuko, a young, unknown actor appeared wearing a tan leather jacket and sang "Alone at a Drive-In Movie." Though vocally untrained, he got through the song, but in the end he wasn't right for *Grease,* and we didn't take him on. We probably did him a huge favor, however, because one year later this young actor had several film/TV credits and was starring in an ongoing TV sitcom.

I doubt that that young actor ever gave much credit to *Grease* for *not* hiring him that day, leaving his schedule clear to begin his meteoric career, but undeniably we did lose out on the services of a superb actor.

Oh, his name? Tom Hanks.

LAURIE GRAFF (*Frenchy*): I got off the plane in LaGuardia Airport and happened to run into my mother's boss, Dr. Cohen. "I hear you're in a Broadway show," he said. "Congratulations!"

Laurie Graff.

I had no clue what he was talking about. I had been away and incommunicado.

"Everyone's trying to reach you," he said. "Call your mother."

Instead I called my answering service. Tons of messages. It seemed Lynne Guerra, the Broadway stage manager, had been trying to reach me through my service, my answering machine, my cousin Randy Graff (then in the show), and my mom. I finally reached Lynne, who told me they were offering me the role of Frenchy in the Broadway company of *Grease*.

"Can you come in tomorrow at 6:00 PM?" asked Lynn.

"Sure. To like settle in and watch the show?"

"No. You're going on."

"But I haven't done it since the third national tour closed, and that was almost six months ago."

"Oh." She paused. "Then can you come in at 5:00?"

SHERIE SEFF (*Understudy*): I swear I didn't hear the alarm going off. All I know is that when I lifted my head and squinted at the clock through the fog of half-sleep, the time read 7:15 PM.

Holy shit! It's my Broadway debut, and I overslept.

I jump out of bed and start scrambling around the apartment. Fast shower. Clothes on. Grab a bagel. Out the door. *Curtain is at eight. Maybe I can still make it.*

I frantically run onto the street and begin waving my arms like a lunatic, trying to hail a taxi. *No taxi! NO TAXI! Come on, people! It's New York Friggin' City and there are no taxis?* I start sprinting down Broadway like an Olympian, my arms pumping at my side, bagel clenched between my teeth—dodging people, dodging strollers, dodging dogs. It's hard to breathe, my heart is pounding, and I'm dripping with sweat. That's when the tears come.

I crash into the stage door and give it a yank. It won't open. I'm pushing, pulling, and banging on the door, but it won't budge. *Hey, hey, it's me! Sherie! Cha-Cha!* Through the door I can hear the preshow music start to roll.

"*One-two-three-o'clock, four o'clock rock! Five-six-seven-o'clock, eight o'clock rock!*"

"I'm here!" I begin screaming. "Open the goddamned door!"

Next thing I know, I'm inside. Before I can say a word, the stage manager, Lynne Guerra, grabs my hand. She drags and shoves me up the stairs.

"*Earth angel, Earth angel . . . will you be mine . . .*"

I run into my dressing room. *Shoes on! Prom gown on!* I tear into the wardrobe room and grab my wig, yanking it onto my head as I barrel back down the stairs. But the faster I run, the slower I move. I look out onto the stage. And that's when I see my castmates—Danny, Peter, Duffy—all of them taking their curtain call!

The curtain call? The show's over? How the hell did that happen? Then all at once my fellow actors turn stage left and point directly at me. Then they begin laughing. Hysterically. I burst into tears and . . .

Buzzz.

I wake up. It's 7:15—7:15 in the morning! My heart is pounding and my sheets are drenched. I collapse back onto my pillow. Oh yeah, they warned me—the classic actor's nightmare. It was October 31—Halloween—my Broadway debut was still intact.

I smiled. In just a few hours, in this joyous musical, Cha-Cha DiGregorio and I were going to win the dance contest, and this overweight, lonely schoolgirl would quietly celebrate having achieved her big dream.

TOM WIGGIN (*Understudy*): One night I was playing Kenickie while Danny Jacobson was on vacation. We ended the first act, and at intermission Lynne Guerra came to my dressing room and said, very calmly and matter-of-factly, "Frank Piegaro (who was playing Zuko) got food poisoning and can't go back on. Paul (Greeno, the other understudy) is going to take over for you as Kenickie, you'll take over for Frank." I just nodded, changed my costume, and jumped in to finish the show as Danny Zuko.

While some of the audience might have been momentarily confused, we delivered the show they had paid to see, two for one, without missing a beat.

REX SMITH: Before I could become a Zuko, like a West Point plebe, I had to suffer from the designation ZIT—"Zuko-in-Training." I was hazed accordingly.

But tonight is my debut on Broadway! I'm excited, nervous, and . . . playing Kenickie! You know those stories where the person just can't get anything right on their debut? That was me. Kenickie's big number, "Greased Lightnin'," was staged with handheld corded microphones. The song ends with the Burger Palace Boys throwing their mics to the stage at the end of the last verse as they fall into the car.

At this performance I threw my mic down on the stage a whole verse too early and, proudly following my choreography to a T, fell into the car doing leg splits. The soundman was caught unaware; the feedback sounded as loud as Jimi Hendrix. This ZIT was eating his humble pie.

Then in the second act came the move into Jan's basement party scene. As the actors did the scene changes, it was like flying with the Blue Angels, everyone moving furniture and props in synchronicity. I grabbed the microphone on a stand at center stage—and too late realized it was Zuko's scene-change track, not Kenickie's. I found myself face-to-face with the then-current Zuko: Peter Gallagher.

Peter gave me the most blistering, incredulous expression I'd ever received onstage. And just at that moment, the sofa I was supposed to move in the blackout snagged the microphone cord. As the lights came up, the actor playing Eugene tripped on it and slid like he was stealing home plate straight across the stage on his chin!

OK, Rex, come out of the dressing room. You have seven more shows this week to get it right.

SHERIE SEFF: Cha-Cha's big moment of glory happens at the prom, when she wins the dance contest with Danny Zuko.

I had always been a pretty good dancer, and for a chubby girl my stamina was surprisingly strong. But "Born to Hand Jive" is a friggin' marathon! Pat Birch's classic choreography looks like a cross between the jitterbug, a hoedown, and Irish step dancing.

Cha-Cha's high kicks, however, were my biggest challenge. One night at the climax of the dance, when I had to swing my leg over Peter Gallagher's (Zuko's) head, my exhausted leg lagged and sagged, and the heel of my shoe clipped poor Peter right across the forehead. I was horrified. When the same action happens just a few moments later, I summoned everything I had, including my inner Rockette, to make sure I cleared Peter's head. Turns out I didn't need to. When my leg swung up, Peter instantly dove to the floor and landed spread-eagle, saving his head and getting a huge laugh in the process.

After the show I ran up to Peter, profusely apologizing for my dance floor assault. "No problem!" he said, affecting that signature Danny Zuko swagger. "Meloche (Patty Simcox) kicked me in the balls! I guess it's just one of those nights."

MARY GORDON MURRAY (*Sandy*): One of my first gigs was working as an extra on *All My Children*, featuring an awesome young actress named Candice Earley, who was also starring as Sandy in *Grease* on Broadway. I couldn't imagine ever being that lucky! A few years later I was cast as Sandy in the third national tour. This was momentous! Unfortunately the tour closed early.

Shortly after coming home from the tour, I was cast on a soap opera—*One Life to Live*—in a role I would play for the next six years, and around the same time, I received a surprise call to be a vacation replacement for Sandy on Broadway. Suddenly I realized, *I am living the unimaginable Candice Earley life!*

So the big day comes. I am going on as Sandy. My entire family has driven in from New Jersey. I sing my heart out during "Summer Nights" and belt my way through "It's Raining on Prom Night." Finally, in the home stretch of Act 2, I begin to make my entrance down the stairs into Jan's basement, record player in hand. But I can't—my foot has become trapped between the steps, and in what seems like slow motion, I am flying down the flight of stairs, landing flat on my face on the floor.

My first performance in a lead role on Broadway and I fell flat on my face. I'm pretty sure something like that would have never happened to Candice Earley.

MARCIA MITZMAN (*Rizzo*): I had been doing the show for around ten months. On this one night I had friends coming to the show, so I may have been trying a little too hard. The second-act prom scene culminates in the showstopping dance frenzy "Born to Hand Jive." I was dancing with Danny Zuko (Peter Gallagher). On the final beat of the music, I was supposed to do a single pirouette into a back bend in his arms.

But I was so excited to impress my friends that I went for a double pirouette instead—so I rushed into the bend before I had completed the turns. *Bam!* My knee dislocated, all the way out. I screamed and collapsed, with my knee sticking out of the side of my leg. And then the show just stopped! For once all the cute alpha males in the cast were at a loss for words. Everyone was just standing around staring at each other. The audience was all abuzz.

The ambulance arrived outside of the theater, sirens blaring, where my friends and what seemed like half the audience ran out to watch me get carried out on a stretcher. "Hi-ho, the glamorous life!"

In the ER, still in full Rizzo makeup, I was parked in the hallway on my gurney waiting for a doctor and trying to stay calm. A few huddled-together nurses were eyeing me and whispering. Finally one of them came over. "Are you . . . in a Broadway show?" "Yes, I am," I answered, hoping this might get me to the doctor faster. She looked relieved. "Oh good! We figured it was either that or you were a hooker!"

"Hang Up My Rock 'n' Roll Shoes"

MEGHAN DUFFY (*Frenchy*): When you are young and naive and fortunate enough to be dropped into your dream, you believe that living that dream will surely vanquish your demons, ghosts, and sorrows. You are mistaken. Performing the show eventually became a job, one that didn't leave room for much creativity.

I left *Grease* a month before it closed. It would have been nice to say I was the last Frenchy, and I tried to stay, but I had been with the show too long and the time had come. It's like knowing that you've reached the end of an intimate relationship, when staying any longer isn't a kindness to anyone involved.

I went back to school, started college at thirty-seven, and now have a PhD—in theater. This beauty school dropout became a doctor of theater.

PATRICIA DOUGLAS (*Jan*): It's the dream of every tour member to get the call that leads to Broadway, and I was no different. This would be the continuation of my wonderful *Grease* journey. But when that time came, it was the day of my mother's funeral.

As always, my *Grease* family had rallied to my side, especially Mary Murray (Sandy) and Michael Corbett (Kenickie), and I was grateful. When I got home that day, I got *the call*. The call to play on Broadway. *Could I cover a vacation for the Broadway Jan?* My heart broke for the second time that day, but I had to say no. I had nothing to bring to the show. I was just too sad. The show would assuredly go on . . . just without me.

JOHN EVERSON (*Assistant Stage Manager/Understudy*): In the late 1970s I got a call asking if I could come in and cover for a week. The second day back I was told I'd be going on for Kenickie that night.

Unfortunately my performance that night resulted in an injury. In the big Act 1 finale, as we were all singing and dancing our hearts out, Marty was standing on the park bench and said quickly to me, "Here I come, catch me." As I caught her, I heard a snap in my right knee. I finished the number and limped off into the wings. With the help of one of the electricians, I taped my knee with duct tape and managed to finish the show, a Saturday matinee. I put ice on it and did the evening performance as well as the Sunday matinee . . . then went home and cried.

Upon diagnosis I learned I had torn the medial meniscus rather badly. I've reflected on that episode over the years, wondering whether or not I should have performed those weekend shows. However, today I take pride knowing that for those three performances, I kept the curtain up and the show went on.

I got a wonderful compliment from Tom Moore, when in a quiet moment he said, "John, you are one of those people who is always there." Those words have stayed with me throughout my career.

40 | Grease Becomes Broadway's Longest-Running Show

December 8, 1979

KEN WAISSMAN (*Producer*): On December 8, 1979, *Grease* played its 3,243rd performance, which made it, at the time, the longest-running production in the history of Broadway.

The summer before, Marilu Henner had called me from her dressing room on the set of *Taxi*. "Last night I dreamt I was on an airplane with the whole *Grease* gang flying to New York for the December 8 record-breaking performance," she said. "So I started thinking . . . since director Tom Moore and so many alumni are out here in L.A., can we get one of the airlines to provide a plane to fly us to New York for the celebration?"

We hired Bruce Lucker and Klaus Incamp to handle our historic happening. They had organized the famous I Love New York campaign. Bruce and Klaus were able to get Pan American Airways to agree to provide a 747 to fly the *Grease* alumni in Los Angeles to New York and back. They even agreed to paint the *Grease* logo on the sides of the plane.

The original cast and the first national tour cast were invited to perform the show on that historic evening. We held the rehearsals in Los Angeles, flying out the few cast members who were still living in New York, plus Pat Birch and Louis St. Louis.

John Travolta, who had played Doody in the first national tour and then on Broadway, wasn't available for the rehearsals. However, he agreed to attend the event and come up onstage. We also invited Olivia Newton-John.

That evening at the Royale Theatre, the first national tour cast, headed by Jeff Conaway, performed the first act, and the original Broadway cast, headed

Rehearsing in Los Angeles for the big NY celebration.

Pat Birch, Tom Moore, Michael Lembeck, and Jerry Zaks.

by Barry Bostwick, performed the second act. Additional alumni filled in for the few original cast members who were unable to participate. The audience was made up of friends, relatives, industry people, investors, and a majority of our *Grease* alumni.

Boarding the plane from L.A. to New York: Ken Waissman, Pat Birch, Jeff Conaway, Maxine Fox, Tom Moore, Marilu Henner, John Travolta, and Ellen Travolta.

Act 1 with Jeff Conaway and the first national tour cast.

Marilu Henner, Rebecca Gilchrist, Ellen March, and
Judy Kaye, in Act 1: "Freddy, My Love."

Act 2 with Barry Bostwick: "Alone at a Drive-In Movie."

Act 2 with the original Broadway cast.

At the end of the show, the current cast, which included a young actor named Patrick Swayze, came onstage along with the original cast and the first national tour cast, and they all sang "We Go Together."

Then Maxine and I came onstage.

Ken Waissman and Maxine Fox introduce the *Grease* alumni.

I started by bringing out Jim Jacobs and Warren Casey. Next I introduced Tom Moore and Pat Birch. Then I addressed the audience.

"As I call out your names, please come up onstage." The band played "Pomp and Circumstance" as the alumni marched down the aisles and up the stairs to the stage.

Then I introduced Sheldon Harnick and Jerry Bock, the composer and lyricist for *Fiddler on the Roof*, whose record we were breaking with that night's performance. Harnick made a very gracious speech and turned the longest-running-show mantle over to us.

Following the festivities at the theater, the celebration moved to adjoining ballrooms at the Americana Hotel, where we had booked rooms for all the *Grease* alumni. Chubby Checker and his band played in one of the ballrooms, and the Hot Nuts played in the second. For those who made it until dawn, special buttons were given out that read I WENT THE DISTANCE WITH GREASE.

BARRY TARALLO (*Doody*): When *Grease* was about to become the longest-running musical in Broadway history, I distinctly remember thinking how cool it would be to have been a part of the cast for that celebration. And then out of nowhere, the phone rang. It was Ken Waissman, who told me that everyone from the first national tour was available for the gala performance except for the actor who had played Doody: John Travolta. "Would you be interested in stepping in?" he asked. My two-word response: "Fuckin' A!"

Our sold-out, one-time-only performance was filled with show-biz celebrities and supportive *Grease* alumni from every incarnation, including the hit movie's own John Travolta and Olivia Newton-John. It was an unforgettable experience.

PEGGY LEE BRENNAN (*Frenchy*): After celebrating all the way across America in our *Grease* plane, we arrived at JFK in New York, exhausted but giddy with excitement. And it continued the day of the big event. I hopped into one of the limos provided for us with my little sister Eileen and my former fellow cast member Buddy (a.k.a. Patrick Swayze) and his wife Lisa. Buddy took charge as our chariot pulled up to the red carpet, surrounded by screaming fans outside the Royale Theatre. He said, "OK, everyone, follow my lead. I will escort each of you out of the car one at a time, and then we will all walk the red carpet together."

When the car stopped, Buddy opened the door and the screaming fans exploded into uproarious adulation. But as Buddy stood up on the curb, the adoring fans immediately turned on the then unknown, mistakenly identified former Danny Zuko with groans and complaints. "It's not Travolta!" And the fickle crowd's attention turned to the next arriving limo.

I was the first to be escorted by Buddy, who had whispered to me as I got out of the car, "Hold your head high and just keep smiling." Once we were inside, we all laughed. Then right behind us I saw John arriving, totally surrounded by bodyguards shielding him from the reinvigorated, screaming fans.

Peggy Lee Brennan and John Travolta.

Barry Bostwick and Jeff Conaway.

JOY RINALDI (*Understudy*): One of those unforgettable events of a life-time was the *Grease* celebration when it became the longest-running musical in the history of Broadway. The night was to be a full-dress major reunion of everyone who had ever been involved in the show over the last eight years.

I was living in Los Angeles by then, as were many of the former cast, so Pan Am Airways provided a jumbo jet to fly us all to New York. I couldn't believe my eyes when I saw the word *Grease* painted in giant letters on the side of the plane! It was a wild party for the entire five-hour flight east. Johnny (Travolta) and several others had already become names by then, but there were no celebrities on that trip; we were all one, celebrating our good fortune.

It was a fantastic night. Although I was disappointed not to be perform-ing that night, watching my dear cast members—who had lost none of their charisma and exuberance—shine was a thrill. The stage glowed with talent, and the audience was thrilled.

TOM MOORE (*Director*): It was my intention to share the exact words that I spoke at the end of that remarkable evening, but when I searched my archive, there was only a single note card with which I had addressed everyone in the Royale that night. You can see me clutching that note card in the photo.

So although I can't share the actual words, I can assuredly share the actual emotion. It was without question one of the most thrilling nights of my life.

After expressing appreciation to everyone you would expect, I talked about the momentous journey we had all taken together and how it had changed each of our lives profoundly. About the passion and affection shared in each and every company, and my pride in having brought them all together. And then I told them about a young boy who loved to pull open his aunt's draw drapes over and over again to make an entrance, and who later staged magic shows in the basement and childhood circuses in the backyard, and the miracle that led him to Broadway and, astonishingly, to become the director of its longest-running show. It was a dream I couldn't have imagined, a fantasy come true. I was overcome with gratitude, emotion, and—no other word for it—joy.

Tom Moore: gratitude and joy.

Barry Bostwick, Patrick Swayze, and John Travolta.

John Travolta, Maxine Fox, Barry Bostwick, and Jeff Conaway.

The party continued the day after with a casual Sunday brunch at the Americana Hotel. Entertainment was provided by Barry Tarallo, David Paymer, and Peter Gallagher (parody lyrics were by Danny Jacobson).

LEFT: Peter Gallagher. RIGHT: A weekend-long celebration. Maxine Fox, Ken Waissman, Marilu Henner, Ellen March, Laurie Graff, and Jeff Conaway.

41

"The Party's Over"

The Majestic Theatre, January 29, 1980–April 13, 1980

JEREMY STONE (*Music Director*): Late in 1979 word came down that we would soon have to vacate the Royale and the show would be moving to the Majestic, a considerably larger house (1,559 seats). To most of us the Royale had been home, and the thought of moving to another theater was deeply unwelcome. Plus there was good reason to worry that the show which had thrived at the Royale would feel lost in such a large venue.

We needn't have worried. During one of our early performances in our new home, while Betty Myers, the associate conductor, was in the pit, I stood in the back of the theater with the director, Tom Moore. From the first scene with the Burger Palace Boys, you could feel yourself being pulled into the story, just like it had been at the Royale. At some point during Act 1, Tom turned to me and said, "This show's like a weed. It grows anywhere!"

MAXINE FOX (*Producer*): The Shuberts, wanting to book a new play into the Royale, had offered to greatly reduce our theater rent if we agreed to move to the larger Majestic Theatre. The show was winding down, and this would lower our breakeven and help us run a little longer. We'd have a larger capacity on the weekends, which still sold out. That seemed to be working until April 1, when New York was hit with a major transit strike. The eleven-day strike devastated our box office, and it didn't recover when the strike was over.

BUDDY POWELL (*Eugene*): Only a couple of weeks after I finally got a chance to join the Broadway show in March of 1980, the one-week closing notice went up.

Closing? The longest-running show on Broadway closing? Now? I just got here!

Doing the final Sunday matinee was bittersweet. We knew that following our bows the set would be coming down, the costumes and props would be packed up, and the cast and crew would part ways. To a one, we were very, very sad.

JoELLA FLOOD (*Patty*): In early January 1980, just one month after the big celebration when *Grease* became the longest-running show in the history of Broadway, the show moved from the Royale to the Majestic. The Majestic was one of Broadway's biggest houses. Compared to the Royale, it was cavernous. It took a lot of energy to project into that huge space. We all felt a bit lost.

April 13, 1980, was the closing performance of *Grease*. It was difficult for all of us. Many of the creative team and staff were there to say goodbye, and Tom, our director, had called from California at half hour with final and ruefully funny "notes." Our feelings of loss were overwhelming. We sobbed and wept as we sang out our final number, "We Go Together."

The ending refrain was repeated as usual over and over. "*We'll always be together . . . always be together . . . always be together . . .*"

And we all exited stage left—for the very last time.

PAUL GREENO (*Understudy*): April 13, 1980, a date we prayed would never come—the day *Grease* closed—performance number 3,388!

I had a dressing room to clean out—nine months of accumulated junk. But I wanted more. I wanted something from the show, a keepsake, a memento. But what? Since I couldn't fit Greased Lightning under my jacket, I would have to settle for something smaller. As it turned out, I took a package of Hostess Snoballs and my Sonny LaTierri sunglasses.

I was finally ready to leave the theater. It seemed like hours had passed since the final curtain; dressing rooms were cleaned, goodbyes had been said, and heartfelt promises had been made to stay in touch. We had to leave. As much as it hurt, it was time to stick a pin in this phase of my life. I was heading toward the stage door when, lo and behold, I spotted the perfect keepsake. There hanging on the bulletin board was the *Grease* sign-in sheet—the LAST *Grease* sign-in sheet! I couldn't believe no one else took it . . . so I did.

Happy trails.

Oh, I ate the Snoballs in 2014. They were delicious.

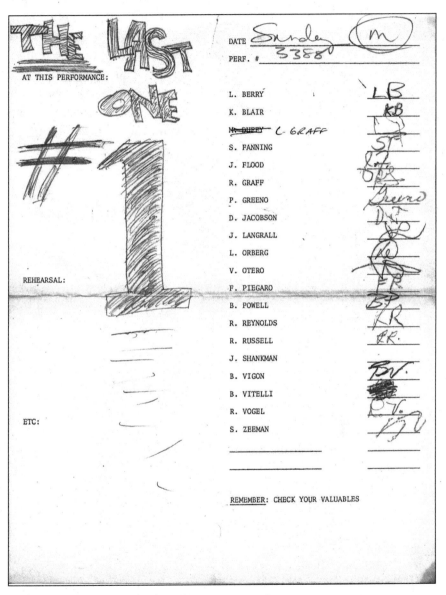

THE LAST ONE

#1

AT THIS PERFORMANCE:

REHEARSAL:

ETC:

DATE Sunday (M)

PERF. # 3388

L. BERRY — LB

K. BLAIR — KB

M̶.̶ ̶D̶U̶F̶F̶Y̶ — L. GRAFF

S. FANNING

J. FLOOD

R. GRAFF

P. GREENO

D. JACOBSON

J. LANGRALL

L. ORBERG

V. OTERO

F. PIEGARO

B. POWELL

R. REYNOLDS

R. RUSSELL

J. SHANKMAN

B. VIGON

B. VITELLI

R. VOGEL

S. ZEEMAN

REMEMBER: CHECK YOUR VALUABLES

Performance #3,388. The last *Grease* sign-in sheet.

TOM MOORE (*Director*): The Sunday afternoon *Grease* played its last performance at the Majestic was a gloomy, rainy day in Los Angeles, and I felt bereft and guilty for not being able to be with the cast and crew to say goodbye. In a rather heroic effort to include me, the production stage manager, Michael Martorella, and the sound team hooked up a speaker connection so I could talk to the cast as they gathered onstage at half hour before curtain.

After playfully giving last notes, I spoke of many things but finished with this: "To those of you who are taking *Grease* across the finish line, the most thanks of all—for it is you who have seen the show through these last tough months. Because of you, *Grease* will go out strong, vibrant, and invincible.

"I will miss *Grease*. And I will miss you!"

EPILOGUE

BARRY BOSTWICK (*Zuko*): The original *Grease* family has stayed close and bonded over all these years. We try for a reunion/party/dinner/drink fest every few years. Friends for life. I think with all the different casts around the world, the feeling is the same. Once a Greaser, always a Greaser. We went together then, and we still go together now.

RICHARD COX (*Zuko*): If I throw out the last notes from "Summer Nights," anyone near is sure to chime in with a joy only reserved for our happiest collective cultural memories. *"Remembered forever as shoo-bop sha wadda wadda yippity boom de boom!"* What a gift!

DAN DEITCH (*Understudy*): I'm at Mount Sinai Hospital for an innocuous test requiring a twilight knockout. My anesthesiologist, Anthony, looks and sounds just like Sonny à la Jim Borrelli. And Anthony can't stop talking.

"Hey, Anthony," I say, "Did I tell you I was in the original Broadway cast of *Grease*?"

"Wow, that's my favorite show of all time," he says as he inserts the IV. "Are you still acting, Danny boy?"

"Yeah, I sing *Grease* songs all the time for my real estate clients, especially at closings."

"Tell you what, my man. When you revive, gimme a few bars from 'Mooning' so we know you're all there."

I did and I am.

CAROLE DEMAS (*Sandy*): Over the years it has been a pleasure for me to work with teenagers in high schools and other theater groups while they are in rehearsal for their own *Grease* adventures. The *Grease* experience always brings them closer together. Their high school friendships are sacred ties, and they are thrilled to know that the friendships we made are still enriching our lives today. *Grease* is a ribbon that ties us all together, and they too become part of the *Grease* legacy.

NANCY ROBBINS (*Assistant to the Director*): My French husband, Michel, compares *Grease* to having been in the French Foreign Legion. The ties are always strong!

COSIE COSTA (*Doody*): I have to thank my wife, Susan—I believe all Greasers need to thank their spouses/partners—for listening to every *Grease* story I have ever told, every time Greasers get together. Every time!

MICHAEL LEMBECK (*Sonny*): When Jerry Zaks and I get together, after nearly fifty years as friends, there is never a time when the conversation doesn't turn to our *Grease* stories. And we laugh at them as family stories, as familiar stories that tie us together. Each time one of us tells the same story, it's like hearing it for the first time . . . again.

GARN STEPHENS (*Jan*): It was late on a hot afternoon and I had some time to kill, so I went into the Apple Pan in west L.A. to get something to drink. The only other occupants were two teenage boys sitting close to me at the counter. I couldn't help but overhear what they were saying. They were excited because they had both been cast in a production of *Grease*. I thought how cool it would be if I told them who I was. It would be fun; maybe they had questions. It could give them an edge up with their fellow castmates. So I leaned over and, with my most dazzling smile, told them I had played Jan in the original Broadway production.

They both froze. And without a word, they couldn't escape fast enough from the crazy bag lady.

NICK WYMAN (*Understudy*): *Grease* gave me that precious imprimatur of professionalism, my Equity card. It was my second Broadway show, and those memories have the hazy, sentimental glow of a first love.

Grease taught me that this is a business, a profession—not a hobby. I learned about professionalism (and lack thereof) from watching my fellow company members. Most of all I learned that *theater is family*.

The experience has served me well in my decades of work as an actor, in Equity's government, and as a proud former president of the AEA (Actors' Equity Association).

CARYN RICHMAN (*Understudy, then Patty/Sandy*): Not long ago, I was shooting a TV series starring Barry Bostwick. We were shooting a Thanksgiving scene with at least twenty other actors sitting at a very long table all decked out for the holiday. The crew was setting up the shot. Then for a moment there was a lull, and all was quiet. Out of nowhere, from the other end of the table,

I hear Barry sing, *"Summer lovin', had me a blast,"* and without thinking or missing a beat I sang back, *"Summer lovin', happened so fast."*

MELODY MEITROTT (*Understudy*): When I was in *Grease*, I was amazed that even though it was then a long-running hit, Tom and Pat brought the same intensity and care to the rehearsals as if the show was just about to open. Those early *Grease* experiences served me well, inspiring me to start my own theater, the Summer Theatre of New Canaan, where I have served as artistic director for the past seventeen years.

In 2013 it was especially cool to direct my son as Danny Zuko in our theater's *Grease*, a show that meant so much to me, and now to him. As we played the show, it seemed like my son's reactions, like those of all Zukos everywhere, just got bigger and bigger and bigger. It made me think in sympathy of Tom, constantly reminding us to please bring it down and *keep it real!*

PHILIP CASNOFF (*Understudy, then Teen Angel / Johnny Casino*): *Grease* was the first time I found what I was looking for without realizing it—a theatrical family.

PETER GALLAGHER (*Zuko*): One of the remarkable things about having been a small part of a cultural phenomenon like *Grease* has been how it has endured. And what has endured are the friendships.

One of my favorite memories is of Danny Jacobson (Kenickie), David Paymer (Sonny LaTierri), and me (Zuko) hanging out onstage just before the curtain went up, singing made-up songs with lyrics like "Our careers have peaked and we will never work again"—because it was hard then to imagine things could get much better. We've been singing that same song together for over forty years . . . all thanks to *Grease*.

RANDY GRAFF (*Understudy*): A full-circle moment: When I was a junior in college, my folks took me to see my cousin Ilene playing Sandy in *Grease* on Broadway; that night playing opposite her was the Danny understudy—*Richard Gere!* When we went backstage, I was in awe. Of everything. For me *Grease* ain't nothin' but a family thing. I was one of three cousins (Ilene, Laurie, and me) who played the Royale. Laurie and I actually got to go on together as Frenchy and Rizzo. The whole family was in the audience, and Laurie and I couldn't stop smiling when we looked at each other and sang *"rama lama ding dong!"* "We Go Together" indeed.

ILENE GRAFF (*Sandy*): *Grease* was much more than a show. It was a way of life. We were so young at the time that for many of us, our *Grease* friends took the place of our high school and/or college friends. We partied together, slept together, traveled together, bowled together, and celebrated holidays together. We were each other's world. We broke each other's hearts and fell deeply and permanently in love. My husband, Ben Lanzarone, and I met during the show—he was the associate conductor—and have been married and making music (and a daughter) together for over forty-two years. So much of the lives we have today started with *Grease*.

SHERIE SEFF (*Understudy, then Cha-Cha*): I struggled with weight most of my life and was told by theater teachers that my weight would limit my opportunities to be a working actor. But I was determined to never let my weight stop me from doing what I loved to do. *Grease* changed my life when I was cast as Cha-Cha DiGregorio at the age of twenty-two. I learned early on that I could do whatever I set my mind to, and that the only voice I needed to pay attention to was my own.

Empowered—absolutely—and the doors swung open in a way I could never have imagined. *Grease* gave me a foundation that I could build upon, not to mention a family that has been present and reliable for decades. *Grease*: the gift that keeps on giving!

SANDRA ZEEMAN (*Marty*): What I learned from *Grease* is always be on time, always be prepared and know your lines, surround yourself with talented people whose company you enjoy, take risks and don't be afraid of failure, take criticism and work to do better, give others praise for work well done, you can easily be replaced, and the show must go on!

CYNTHIA DARLOW (*Jan*): When Patrick Swayze was going to audition for Danny Zuko, I was glad to help coach him for the dance audition. And *of course* he got the job! In those days he used to support himself by doing fine carpentry work, and to thank me for coaching him, he and his wife, Lisa, helped me build the sleeping loft that stands in my apartment to this day. Recently I had a little brass plaque made for it. DESIGN: CYNTHIA DARLOW, CONSTRUCTION: PATRICK SWAYZE, LISA NIEMI, 1977.

STEVE YUDSON (*Teen Angel / Johnny Casino*): After my journey with *Grease*, I went back to college and became a licensed occupational therapy assistant. I found it incredibly rewarding doing hands-on treatments for patients with stroke, brain, and spinal cord injuries. I created a music program for the patients, and the music of the 1950s was always their favorite.

They loved it when I brought in a karaoke version of "Summer Nights" and were thrilled when they got the chance to play Sandy and Danny and all the other parts. It proved exceptionally therapeutic for them to use their long-term memory as a pathway to recovering their speech. I cannot tell you the pleasure I got from the universal joy on those appreciative faces.

As fate would have it, I am living with Parkinson's disease now, but I continue to sing and, yes, meditate for my own personal therapy. And often I can't help but break out into "Beauty School Dropout." *Grease*, as always, never disappoints.

LISA RAGGIO (*Frenchy*): Throughout my life I always had tapes playing in my head. Most times they were my favorite songs, but other times they were the broken records that belonged to other people . . . family members, my mother. Her voice was strident, critical, defeatist, and negative. She was on my hit parade and her technique worked, but those tapes needed to be erased and permanently ejected. I had little confidence and never trusted myself. So it's no wonder that my first professional job in *Grease* shook me to the core.

During my most challenging moments in previews, I could hear my mother's mantra of defeat and fear: "Don't expect too much, 'cause you're not gonna get it." Tom offered me a different narrative: "Just go out there and trust yourself. I know it will be all right." I had never heard anything like this. I never knew that I had any real power over the situations in my life. It was clear right then and there that Tom was definitely not Italian, because he was filled with hope and belief in me. His statement turned me around.

I now had a new mantra—one that would get me through my career and my personal life. Success would be mine if I embraced each experience and owned it. I had to trust myself and take the leap. And leap I did. I continue to reinvent myself as a direct result of my experiences in *Grease*, and I still view life and career through the lens of that heartfelt advice given me back in 1974. "Just go out there and trust yourself. I know it will be all right." I do and it is.

LORI ADA JAROSLOW (*Understudy, then Jan*): It was fifteen years after *Grease* when I realized why my life was unraveling, and I finally figured out that there was a solution to my problem. I ended up in an AA meeting, and that was the start of my life with a new pair of glasses.

Thirty or so years after my first audition for *Grease*, and sixteen years into my sobriety, a friend called me. "Hey, the theater teacher at my kid's elementary school was found facedown, drunk in the janitor's closet. They're just beginning rehearsals for a production of *Grease*. Could you step in and direct it?" I started working the same day. I had 110 children to fill out four casts. One hundred and ten children, ages six to twelve, doing two separate tracks in four casts. No wonder the director was found passed out in the closet.

The show was approximately half cast when I arrived on the scene. In addition to the fact that I had never set eyes on these children, this school was in L.A.; not surprisingly, half the kids had Mama Rose mamas—the pitching, the begging, the wringing of hands. "You must see my daughter for Rizzo; she has worked her entire life for this role." *What entire life? She's ten!*

What saved me was that I remembered every inch of blocking, staging, and choreography from the original company, and I was ecstatic to share all of it. They were great kids, and several of them were talented too.

All four casts crushed the show. What a gift to be able to pass on my experience of this iconic show to another generation of actors and have an opportunity to make amends by proxy for whatever stupid shit I did in my young *Grease* years. Some of my students stay in touch and tell me that I changed their lives. The feeling's mutual.

I've now been sober for twenty-seven years!

SCOTT ROBERTSON (*Roger*): Soon after my Broadway run in *Grease*, something happened that changed my life in another way. On a gorgeous spring day, I was walking down the street near my little apartment in the East Village when I began to feel tears falling down my cheeks. I then began sobbing and I could not stop. I had no idea what was going on, but I knew I needed help.

I started seeing Al, my very tall Italian therapist, and for the next three years I slowly began the process of grieving for my dad, my best friend in the world, who had died when I was fifteen and he was forty-nine, five years before I was cast in *Grease*.

So what does the loss of my dad have to do with *Grease*? When my dad passed, I filled the void with numerous substances and not-so-healthy activities. My teen years disappeared. I was able to graduate but missed the high school experience almost completely.

Where was that high school gang I so wanted to be a part of? The laughs? Hanging out at the drive-in, the Dairy Queen, the school football games, and the prom? I became the man of the house when my dad passed. I skipped it all.

Then I was cast in *Grease*. I found something in my years with *Grease* which I had lost at fifteen. I found that kid. The kid who wanted to be part of a gang. Who wanted to know what camaraderie felt like. Who wanted to hang out and laugh, tell stupid jokes, and have a pizza party for more than one. Who wanted to sing too loudly in the street and go to a dance.

Grease filled that void. My first prom was in the Rydell High School gym, "Shakin' at the High School Hop." With hard work and dedication, *Grease* gave me back some of those lost years. Gratefully, I just celebrated twenty-five years of sobriety.

Grease gave me a second chance at fun—and a lifetime of joy. I'm a lucky kid!

TREAT WILLIAMS (*Understudy, then Zuko*): After a performance I would often be the last one out. On my way I'd always stop stage center, near the ghost light, and I'd look out into the dark house. I could still feel a vibration of the energy that had exploded on the stage with the love of eleven hundred people for this odd and magical thing called *Grease*. And we onstage had been vibrating right along with them.

Grease was a remarkable training ground for all of us young actors. How to do eight shows a week. How to sing through a cold. How to bring the energy on a day you didn't feel any energy at all. To say to yourself, *Buck up, just get out onstage and it'll come.* And then to feel that wave of energy from the audience, so no matter what you were feeling before, the adrenaline flows and you not only get through it, you triumph!

Each night I would just stand there thinking what a lucky guy I was to be playing this iconic role in this super-hit on Broadway. I was all of twenty-one years old, and I knew then that this was and would be one of the greatest experiences of my life. I was grateful. *Grease* was the remarkable beginning of my professional career, and it remains a high point (if not the highest) by which all others have been measured.

TOM MOORE (*Director*): When *Grease* opened inauspiciously at the Eden Theatre to those decidedly mixed reviews, one of New York's most acerbic critics, despite his generally negative review, recognized a special key to the *Grease* success when he called Pat Birch "the jewel in the toad." As much as it pains me to praise John Simon, he was remarkably acute in his early recognition of Pat.

Pat was a collaborator nonpareil, and the *Grease* the world knows would not have happened without her. Because Pat puts her whole petite being into every project, she infuses it with her energy and spirit. Although Pat conceptualizes, researches, and plans more than she will admit, the magic comes from her watching the actors and then perceptively designing the movement around them and from them so that, much as a good director lets the actor find the part, she finds the dancer in them and works from there, so that when it is realized, it is of them as much as her.

It is magical to watch, if sometimes a little nerve-racking, as you never know quite where she is going until she does. To watch the actors' fears and trepidation turn to confidence, if not downright giddy bravado, as they dance is one of my favorite memories of our work together. The *Grease* choreography is iconic for a reason. Sixteen reasons—each and every role.

In some of these stories, the actors describe their process in learning to dance from Pat, but what they can't tell you is what a fantastic partner Pat is to the director. Our preproduction, auditions, rehearsals, and previews were never less than a constant dialogue and collaboration. Together we determined the best actors for a part, the substance of the scenes, the styles of the songs, and the proper way to introduce them. We freely shared each other's work, were open to each other's suggestions and criticism, and quickly recognized wrong turns—joyful and happy at almost every turn. Our only battle was in the division of rehearsal time scheduled for scenes and musical numbers. And that was unending.

Pat is fond of calling me her brother, and I call us soul mates. A singular collaborator, and a singular friendship, happily steadfast and unbroken for over fifty years.

Our first *Grease* reunion, 1989.

The *Grease* gals gather in New York for an early twentieth anniversary reunion, January 1992.

Photos of our twentieth anniversary celebration, Los Angeles, 1992.

Jeff Conaway, Mews (Marya) Small, Tom Moore, at a book signing for Lynne Guerra, 1996.

Barry Bostwick and Joy Rinaldi celebrating thirty-eight years of friendship at a 2010 L.A. reunion at Joy's house.

Tom Moore and Adrienne Barbeau, 2010.

Tom Moore, Ken Waissman, Tom Harris, and Don Billett, 2010.

Katie Hanley Storer, Tom Moore, Carole Demas, Mews (Marya) Small, and Joy Rinaldi at our fortieth anniversary celebration, 2012.

Reunion at Ilene Graff and Ben Lanzerone's house, 2013.

Mews (Marya) Small, Garn Stephens, Ilene Kristen, Denise Nettleton, and Joy Rinaldi at an impromptu reunion, 2018.

Alan Paul, Mews (Marya) Small, Ilene Graff, Ben Lanzarone, Garn Stephens, Jay Donohue, Joy Rinaldi, Barry Bostwick, Bob Garrett, Ilene Kristen, and Tom Moore at the impromptu reunion, 2018.

In Memoriam

Jerry Barkoff
Shelley Barre
Frances Bay
Shirl Bernheim
Bill Beyers
Imogene Bliss
Sudie Bond
Marjorie Bowman
Dodie Boyhan
Stephan Burns
Warren Casey
Leo Cohen
Jeff Conaway
J. Curtis Crimp
Eddie Davis
John Delaat
Karren Dille
Candice Earley
Mike Falk
Char Fontaine
Larry Forde
Joy Garrett
Lynne Guerra
Peter Hammer
Peter Heuchling
Larry Horowitz
Betty Lee Hunt
Mark Immens
Geoffrey Johnson
Matt Landers

Jim Langrall
Dorothy Leon
Mickey Leonard
Joene Lewis
Bill Lieberman
Vinnie Liff
Linda Lyons
Timothy Meyers
Bob Minor
Kathi Moss
Peter Mumford
Frank O'Brien
Vince Otero
Maria Pucci
James Rebhorn
Paul Regina
Michael Riney
Ruth Russell
Buddy Saltzman
Linda Scoullar
Tony Shultz
Jimmie Skaggs
Tommy Smith
Louis St. Louis
Patrick Swayze
Chick Vennera
Billy Vitelli
Andrea Walters
Dan Woodard
Pete Yellin

ACKNOWLEDGMENTS

Tom Moore

It seems appropriate to start with appreciation to my editing collaborators. To Adrienne, not only for her superb editing skill and exacting attention to detail but especially for her constant encouragement during some *difficult* times on the project. To Ken for his "overview" and humor and for his remarkable memory for everything *Grease*; and gratefully and forever, for taking a chance on a very much unknown director back in 1971. Without Jim Jacobs, Warren Casey, Maxine Fox, and Ken Waissman there would have been no book to write.

To our agent Jane Dystel of Dystel, Goderich & Bourret, who fought the good fight and found us the perfect publishers in Chicago Review Press.

To Devon Freeny of CRP, who shepherded the book to release, and Jerry Pohlen, who guided us every step of the way. In a fateful moment when it seemed the book would have to be severely truncated, cutting out many of our contributors, Jerry miraculously marshaled the forces at CRP, allowing us to make the book we had always hoped to write.

To Marilu Henner, who gave us excellent advice as we embarked on this adventure, even giving us the title. And to a team of theater artists—Charles Dillingham, Gary Dontzig, Asaad Kelada, Art Manke, Duane Poole, and Jim Pentecost—who took the time to read our first draft, helping us, in the words of Stephen Sondheim, "finish the hat."

And, most important, appreciation to all those *Grease* alumni who contributed to this look back at our magical *Grease* era. The work and collaboration with each of you as these stories came to life felt almost like we were back in rehearsal again. Our virtual time together was a fantastic antidote in the years of the COVID pandemic 2020–2021.

Adrienne Barbeau

My thanks, first of all, to Jane Dystel of Dystel, Goderich & Bourret, who sparked to this idea the moment I mentioned it. "I can sell that," she said, and she did.

And to Jerry Pohlen, Devon Freeny, and everyone at Chicago Review Press. Without Jerry's patience and guidance, this book would never have come to be.

Thanks, too, to Duane Poole, Billy Van Zandt, and Alan Kelly, who, along with Tom's support crew, read the first draft and offered invaluable notes and insights that made what we had so much better.

And to my son Cody, who walked the dogs on the days I started work early, brought me dinner on the nights I finished work late, and, along with my sons William and Walker, listened to me let off steam in between.

Ken Waissman

Thanks to literary agent Jane Dystel of Dystel, Goderich & Bourret, and to Jerry Pohlen and everyone at Chicago Review Press. You got this "show" on!

Thanks also to my collaborators Adrienne Barbeau and Tom Moore. Despite various differences in opinions, we and our friendship survived the process.

Thanks also to Marilu Henner, who came up with the book's perfect title.

And a very special thanks to my former college roommate Phillip Markin. Without his phone call to me in August 1971, Broadway's *Grease*, the world phenomenon that resulted, and the stories in this book might never have happened.

CREDITS

Photo Credits

Unless otherwise indicated below, all images are courtesy of Waissman & Fox. "I#" indicates a color insert page. The editors have made every effort to secure permissions for the images in this book. They would welcome information concerning any inadvertent errors or omissions.

p. 2: Courtesy of J. Jacobs

p. 4: Courtesy of J. Canning

p. 13: Photo by M. Childers, courtesy of T. Moore

p. 17: Courtesy of D. Schmidt

pp. 42, 67, 87, 101, 125 (bottom), 135, 137, 148 & I8 (center, bottom): Courtesy of B. Bostwick

pp. 47, 94, 95, 145, 266, I3 (bottom), I4 (top) & I10 (top): Courtesy of J. Canning

pp. 51, 62 (top), 85 (both): Courtesy of K. Storer

pp. 55, 60, 61 (both), 62 (bottom), 77, 82 & 96: Courtesy of D. Douglas

pp. 78, 167, 175 (top left), 183, 204, 206, 281 (all) & 285: Courtesy of F. Piegaro

pp. 118 & I7 (both): Courtesy of R. Gilchrist

p. 129: Courtesy of J. Sullivan

p. 130: Courtesy of V. Fineman

p. 134: Courtesy S. Van Benschoten

pp. 142 & 149: Courtesy of I. Graff

p. 165: Courtesy of D. Kucsak

pp. 171, 173 (all) & 174 (bottom): Photo by Friedman-Abeles, courtesy of Waissman & Fox

p. 180: Courtesy of I. Kristen

pp. 188, 193, 194, 196 (both) & 201 (bottom): Courtesy of L. Raggio

p. 191: Courtesy of M. Kennedy

pp. 195, 199 (all), 200 (both), 202 (both) & 258: Photo by R. Fisher, courtesy
    of Waissman & Fox
pp. 201 (top), 270 & 271: Courtesy of M. Landers
p. 205: Courtesy of K. Morse
p. 217 (right): Courtesy of T. Williams
p 218 (left): Unknown
p. 218 (right): Courtesy of J. Lansing
p. 219: Courtesy of E. March
pp. 234 & 255 (right): Courtesy of K. Meloche Ricardo
p. 248: Courtesy of C. Costa
pp. 272, 333 (top), 336 (bottom), 337 (bottom), 338 (both), 339 (both)
    & I14 (bottom): Courtesy of J. Rinaldi
p. 276: Courtesy of R. DeMattis
p. 288: Courtesy of J. Shankman
p. 299: Courtesy of L. A. Jaroslow
p. 301: Courtesy of P. Greeno
p. 302: Courtesy of L. Graff
pp. 315 (bottom), 333 (bottom), 335 (top) & I14 (center): Courtesy of P. L. Brennan
p. 323: Courtesy of P. Greeno
p. 334 (bottom): Courtesy of K. Waissman
p. 335 (bottom): Courtesy of S. Seff
pp. 336 (top), 337 (top): Courtesy of T. Moore
p. I2 (all): Courtesy of C. Robbins
p. I4 (bottom): Courtesy of N. Small
p. I8 (top): Courtesy of J. Sullivan
p. I10 (bottom): Courtesy of S. Boccieri
p. I14 (top): Courtesy of J. Becker
p. I15 (both): Courtesy of S. Seff
p. I16 (top): Photo by P. J. Zielinski, courtesy of Waissman & Fox
p. I16 (bottom): Courtesy of Whitney Browne

Other Credits

The memories from the late Kathi Moss were contributed by her husband, Tom Quinn, recalling Kathi's many stories from her years with *Grease*.

Matt Landers's memory of the Richard Burton / Elizabeth Taylor visit to *Grease* in chapter 34 was written by Matt as a complete personal story and was discovered in his papers when he died. Permission to use it in this book was given by his daughters, Fiona and Lily Landers.